Godfaring

Godfaring

ON REASON, FAITH, AND SACRED BEING

Francis Clark

The Catholic University of America Press
Washington, D.C.

Copyright © 2000

The Catholic University of America Press

All rights reserved

Printed in the United States of America

The paper used in this publication meets the minimum requirements

of American National Standards for Information Science—

Permanence of Paper for Printed Library Materials, ANSI Z39.48-1984

LIBRARY OF CONGRESS CATALOGING-IN-PUBLICATION DATA

Clark, Francis, 1919–

    Godfaring : on reason, faith, and sacred being / Francis
Clark.

       p.   cm.

    Includes bibliographical references and index.

     1. Faith and reason—Christianity.   2. Catholic Church—
Doctrines.   3. Natural theology. I. Title.

BT50.C55   2000

231'.042—dc21

99–36505

ISBN 0–8132–0959–5 (pbk.: alk. paper)

To my wife, Pauline,
loving and beloved guide
in our shared wayfaring to God

Contents

✵

Introduction
Wayfaring and Wondering

As a small child I first heard, in catechism class, the fundamental question that confronts all humanity: "Why did God make you?" I duly learned to recite by rote the required answer: "God made me to know him, love him, and serve him in this world, and to be happy with him forever in the next." In the school of life the meaning of that trite formula, construed by faith, became my central certainty, giving direction to all my wayfaring despite all my waywardness.

I have been spared trial of faith in the crucible of doubt. Yet my life, while ruled by the certainty that my purpose and fulfilment lies in knowing, loving, and serving God, has been, and still is, an urgent quest to find him, a quest that is still a questioning. Nearing the end of my long pilgrimage, looking back on joyous discovery and woeful backsliding, still I ponder with wondering awe on the omnipresent mystery of the Holy, which gives meaning to human existence and which has been the lodestar of my journey.

Some of the questions that arise in my mind lead it into clearer light. Others voice my incomprehension of mystery beyond my ken. I am still, as in the catechism class of my now far-distant childhood, seeking deeper understanding both of the questions I ask and of the answers I hear. I apprehend with joyful hope the evidences of God's design of wisdom, power, and loving purpose in the world that he has created, and that he has transformed by becoming incarnate in it. I am certain that the purpose of my own life, as of every human life, is to be conformed to that master plan of divine love, revealed in Jesus Christ. Yet my mind also finds in this world of created and redeemed reality strange, perplexing riddles. To some of them it can give at least a conjectural explanation. To others, beyond its comprehension, in particular the dark enigma of evil, the only conclusive answer it can give is submissive faith and adoration of the all-holy God, whose omnipotent goodness cannot contradict itself.

The memory of my lifetime is a pilgrim's sack, containing baubles and dross picked up by the wayside as well as records of the journey and some precious gages of eternal treasure found in holy places. There, amidst the mingled clutter in my sack, are partly faded but ever legible documents registering good and ill. Among them are ledgers of loss and gain, temporal and spiritual. Past arraignments for sins of commission and omission are there, together with dockets of merciful quittance. Words of prayer and of Scripture are written on those tattered scrolls, psalms of yearning and of thankfulness, of sadness and of happiness. There are portraits of beloved faces and mementoes of family joys and cares, of friendships, of travels, and of shared tribulations. Diaries scribbled on the battlefield and in the wilderness are bundled with worksheets listing long years of toilsome endeavor. There is an indelible certificate of sacerdotal ordination, with records of pastoral ministry. A solemn profession of religious vows, revoked by papal indult, lies there, and over it an irrevocable profession of marriage vows. Love letters from both heaven and earth are bound together with love poems telling of time and eternity. There are also listed other scrolls, as yet undeciphered, that are stored elsewhere. Among those, I trustfully surmise, are title-deeds to the pearl of great price and to the treasure hid in God's far field.

Is there also to be found in my ragged sack any store of wisdom, grains gleaned during my pilgrim wayfaring? If so, should I try to retrieve those grains, to winnow them from the chaff and even to sow them anew in the hope that others may reap some benefit from them? Or is it spiritual presumption that prompts an aged pilgrim to set before others his meditative musings on the ultimate questions of life, on divine purpose and human awareness of it?

The reflections contained in this book do not put forward any new wisdom. They are my jejune attempt to discern and distil something of what I have learnt from the ageless wisdom of Scripture, saints, and sages. I also articulate here the riddles that I find written in the structure of the created world and in the human mind itself, to which I seek to find some answer from reason enlightened by faith.

For Christian believers reason and faith are not in conflict but in harmony; they do not offer alternative paths to God, but come together in one sacred pathway. Our faith is, as St. Anselm testified in a timeless phrase, *fides quaerens intellectum*, the faith that seeks understanding. It not only leads us to deeper insight into the meaning of the divinely revealed truths that it affirms, but it also confirms and illuminates by its own higher light our rational understanding of ourselves and of the created world in which we live. Conversely, the wisdom of right reason is preparatory to and concomitant with the divinely revealed wisdom of Christian faith. Natural theology not only serves as the forerunner and handmaid of revealed theology, but is elevated and supernaturalized by it. Implicitly natural theology is *intellectus quaerens fidem*, rational understanding seeking fulfilment by faith.

In my quest for clearer comprehension, I accept as God-given the light that comes from Scripture and the corporate faith and teaching of the Catholic Church.[1] As well as the light of revelation, I also call in aid "that perennial tradition of philosophy which is able to transcend the limits of time and place," and which makes explicit the implicit philosophy of human reason seeking the source and meaning of our existence and experience. To that common fund of rational wisdom, that "body of known truths recognizable as a general spiritual patrimony of mankind,"[2] many contemplative sages and philosophers of diverse cultures in East and West have witnessed through the ages. With many another, I find the most profound expression of that *philosophia perennis* in the thought of St. Thomas Aquinas, who was heir to the philosophical legacy of both Christian and pre-Christian antiquity and who combined it, in a unitary worldview, with the higher truth bestowed by revelation.

That sapiential heritage is rejected and ridiculed by critics who are reputed as philosophers. However, I do not propose to encumber these pages with discussion of their views, a pursuit that has taken up too much time in my fleeting life-span. Philosophy means the love of wisdom, but the word is also inappropriately applied to sterile systems of thought that ultimately negate true wisdom. One could use the terms "pseudosophy" or "antisophy," sham wisdom or anti-wisdom, as better names for such destructive thought systems. There is a theist and life-fulfilling worldview that accords with the deepest wisdom of the human race; and there is an

atheist and life-emptying worldview that opposes it. Though stridently as-
sertive in recent times, the pseudosophical philosophers and their disciples
who propound their nihilist creed are in fact a small minority in the history of human thought and experience. As will appear from the following
chapters, I see the radical opposition between those two incompatible
worldviews as arising not simply from a difference in evaluation of logical
arguments in the sphere of the speculative reason, but more ultimately
from a difference of choice in the sphere of the practical reason, the
sphere of conscience and willed life orientation. That choice, seldom explicitly articulated in philosophical discourse, is either to follow or to refuse the supreme moral imperative innate in human rationality—which is
to seek ultimate divine goodness and to conform our life to it. In saying
this, I do not suppose that all who profess themselves atheists are necessarily making conscious and culpable choice to reject that ultimate divine
goodness.

The reflections I voice in these pages will, I like to think, receive sympathetic hearing from many in other churches and Christian traditions. Much
of what is said here about the religious quest of humankind would also be
commonly said, in different idioms, by adherents of all the world religions.
Such common interreligious agreement would not be extended, evidently,
to those passages in this book in which I rely on the premises of Christian
faith to elucidate those universal truths.

In our age Christians and adherents of other faiths are more and more
coming together in joint and reverent acknowledgment of the common
religious and ethical patrimony that we all share as fellow members of the
human family. The development of theological respect for and understanding of the God-given good to be found in other religions is a surpris-
ingly recent development within Christianity, quickening especially in the
Catholic Church since the Second Vatican Council. The horizons of Christian theology are being progressively widened by that development. One
may say that in the narrower perspectives of the past there was so absolute
an emphasis on the uniqueness, finality, and otherness of the Christian
revelation that the truths and values enshrined in the religious quest and
experience of all humankind were undervalued by Christian theologians.
There is still need to redress the balance. This book puts forward further
reflections, within those newly clarified perspectives of Catholic theology,

on the sacramental relationship of nature to grace, of God-seeking reason to faith, of human religion to divine revelation.

⚘

After the manuscript of my work had been substantially completed there appeared a major document of the papal magisterium which bears directly on its subject matter. That document is the encyclical letter of Pope John Paul II *Fides et ratio*, the English translation of which is entitled *On the Relationship between Faith and Reason*.[3] While I did not find in the encyclical anything that required me to correct what I had written, I proceeded to revise and amplify my manuscript to signal the direct relevance of the papal document to the themes discussed in this book. I have added a number of relevant citations from it to supplement the treasury of corroboratory texts and testimonies cited here from Scripture, from the writings of the Fathers and doctors of the Church, and from previous documents of the magisterium. The encyclical *Fides et ratio* begins with a statement of its central theme:

Faith and reason are like two wings on which the human spirit rises to the contemplation of truth. It is God himself who has implanted in the minds of men the urge to seek knowledge of truth—which, ultimately, is the urge to seek knowledge of himself—so that, by knowing and loving him, they may thereby attain to the full truth about themselves.

In the encyclical the Pope gives to the Church and to the world a profound statement on truth itself and on the manner in which those "two wings of the spirit," faith and reason, are coordinated in God's plan for humankind. He devotes special attention to the vital role of autonomous human reasoning, both in reaching truth about reality and about our life's purpose, and in facilitating and developing our understanding of the divinely revealed truths. He reaffirms, in a postmodern age afflicted by corrosive scepticism and by "a crisis of meaning," the value of true philosophy: not the partial and flawed philosophies of individual thinkers and systems, but philosophy, defined as that "universal wisdom and learning" that articulates and reflects on the fruits of humanity's collective reasoning about its experience of reality and is open to higher awareness of metaphysical and transcendent reality.

That universal philosophy of human reason validates the "natural theology" and "natural religion" upon which I reflect in this book. The encyclical *Fides et ratio* illumines anew, with concentrated light, the central themes discussed here. The English translation of the papal encyclical gives its title as *On the Relationship between Faith and Reason*. The word rendered as "relationship" is, in the Latin original, *necessitudo*, which may be construed in a stronger sense as asserting a "necessary interconnection" between faith and reason. It is in this sense that I discuss, especially in my fifth and sixth chapters, the relationship between natural and revealed knowledge of God. I have good hope that my own lowly and lengthier reflections on the relationship between faith and reason, written before the publication of the encyclical, will be seen to be in concord with, and to receive powerful support and actuality from, the papal teaching on that subject.

At the conclusion of his encyclical the Pope has exhortations for both theologians and philosophers. His wish for the former is that, "with singular intentness of mind, they may discern the philosophical implications of the word of God, while grounding their search for understanding in that [revealed truth] from which the speculative and practical excellence of theological science derives."[4] The Pope's wish for philosophers and those who teach philosophy is that, "in the light of the philosophical tradition that remains enduringly valid, they may affirm anew the principles of a philosophical discipline that embraces authentic wisdom and truth, metaphysical truth included." As one who has been engaged for many years of my life in the study and teaching of theology (and of metaphysical philosophy withal) I take to my heart those papal exhortations.

⚜

I use the unwonted but evocative word *Godfaring* as the title of this book, not because of its incidental (though not inappropriate) assonance with the traditional word "God-fearing," but because it has other semantic echoes that resonate with my theme. It can be taken as a compact form of the title I first thought of for the book, namely, "Godward Wayfaring." I vest it here with further connotations: namely, that our pilgrim wayfaring not only is taking us towards God but has its starting point in God; that it is God himself who empowers us at every moment with strength to fare onwards to the goal; that the created universe, which is the terrain of our wayfaring, is translucent with the creative light of God, presaging his full revelation of himself; that all that we encounter and experience on the way, whether we here fare well or ill, comes from God, tells us of God, and calls us to God; and, beyond all our imagining, that God the Son has himself taken human form and stepped into time to join us on the way, where, his pilgrim staff a cross, he fares forth with us on the journey as our brother, guide, and savior; and that he is not only with us in our Godward wayfaring but is himself the Way and our journey's end.

The thoughts that I now formulate anew in these pages I have shared with many others in the past, both by word of mouth and in writing,[5] in the long years (still continuing, *Deo gratias*) during which I have been privileged to study and teach theology and the history of religion. In those exchanges with younger and worthier fellow pilgrims I have had the joy of sensing that in their hearts and in mine the same divine melody was resounding. I here express these thoughts in new form in the hope that at least some of them may yet have usefulness as waymarks for other wayfarers at earlier stages of our common journey—whether they be striding vigorously in the freshness of morning, laboring in the heat of noon, or attempting to quicken their steps with the approach of eventide.

For my own part, I hope that this writing will serve to reinvigorate my own resolve and limping steps in the final stage of my pilgrimage to the God of mercy and love. Divine treasure may be carried in earthen vessels— even in an earthen vessel that is chipped, time-worn, and base. While the timeless truths that I venture to explore in these pages are the common patrimony of all men and women, my perception of them is inevitably colored by the circumstances and experiences of one chequered and undistinguished life. For any reader who may wish to take account of that autobiographical coloring, I summarize in "Appendix I: An Autobiographical Endnote" the stages of my life's course and major turning points in it. In later chapters I will also refer incidentally to particular events and experiences that during my long life have confronted me personally with the ultimate questions that are the subject matter of this book.

Through thought and word, through hearing and reading, through prayer and meditation, we wayfarers seek a route map that will lead us to our home in God. Christians find the God-given chart for our wayfaring in the Scriptures inspired by the Holy Spirit. There we read warnings that all our study and knowledge, even the loftiest theological speculation, will prove unavailing to guide us to our journey's end if it remains merely a loveless intellectual pursuit. "He who does not love does not know God: for God is love" (1 John 4.8). St. Paul exclaims likewise:

If I speak in the tongues of men and of angels, but have not love, I am but a booming gong or a clashing cymbal. And if I have prophetic powers, and understand all mysteries and all knowledge, and if I have full faith so as to remove mountains, but have not love, I am nothing. *(1 Corinthians 13.1–2)*

It is not knowledge alone or even love alone that is the ultimate value, but a divine blend of knowing and loving in which love has primacy, the love of God and the love of his children that issues from it. *"En la tarde, te examinarán en el amor."* The haunting words of St. John of the Cross carry a message for everyone undergoing the probation of this mortal life. They have a special urgency for those of us who have worn the trappings of scholarship in the corridors of academe. His terse axiom should be fixed on our work desks and in our hearts. It can be paraphrased, "In the final examination at the end of the course—the only examination that really matters, to fail which is to lose all and to pass which is to gain all, the subject on which you will be assessed is how you have loved."

Godfaring

Chapter 1

Knowing God by Reason and by Christian Faith

For what can be known about God is plain to them, because God has shown it to them. Ever since the creation of the world his invisible nature, namely, his eternal power and deity, is clearly perceived in the things that have been made. So they are without excuse; for although they knew God they did not honor him as God or give thanks to him, but they became futile in their thinking and their senseless minds were darkened.

St. Paul's Epistle to the Romans *1.19–21*

Human intelligence is indeed capable of surely finding a response to the question of origins. The existence of God the Creator can be certainly known through his works by the light of human reason; this knowledge, however, is often obscured and deformed by error. That is why faith comes to confirm and enlighten reason in the right understanding of this truth.

Catechism of the Catholic Church, § 286

We human beings, looking outwards on the world in which we are embodied and reflecting inwards on ourselves, come to infer that there is, beyond this reality that we directly experience, a more ultimate reality, the purposive origin and cause of all things, to whom our lives and deeds have relation. Those intimations of divine presence and purpose in cosmic nature are the foundation of a natural religion common to all humankind. Even when obscured and frustrated by human fault and folly, the innate capacity and yearning of the human mind to know of God remains ineffaceable.

Linked with that primary truth about the religious quest of humankind is another, incomparably greater, which the believing mind perceives not by the light of its natural reason but by the light of Christian faith: namely, that the tidings of deity apprehended in our experience of the world and of ourselves are immeasurably enriched and surpassed by immediate revelation of God himself, incarnate in human life and history. The Word made flesh has disclosed to us knowledge of God's own life, the divine Unity in the Trinity of interpersonal subsistent relations, Father, Son and Holy Spirit, and also knowledge of the manner in which God destines and enables us to share that life.

What is the relationship between those two different but connected modes by which the mind has access to knowledge about God—one by natural reason which discerns his veiled imprint in creation and which hears the echo of his law in personal conscience, the other by faith which finds him directly revealed through the life, teaching, and saving work of Jesus Christ? Are those two modes of God-knowledge separate and alternative? Is the former uncertain and unavailing, needing to be replaced by the latter? Or is it the latter that must depend upon the former to supply a rational and experiential basis lacking in itself? How are those two modes conjoined in God's all-encompassing salvific plan?

Differing answers to these questions have been given by Christian thinkers. At one extreme, there are those who so exalt divine revelation that they deny religious and salvific value to man's natural knowledge of God. This was the position of the sixteenth-century Protestant Reformers, who judged as necessarily false any claim of fallen human reason to be able to reach true knowledge of God by its natural power. Martin Luther dismissed the rational theology honored by Catholic tradition as a vain and culpable attempt of sinful man to rise above his station. Only God's merciful revelation through Christ, proclaimed in the Scriptures and received by saving faith could bring true knowledge of him. Luther denounced Dame Reason as a harlot, leading men away by deception and seduction from the sole biblical path to divine truth and grace. "Frau Hulda" (as he called her) was "the devil's whore" when she attempted to theologize. He asserted:

In godly affairs—that is, in those that have to do with God, where man must do what is acceptable to God and be saved thereby—nature is absolutely blind, so that it cannot even catch a glimpse of what those things are.[1]

In general accord, the other Protestant Reformers agreed with Luther in rejecting the medieval scholastic synthesis of reason and revelation. John Calvin's denunciation of the religious pretensions of fallen human reason was expressed more moderately. He admitted three senses in which it could be said that natural inklings of God were available to the human mind. He allowed, namely, that "a sense of the divine is written in every heart"; that "God daily discloses himself in the whole workmanship of the universe"; and that the human conscience gives testimony of the Creator.[2] But he too insisted with Luther that those natural inklings of divinity had been radically vitiated by sin, and were utterly otiose and unavailing to bring men to God; only revealed knowledge of God the Redeemer and faith in his pardon could avail for salvation.

The influence of Reformation fideism can be traced in the mistrust of reasoning about God to be found in the thought of later philosophers formed in the Protestant tradition, notably Kant, Schleiermacher, and Kierkegaard, and in more recent times Heidegger and Jaspers. The Reformation protest against natural theology has been repeated by Protestant theologians during the centuries since that time,[3] most forcibly in the twentieth century by Karl Barth and his school. The implications of that protest are further discussed in later pages. Piously intended though it be, that protest nevertheless entails denial of the necessary substrate upon which our apprehension of Christian revelation itself is divinely based, as I shall argue more fully in Chapter 5.

Here I observe, proleptically, that the Protestant divines' rejection of natural theology, and their insistence that scriptural revelation is the sole source of true knowledge of God, is necessarily linked with their rejection of "the analogy of being," that is, of the mysterious participative link between created beings and the creative Being who is their source, which makes it possible for the human mind to know God from his likeness in his works. In later pages (especially in Chapters 2, 8, and 14) I will return often to the fundamental importance of the analogy of being in the Catholic perception of ultimate reality and of the relation between creatures and their Creator.

An affinity may be marked between the position of the Protestant Reformers and that of some Jewish and Muslim metaphysicians and theologians who have likewise asserted absolute separation of God from the world created by him, and consequently humankind's absolute dependence on his revelation, transmitted by scriptural word, for knowledge of his being and his will. According to this perception, even from divine revelation human beings can have no knowledge of the nature of God in his hidden self, but only knowledge of the ways of religious thinking and acting that he has decreed for them to observe.

At the other extreme from fideism is religious rationalism, or Deism, which was especially influential in England and France in the age of the eighteenth-century Enlightenment.[4] Deists held that while knowledge of God by reason is sure, the mysterious and unprovable dogmas of faith are not. They asserted that the former alone has objective foundation in rational argument based on the evidence of the physical world, whereas the latter they decried as unproven and irrational, demanding a subjective and unjustified leap in the dark. Their ideas were countered in a moderate and widely influential defense of rational theology within the context of revelation written by the English divine Samuel Clarke in his published lectures, entitled *Demonstration of the Being and Attributes of God, the Obligations of Natural Religion, and the Truth and Certainty of the Christian Revelation.*[5]

Enlightenment Deism in France was often secularist and hostile to the Christian Church and its doctrines. Assertion of natural religion, as opposed to the religion of revelation, was partly a protest against the ecclesiastical system of the *ancien régime.* For some, Deism was a stepping-stone to agnostic humanism. Nevertheless, the writings of the Deists (Rousseau, especially) contain firm witness to the inborn drive in human reason to acknowledge God from his evidences in the natural world and in the religious imperative of conscience. Anti-dogmatic natural religion persisted after the French Revolution in various forms. It is still a diffuse sentiment in post-Christian Western society—indeed in many who regard themselves as Christians in a general sense.

In the nineteenth century some thinkers within the Catholic Church, reacting against Deism, propounded the theory known as "Traditionalism," according to which a primitive revelation of God, prerequisite for any human knowledge of divine truth, has been handed down through all generations since the origin of the human race. In reaction against what they saw as excessive religious rationalism, they veered towards the fideist denial of the natural power of human reason to have reliable knowledge of God and of his law.[6] Contrariwise, some other Catholic thinkers were suspected of tending towards an unorthodox "ontologism." That is, they were accused of so unduly vaunting the reach of the human mind as to claim for it the power to apprehend the very being of God, and thereby to attain direct knowledge of ultimate divine truth without need for revelation and faith.[7] Both of these opposing tendencies were censured by the magisterium of the Church.

Between the two extremes of ultra-fideism and ultra-rationalism lies the orthodox Catholic doctrine, which affirms the place in human knowledge of God of both natural and revealed theology, while declaring that the latter immeasurably excels the former. In 1870, in its *Dogmatic Constitution on the Christian Faith*, the First Vatican Council solemnly defined a dogma that accords both with the general conviction of humankind and with the basic Deist premise: "God, the beginning and end of all things, can be certainly known by the natural light of human reason, from the things that have been created."[8] It follows from this dogmatic definition that the human mind is capable of attaining true inferential knowledge of the existence and creative sovereignty of God independently of Christian revelation and dogma. Such knowledge is therefore open to all human beings through use of their natural reason, whether they are Christians or belong to that majority of the human race who are not.

In the same passage Vatican I went on to state the limitations of human reason's natural grasp of religious truth. In the present condition of humankind, it explained, divine revelation aids and enhances the light of reason so that such truth about God as lies within the scope of reason "may be known by all, easily, with firm certitude and without admixture of error." Moreover, the Council declared, revelation is absolutely necessary to enable human beings to attain the supernatural end that God has ordained for them, and thus "to participate in that divine good which altogether exceeds the understanding of the human mind."[9]

Plainly Shown, Clearly Perceived, Certainly Known?

In the primary scriptural text relating to natural theology, cited at the head of this chapter, St. Paul says that what can be known of God has been

shown plainly to men, and that "his invisible nature, namely his power and
deity, is clearly perceived in the things that have been made." The certainty
of such natural knowledge of God is emphasized in the definition of Vatican I. But how can it be said that humanity is given sure evidences of God
in the created world when so many human beings are unsure about those
evidences? If knowledge of God from his works is plainly shown to men
and clearly perceived by them, how is it that some doubt or even deny the
existence of the absolute divine reality, and many others have diverse conceptions of its nature? This objection was expressed, flippantly, by the agnostic philosopher Bertrand Russell when someone once asked him, "Supposing, after you die, you find there is another world and you meet God,
what would you say to him?" Russell replied, "I would say—'Well, why on
earth didn't you give better evidence of your existence?'"

The encyclical letter *Humani generis* of Pope Pius XII addresses this question of the failure of many minds to acknowledge God from the evidence
of his creation:

Although, speaking generally, human reason is truly capable of attaining, by its
own natural power and light, to a true and certain knowledge of the one personal
God who watches over and controls the world by his providence, and also of the
natural law inscribed in our hearts by the Creator, yet there are many things which
impede reason from making effective and fruitful use of this innate capacity. Truths
that pertain to God and to the relations between man and God wholly transcend
the order of things perceptible to sense; and putting those truths into practical effect to transform human life demands dedication and abnegation of self. The
human mind is beset with difficulties in grasping such truths, both because of the
sway of the senses and of the imagination and because of the disordered appetites
that are the consequences of original sin. So it happens that in such circumstances
men easily persuade themselves that what they would not like to be true is false or
at least doubtful.[10]

Thus we find that human reason, created to find and follow the path to
God, is yet prone to deviate from it. The impediments to perception of
God from his works that arise from the human condition are both moral
and physical. There are the moral impediments of sinfulness and wilful
folly, which may corrupt natural religious awareness both in individuals
and in whole communities. Physical impediments arise from the manifold
necessities and tribulations of human life; for many, they may weigh so
heavily on both body and mind that they impede or exclude opportunity

for meditative reflection on the meaning of life and deaden sensitivity to spiritual truth and moral values. Those difficulties besetting men's perception of the naturally knowable truths about God and his law are cited by Aquinas as congruous reasons for the divine bestowal of clearer knowledge of such truths by supernatural revelation.

Not only can the perception of deity from the evidence of the created world be darkened by culpable obtuseness and by physical and psychological obstacles, but in the showing of that evidence there is a certain enigmatic challenge which is both an invitation to and a test of human response. There is indeed translucence in that showing, but it is a *chiaroscuro* interplay of light and shadow, a theophany through veils. Our mind's inference of divine reality is not simply a theoretical conclusion from a process of logical reasoning. Our Godfaring engages the whole person—not intellect alone, but also the free will, affectivity, and moral life stance of each. We are implicitly called by our conscience to acknowledge God not simply as a mysterious first principle of creation, but as holy Lord who is the meaning of our lives, whom we must acknowledge not only in thought and word but also by godly conduct. That acknowledgment may be negated by the latent *non serviam* of recalcitrant human will. "I will not serve" can subconsciously translate into "I will not see." As Pius XII observed in the passage cited above, denial of God may be obscurely motivated by unwillingness to accept the obligations that would follow from acknowledging him and his holy will. Pope Pius's words, incorporated in the *Catechism of the Catholic Church*,[11] are also paralleled by those of Pope John Paul II in his encyclical *Fides et ratio*:

If a man does not attain, by application of his intellect, to acknowledgment of God as Creator of all, that must not be attributed to defect in the instrument that he applies but rather to an obstacle put in the way by his free will and his own sins. . . . It can come about that a man flees from the truth as soon as he begins to recognize it because he fears its demands.[12]

The ascent of the mind to God by the ladder of created things is a continuing process. Recognition of the divine impress in the world, which may at first be obscure and fitful, grows progressively clearer and deeper in one who lives and loves aright, until it is a habitual state of soul. In the life of grace, the intellect's natural inference of God from his works is elevated to become the Holy Spirit's infused gift of wisdom.

Is Knowledge of God by Reason Made Obsolete by Revelation?

To say that human reason's natural inklings of the divine still retain deep religious significance, even after the human condition has been transformed by divine grace and revelation through Christ, seems disconcerting and dubious to some Christians, especially to those who continue the Reformation protest against natural theology. Some others would object, less absolutely, that even though a modicum of religious truth can be seen by the dimmer light of natural reason, surely it is pointless to look to that source for knowledge of God and of his law once we are illumined by the full light of faith. When sunlight comes, starlight fades. Why then labor to extol those fainter notions of deity in the religious consciousness of humanity when they have been superseded by higher divine truth revealed through the incarnate Word of God himself and recorded in divinely inspired Scripture? In any case, it may further be argued, most Christian believers come to acknowledge God through being taught in childhood revealed truth about him, and they may go through life without explicit realization that a distinction can be made between what can be known of God by faith and what can also be known by natural reason. How then can reflection on that distinction have importance for Christian life?

Nevertheless Christian doctrine itself leads us to recognize that those two modes of knowing God are included and interconnected in the divine plan of love for humankind. The hidden God whom we glimpse through the veils of created being and the all-holy and all-loving God whom we know through the revelation of the incarnate divine Word, Jesus Christ, is the selfsame God. He, whose reflection in this world of his making is distantly visible to all human beings by the light of reason, calls us to know him more surely and to be united with him more intimately by the gift of faith. Through the grace of Christ we are brought into a communion with God beyond the capacity of all our natural powers to attain; yet with the coming of the greater light of faith the knowledge of God and his will given by the lesser light of reason is not extinguished or rendered obsolete.

From the Church's own teaching, it can be affirmed that the higher revelation we have of God through grace and faith *presupposes, transforms,* and *fulfils* the aboriginal revelation we have of him through nature and reason. In my fifth and sixth chapters I set out more fully the reasons that justify this threefold affirmation. To reflect more deeply on the interrelation of natural and revealed religion is then not mere speculative curiosity. It is a profoundly theological question, exercising the faith that seeks understanding. Its importance has not always been apprized in the teaching and study of theology. Catholic theologians have duly professed the natural capacity of human reason to know of God as a truth based on scriptural authority and dogmatic definition by the Church; but in writing their textbooks they have often tended to treat natural theology as little more than a footnote in the study of revealed theology and to remit it to the separate sphere of metaphysical philosophy. This tendency has been accentuated in recent years by some who argue the need for theological study to take account of the riches of the human sciences and to shun the aridities of metaphysics. Teachers of metaphysical philosophy in their turn have tended to limit the scope of "natural theology," concerning themselves more narrowly with subtle critiques and debates about the formulation and logical force of the various "proofs for the existence of God."

Today these questions appear in new light. The twentieth century has brought a major advance in Catholic theological understanding of the relationship between the natural and the supernatural in God's revealed design for bringing humanity to himself. It is now understood more clearly that there do not exist two different and separate spheres in which man stands before God, one a sphere of supernatural grace, the other of merely natural goodness; rather, there is one existential order, in which all that is good in the being and action of humankind is related to the transformation of human nature consequent upon its assumption by God in person and upon his saving work in all humanity. Of major influence in furthering understanding of this simultaneity and symbiosis of grace and nature have been the writings of Henri de Lubac and Karl Rahner, which bore fruit in the deliberations and decrees of the Second Vatican Council. In later chapters I reflect repeatedly on the implications of that truth. With the coming of these deeper insights, and especially in the light of the teaching of the Council, the way is open and is still widening for deeper theological appreciation of the relationship between natural and revealed religion.

A protracted doctrinal development has eventually led the Church to declare, through the decrees of Vatican II, that eternal salvation lies open to the non-Christian majority of humankind, and to acknowledge, as never before, the God-given truths and values to be found in non-Christian religions. The same doctrinal development also points the way to deeper understanding of the place, in the divine economy of salvation revealed through Christ, of the natural outreach of the human mind towards ultimate divine Being. Pope John Paul II's encyclical *Fides et ratio* has brought a powerful reaffirmation of the essential place of reason, true philosophy, and natural theology in the Christian understanding of God's revealed plan for humankind.

In these newly widened horizons of theology, the natural acknowledgment of God—to which all are prompted by reason and which demands right willing and acting as well as right knowing—may be seen as an analogue of supernatural faith. Natural religion may now be seen as a kind of sacramental medium making possible, in a mysterious manner, the reception of Christ's grace and salvation by that greater part of the human race who live and die outside the visible bounds of his Church.

In later pages I discuss more fully that basic question of the relation, in the divine plan for human life, between our two modes of knowing God: that is, between reason and faith, between natural and revealed theology. In the two immediately following chapters I reflect on the antecedent questions concerning the possibility, sources, and content of natural theology considered in itself. How can our finite minds have knowledge of infinite God? How can human concepts and language, based on the data of the senses, have true reference to transcendent spiritual reality? If there is a theology written in the runes of cosmic nature for the human mind to read, how can we decipher those runes and verify their meaning? How has human reason speculated on divinity in the course of ages? Can we formulate the content of natural theology?

Chapter 2

How Is Natural Theology Possible?

From earliest ages until the present day, there is found among the different peoples a certain awareness of a hidden power present in the rhythm of nature and in the events of human life, which indeed is at times recognized as supreme divine reality, even as Father. This awareness and recognition imbues their life with a deep religious sense. As cultures develop, the religions associated with them endeavor to give answers to those questions through subtler concepts and language.

Second Vatican Council, Nostra aetate, §2

The world, and man, attest that they have within themselves neither their first principle nor their final end, but rather that they participate in the Being [Esse] which alone is without origin and end. Thus, by following various "ways" of reasoning, man can come to knowledge of the existence of a reality which is the first cause and final end of all things, "a reality that everyone calls 'God.'"

Catechism of the Catholic Church, §34

Although many of the religious cultures of humankind have postulated a plurality of divinities or spiritual powers, they commonly acknowledge with awe one supreme spirit or principle who is divine in a unique sense, "a reality that everyone calls God." Those concluding words in the second passage cited above are taken from the *Summa theologiae* of St. Thomas Aquinas.[1] He calls that reality by the Latin word *Deus*, and he means that all peoples have a name to refer to it. Evidently the linguistic

forms by which they name God are very diverse, according to the diversity
of their nations and languages. Even in polytheistic societies we commonly find use of a universal name for deity or heavenly power, current
together with use of specific names for particular gods or manifestations
of that power.

The ancient Hebrew name *Elohim*, frequently used in the Pentateuch as
the name of God (as well as the unique name YAHWEH revealed to Moses
on Mount Horeb),[2] was akin to similar divine names used in other
branches of the Semitic family of languages. Plural in form, *Elohim* is, in
the context of inspired and monotheistic Scripture, explained by biblical
commentators as "a plural of majesty." Even in polytheistic cults, use of
similar linguistic forms would have reflected an overarching concept of
deity as such, applicable to all manifestations of the divine.

Within the Greek- and Latin-speaking branches of the Indo-European
family of languages the cognate divine names *Theos* and *Deus* were in use
from remote antiquity (the etymology of both terms is thought to be
linked with an Aryan root signifying "to shine"). The Greek-speaking Jews
who completed the Septuagint translation of the Hebrew Scriptures in the
second century BC adopted that traditional Greek word for deity, *Theos*, as
equivalent to the Hebrew name *Elohim*, and thus as fitting to designate the
one true God who had revealed himself to his chosen people. The New
Testament writers continued the same usage, likewise calling by the name
Theos the triune God who revealed himself through Jesus Christ. As the
Christian Church spread from the Levant throughout the Mediterranean
basin and beyond, it invoked and worshipped God by that Greek name, and
soon, in the West, by the corresponding Latin name *Deus*. When the Ro-
manized nations of the Western Empire were brought into the Christian
fold they likewise called on the God revealed by Jesus Christ by continuing
to use that traditional Latin name, with its various derivatives in the emerging Romance languages.

Similar usage can be observed in the process by which the barbarian
tribes who pressed into Western Europe as the Roman Empire declined
were progressively Christianized. The English word "God" with its cognate
forms in other Teutonic languages (thought by etymologists to derive from
an Aryan word form denoting adoration or sacrifice) had likewise been in
use from remote pre-Christian times. Those word forms were adopted

with continuity of meaning by the Christian missionaries to the Anglo-Saxons and to the other Germanic tribes.

The same God whom those peoples named and distantly knew through natural religion they came to know in a higher and clearer manner through the Christian revelation now brought to them. So it was everywhere in the great missionary outreach of the Church throughout the world. The nations of the earth heard the preachers of the new faith speaking to them as messengers of the heavenly power whom they already named and invoked in their own mother tongues. The Christian missionaries, while never applying to God (but rather avoiding with abhorrence) specific names that they saw as associated with polytheistic or idolatrous cults—such as Zeus, Jupiter, Thor, or Siva—readily adopted the generic name and title that was in general use in the language and religious culture of each pagan people to designate supreme deity. Such names were Christianized by their adoption in preaching, worship, and translations of the Bible. Their baptism by the Church implicitly testifies to its conviction that humankind's natural cognizance of God by reason is precursory to and fulfilled by the Christian revelation and faith.

But how can natural theology be valid? Agnostic objections are brought to argue that knowledge of God from nature is impossible. Since spirit and matter are by definition distinct and incommensurable, and since an impassable gulf lies between the finite and the infinite, how can God, proclaimed to be supreme spirit and infinitely other than his creatures, be known from this finite world of matter which provides the data for human reason? Since human language expresses finite concepts drawn from human experience, how can our words ever truly refer to that infinite and unknowable Other?

Does not natural theology therefore involve an inherent contradiction—namely, the claim that the human mind can know what is in principle unknowable to it? How can any human words about transcendent divine mystery be anything more than wishful metaphors, telling us nothing meaningful about what must inevitably remain for finite minds an unknown "X"? The same radical objections are brought against the possibility of revealed theology, which uses the same earthbound conceptual language as natural theology.

Those agnostic objections notwithstanding, human reason itself testifies in all ages that it does gain awareness of the divine from the world of experience, and expresses that awareness by religious words and rites. *"Ab esse ad posse valet illatio*": from the fact that something does happen we have proof that it can happen, even though we may find it difficult to give a clear philosophical explanation of how it is possible. Moreover reason itself, reflecting more deeply on its own processes, can see that the objections cited above are not cogent.

Epistemology as Antechamber to Higher Wisdom

Epistemology, the study of how we know, provides an antechamber to the higher wisdom of theology. I here sketch an outline of the epistemology of the perennial philosophy, especially as presented by St. Thomas Aquinas, and of the answers it gives to the objections outlined above. In so doing I take passing account of antisophical theories currently in vogue which would deny any stable certainties in human thinking. However, no detailed engagement with the subtleties of postmodernism, deconstructionism, poststructuralism, and other similar "isms" will be found in these pages.

Human beings come to rational consciousness with no innate knowledge or preformed ideas, even of God. Although to know him is the central purpose and ultimate goal of our rational nature, our natural knowledge of him must, like all human knowledge, be acquired through a process of learning and discovery. That process is rooted in sense-knowledge. Empiricism is in truth the necessary starting point of epistemology. Our mind has no direct access to spiritual reality independently of the material world in which we are embodied.

The epistemological first premise of Aristotle, Aquinas, and other great metaphysical realists is in agreement with that of modern proponents of atheistic materialism in asserting that there is nothing we know rationally that does not depend on what has first come through sensory experience of our material environment. "Our knowledge even of the first principles of reasoning takes its rise from the senses," St. Thomas affirms.[3] Yet the collective wisdom of humankind refutes doctrinaire materialists when they assert that matter is the only reality, and that our rational consciousness itself, and the universal truths and values that it apprehends, are merely by-products of matter and its energies.

The scope of the human intellect is clearly distinguishable from that of the senses and sensory imagination that we share in common with the irrational animals. Although sense-knowledge provides the basic data for all its operations, the intellect has a reach far above and different in kind from that of the senses, which record only the phenomena of bodily experience. In coming to that higher cognition through rational search and intellectual discovery, and in retrieving it from memory, the spiritual life-principle of the human person is indeed completely dependent on the functioning of the biological processes of the body that it animates. Physical science can tell us much about those processes, but since its scope is limited to investigation of the properties of matter, it can say nothing, whether in proof or disproof, about the stupendous power of the human mind to discern, in the material world apprehended by the senses, non-material meaning, truth, and spiritual values. The proof of that power cannot be found in physics and chemistry, but may be directly apprehended in the personal experience of intellectual consciousness itself. Aquinas thus states the proper limits of empiricism:

Intellect is so called because it knows the inwardness of things. For to know by intellect is, as it were, "to read within" [*est enim intelligere quasi "intus legere"*]. Sense and imagination know only exterior phenomena; intellect alone penetrates to the essential reality . . . When we say that our mind's knowledge has its origin in sense, it does not mean that sense apprehends what the mind knows, but that from the data which sense apprehends the mind is led to what lies beyond sense.[4]

The basic axiom of empiricism, *"nihil in intellectu nisi prius fuerit in sensu . . . ,"* must then be clarified by the addition of an explanatory clause: *". . . nisi ipse intellectus."* That is, anglicized, "There is nothing in the intellect that was not first in the senses—*except the nature and function of the intellect itself.*" Sense-knowledge provides the material data, but it is only the non-material intellect that has the stupendous power of abstracting from that data true knowledge of universal reality.

Yet the question returns: how can that be? How can bodily sensations and sensory images drawn from matter provide the basis for such universal intellectual knowledge? How can a spiritual soul discover higher truth through the neural processes of an animal body?

The answer of the perennial philosophy to these questions may be summarized as follows. The one incomposite soul within the human organism is both the animating principle of an individual body, coordinating all its physiological and sensory processes, and an immortal spirit whose rationality opens the human person to awareness of universal reality. In the essential body-soul unity, that unitary life-principle activates and unifies sense-perception, imagination, emotions, and memory all under the primacy of reason. As immaterial intellect, it draws meaning from the manifold of sensory data which, as biological life-principle, it has coordinated into connected images and memory traces in its cerebral sensorium, by means of intricate neural processes on which modern science progressively throws greater light. Physiologically, this sensory system, though more complex, is not essentially different from that possessed by the irrational animals. In human life, however, it provides the medium from which the intellect draws the data for its rational cognition of all reality, corporeal and incorporeal.

The Preconditioned Structure of the Human Intellect

In the process of rational cognition itself there are to be distinguished two stages or aspects: first, the assimilation and classification of the data of experience in meaningful conceptual molds; and second, the synthesis and interpretation of those conceptual patterns of thought by discursive reasoning, leading to judgment on the reality that they manifest.

Under the first aspect, our intellect apprehends and collates the manifold of sensory and imaginative data according to certain predetermined categories or patterns of thinking within itself. Those conceptual patterns are reflected and expressed in the linguistic patterns of human vocabulary, grammar, and syntax. The grammatical parts of speech common to all the languages of humanity correspond to those *a priori* categories of mental apprehension, which in turn correspond to the structure of extra-mental reality. Thus, for instance, nouns and pronouns denote substantive entities; adjectives denote their properties and states, transient or permanent; prepositions denote the relations between them; verbs denote their acting and interacting, and adverbs the manner of such activity. The moods of verbs—indicative, subjunctive, interrogative, optative, imperative, infinitive—reflect the different modes and parameters of the intellect's exploration and grasping of reality in act. The ordered structure and sequence of syntactic discourse corresponds to the intelligible order discernible in the universe of experience.

Under the second aspect of our rational cognition, that of synthesis and interpretation of the conceptual data, our intellect, from its initial grasp of reality according to those innate conceptual categories, proceeds to make true inference and judgment about it in accordance with the operative norms of judgment, likewise innate, which we call the first principles of reason. Here too, our very experience of logical thought reflects the prior operative processes by which the intellect naturally interprets and judges what is true or false. The primary and dynamic sense of the expression, "the first principles of reason," must be distinguished from the consequent sense in which that expression is used to refer to axiomatic propositions formulated as premises for logical argument. It is only because of our intellect's pre-established potency to judge truly and surely what is or is not in conformity with universal reality that we are consequently able to formulate and express in words true propositions applicable to the logical exploration of that reality, such as the principles of contradiction, of causality, of finality.

Aquinas dwells on the distinction between those two phases in the mind's operative grasp of truth, namely, between the attainment of intellectual understanding and the discursive reasoning that precedes and leads to it:

> What we directly and naturally apprehend is said to be grasped by intellectual understanding. Thus intellect itself is said to be the permanent possession of first principles. Human souls are called rational inasmuch as they acquire their knowledge of truth by a discursive process. Such process is needful because of the weaker intellectual light within them: for if (like the angelic spirits) they had plenitude of intellectual light, they would, by immediate grasp of those first principles, comprehend their total potential, grasping by direct intuition all that could be deduced from them.[5]

Thus the term "rational" is applied more precisely to the discursive process of reasoning by which the intellect collates and appraises the intelligible data drawn from sensory experience. The conclusive act of intellect, Aquinas explains, is its explicit recognition and affirmation of the truth implicit in those data, achieved when it judges according to the predetermined first principles which govern its operation. "To understand [*intelligere*] is to grasp truth directly; to reason [*ratiocinari*] is to proceed from one intellectual truth to another . . . Thus ratiocination relates to intellectual understanding as movement towards a term relates to arrival there, or as seeking relates to possessing."[6] Reasoning and intellection are not two diverse powers but two distinguishable phases of the unitary operation of the human intellect, as can be realized by reflection on our processes of knowing.[7] In its intellective act of judgment the mind intuitively certifies what it has discovered by its preliminary process of discursive reasoning.

Philosophers as culturally diverse as Aristotle, Aquinas, and Kant have attested and pondered deeply on the basic epistemological fact that all human beings are preconditioned to think within the same rational framework of categories of perception and principles of reasoning. Kant's critique of the processes of human knowing, deeply perceptive though it was, was limited by his agnostic premise that the speculative reason cannot directly reach reality itself, but only the data of consciousness as perceived according to the innate categorical molds of our rational consciousness. Those who are not constrained by that premise can ask and find answer to the deeper questions: what is prior to those *a priori* categories and principles in our mind? How can it be that they govern all our thinking, and all its linguistic expression? In our search for the meaning of life and universal reality, what are the implications of that pre-programming of the structure and processes of our intellect?

Kant himself, though he held that in the sphere of pure reason we cannot know reality as it is in itself, but only as conditioned by the *a priori* postulates of the mind, considered that in the sphere of the practical reason the "categorical imperative" of moral duty is an experiential postulate of the highest significance in human life.[8] He found in awareness of the absolute imperative of conscience not a rational proof of the existence of God, but a higher bidding to make fideist assent and submission to God. He expressed this basic life-attitude in a celebrated dictum: "I had to remove knowledge to make way for faith."

Subtle wordsmiths in the present age who reduce philosophy to analysis of the meaning of logical propositions do not usually concern themselves with the first foundations and preconditioned structures of human thought. Bertrand Russell, who considered it possible to reduce the prerequisites for logical thinking and argument to five generally accepted "postulates," did speculate in passing on their origin. He thought it plausible to explain them thus: "Psychologically, they are the end of a long series of refinements which start with habits of expectation in animals."[9] A more recent school of "sociobiological" theorists, who likewise assert that what we take to be objective rational truth is a mere product of evolutionary utility, develop their dogma to reach the conclusion that even our conviction of the laws of physics and mathematics is such a product, which has become ingrained in our cerebral tissue because of its superior survival value. A guru of that school explains, "Those proto-humans who believed in $2+2=4$, rather than $2+2=5$, survived and reproduced, and those who did not, did not."[10]

Immune from such sophistries, those who reflect more deeply on the cogent force of the antecedent patterns and principles governing all our rational thinking, and on the universal character and self-authenticating certainty of our grasp of reality, find there a pointer to true wisdom.

The Noetic Ladder between Earth and Heaven

The first rung of the ladder of human knowing that leads upwards to God is, then, the abstractive power of the human intellect to formulate general concepts from its prior sensory perception of material objects. Not only does it thereby form concepts that are applicable to all the concrete individuals of a class, but it discerns and conceptualizes the regularities in the world of experience that we call the laws of nature. By more searching mental investigation it can come to discern in those regularities the principles of logic, of mathematics, of the physical sciences, and of speculative philosophy.

Moreover the intellect, unclouded and unimpeded, can by direct reflection on its own activity apprehend its innate power to pronounce certain judgment on truth or falsehood according to those rational principles that are universally true for all, everywhere. Exercise of that power is self-authenticating. In judging reality, the human mind is implicitly aware (and by deeper introspection can be explicitly aware) of its own pre-established harmony with the real. In a concise and penetrating passage, Aquinas sums up this fundamental truth of epistemology:

Truth is known by the intellect inasmuch as it reflects on its own act—that is, not only as knowing its own act but as knowing its correspondence with reality. Now this cannot be known unless the nature of the act is known. This again cannot be known without the nature of the original power from which it proceeds being known: and that is the intellect itself, the nature of which is to be in conformity with reality.[11]

The insight expressed in that passage resolves—and dissolves—the so-called Critical Problem which has loomed so large in Western philosophy since the time of Descartes. It is not necessary or possible to construct by deductive argument a logical bridge validating the objectivity of our knowledge of the non-self. Such validation does not depend upon logical argument; it lies in the very exercise of rational understanding and judgment. We have certain awareness of it by experiential reflection on our power to judge truly. *"Leges entis sunt leges mentis"*—"The laws of being are the laws of mind." That is a truth that we grasp in the experience of knowing before we express it in logical statement.

Thus human beings in their rational knowing bring the manifold of empirical data into conscious and coherent unity. By virtue of their inborn power to reason and to judge surely according to universally valid principles, they are able not only to attain practical ends for ensuring survival and livelihood for themselves and others, and to pursue crafts, arts, and natural sciences, but also to seek the meaning of the world and of their life. The practical and speculative knowledge that they draw by abstraction from experience of the material world is expressed in conceptual language which has corresponding meaning in their many different tongues. Their collective conclusions are distilled into the various thought-systems and cultures of the earth.

Exploring the intelligibility inherent in the world of matter is then the primary sphere of activity of the intellect, proportioned to the nature of the human soul as spirit-in-matter. But the intellect is also possessed of a higher potentiality, extending beyond that proportionate sphere and enabling it to have knowledge of reality that transcends matter. Inclined by its very nature to do so, it eventually infers the existence of the ultimate divine reality that encompasses all beings and is the meaning of its own existence. It concludes that the pure perfections and values which it discerns in its experience of this world have higher reference to that divine reality. It is from that intellective process that the natural theology of humanity is derived, to be thereafter expressed in a common pattern of religious language—language which eventually becomes the vehicle of God's higher revelation of himself.

So we come to realize that in the data of our senses and imagination, drawn from and dependent on matter, lies latent the spiritual treasure which it is our life's purpose to discover. We recognize the similarities and the essential difference between ourselves and the irrational animals. We share with them the physiological processes that sustain bodily life. Evidently, too, there is similarity between our sensory and imaginative consciousness and that of the higher animals. As in all animal life, our emotions, passions, sensibilities, and natural propensities are essentially conditioned by physical, chemical, and genetic factors; but uniquely in human life they are suffused with the rationality of the spiritual life-principle which actuates them. In the unity of human consciousness our imaginative and affective awareness shares the Godward dynamism of the rational soul that animates the body. "Lord, you have made us for yourself, and our heart is restless till it rests in you."[12]

Possession of rational consciousness, though its exercise can be impeded by physical factors, belongs to the very identity of the human self, to the vital principle that individualizes each of us as a person. The spiritual self is not a direct object of our knowing, for it is the prior subject of all our knowing. Yet in the exercise of reason there is concomitant certainty of the reality of the knowing self, of the "I" who thinks, judges, and acts. I have experiential certainty that it is the same "I" who acts and suffers from infancy to old age, who digests and dreams, who laughs and limps, who aches and meditates, who sweats and mourns, who breathes and bleeds, who craves nourishment for both body and spirit, who thinks and loves and seeks the meaning of life.

Memory gives purposeful continuity to the intellect's grasp of reality and enduring witness to our personhood. There is heavenly wisdom also to be found in reflecting on the mysterious fact and immediate experience of memory, as St. Augustine testifies with reverent awe in the tenth book of his *Confessions.* Our memory links our life's rational experience in a unity, certifying at every moment the enduring identity of our self through all life's journeying. As the conscious continuity of our intellective and spiritual life, rational memory is incorporeal, pertaining to the soul as immortal spirit; but, like all our rational activity, it is essentially dependent for its exercise on the processes of the body animated by that spirit. Just as our intellectual cognition depends on the brain's collation of sense data, from which it abstracts rational meaning, so, for the recall and reuse of its previously acquired knowledge, our intellectual memory likewise continuously depends on our bodily sensorium, which in a complex store of cerebral memory traces preserves records of sense-data perceived and collated in past experience.

The questing mind that rises from matter to spiritual awareness, reflecting on its own pre-established conformity with extra-mental reality, truth, and goodness, comes to infer, with reverent awe, that this conformity has been pre-established by the One who is the origin of all matter and mind, of all reality, truth, and goodness. The source and author of this stupendous marvel of our intellect, by which we are open to all reality and by which we are conscious of our own personhood, must himself be supreme intellect, supreme reality, supremely personal. In his holy and mysterious creative plan he has made us as we are, in a state of wayfaring and searching. He has so ordained our life's probation that by a mediate process of discovery we are to rise from lowly sense-bound experience to a knowledge of universal reality and ultimately of himself. This pilgrim's progress of our mind is essentially linked with his call to live out our span of bodily life in conformity with his loving will. Not natural reason but only God's self-disclosure in Christ reveals to us that this pilgrim journey of human life towards himself is encompassed in a supernatural destiny that far surpasses the capacity of our reason to discern.

The Analogy of Being, Bridge across Infinity

What of the radically agnostic objection, already sketched above, which is brought against the very possibility of a meaningful idea of God? Since there must necessarily be an infinite gulf between finite human knowers and the postulated divine object of their knowing, surely it follows that there must be discontinuity of meaning in that process of reasoning from creatures to Creator, which is claimed as the basis of natural theology and as the precondition of revealed theology?

True it is that our reason cannot adequately comprehend how there can be such a bridge across infinity, since it cannot penetrate the mystery of creation; but reverent reflection brings a measure of understanding. Underlying all its conceptualizing and reasoning is the intellect's basic awareness of *being*, which is indefinable because it precedes all definition and grounds all knowing. Created being, from which the human intellect draws knowledge of its transcendent source, must necessarily have some existential correspondence to the source from which it proceeds and on which it depends. It is because of that ineffable relation, necessarily and intrinsically linking created beings to the creative Being (though not him to them), that human minds, which are made to be conformed to universal reality, can have true concepts about God, immeasurably inadequate though those concepts must be. The language of natural theology in which those concepts are expressed, and which revealed theology adopts and perfects, does consequently express truth about him.

If there were no such intrinsic relation, no participatory likeness in the very being of created things to the creative Being from whom they continuously draw existence, God would indeed be for us an unknown and unknowable "X." Human thoughts and words, which are all grounded in our experience of finite being, could have no meaningful reference to him. What Catholic philosophers call *analogia entis*, "the analogy of being"— namely, the existential relationship of created beings to creative Being which our mind is preconditioned to apprehend—is the basis of all truth and meaning in human thinking and speaking about God. It is especially from our knowledge of what is true and good in the human spirit that we can have analogical knowledge of the truth and goodness of the supreme divine Spirit.

In Chapters 8 and 14 I shall return to reflection on that mysterious analogy of being, the cognitional basis of all theology, both natural and revealed. This book is subtitled, *On Reason, Faith, and Sacred Being*. The relation of finite beings to infinite and all-holy Being is its ever recurring theme. On a later page I make further mention of a current of postmodernist, deconstructionist, and anti-metaphysical thought, influenced by the writings of Nietzsche and Heidegger, which may fairly be described as a philosophy of anti-being. In one form, as in the writings of John Paul Sartre, it is a defiantly proclaimed atheist creed. In another form an attempt is made to present it as a Christian apologetic for a fideistic life-stance that spurns the philosophical wisdom of ultimate Being by which traditional Catholic theology has been supported, and which has been trenchantly reaffirmed by Pope John Paul II in his recent encyclical *Fides et ratio*. A book has even been written with the title, *God Without Being*.[13] I make further mention of this endeavor on a later page.

By its innate possession of the primary categories and operative principles of thought, the spiritual intellect precontains in itself potential possession of all that is. Thus Aquinas can write, "in a manner, the mind is all being," and, "in one who is taught, what is learned already pre-existed."[14] In another pregnant phrase he sums up the latent orientation of the intellect to God: "Every knower is implicitly knowing God." Knowing is a grasping of being, and being is ultimately God-likeness, imprinted in all things by the influx of the creative power that holds them all in existence and empowers them to act.

As our intellect is naturally ordained to know God, so also is our will naturally ordained to obey him, to love him, and to find happiness in him. Whoever wills good is implicitly willing God's will; whoever loves aright is implicitly loving God; whoever longs for true happiness is implicitly longing for God.[15] The goal of our earthly pilgrimage is to make explicit what is implicit in such knowing, willing, loving, and longing.

Thus the proclivity we have by nature to find our way to God in and through the world of his making is not merely a prompting to infer his existence by a logical process in the mind. It engages our whole self, our intellect and will, and all our affective consciousness and striving. Under the sway of right reason, our emotions and affections are drawn to higher good in the living of our lives. The ascent of the soul to God by the ladder of created things is energized by yearning and love, and by the sense of awe and wonder that is evoked in us by the beauty, harmony, peace, and purposiveness of the universe in which we are embodied and which mirrors him. We acknowledge his holy presence not only by intellectual assent but also by the living liturgy of our joys and sorrows, by music and song, by service and self-offering, by joining in the fellowship of love that is his earthly kingdom.

Our Godfaring is then a lived experience, not simply a process of philosophical speculation. Rational arguments from creatures to Creator, from caused to First Cause, from image to Exemplar, from purposive order and design to divine Designer, are indeed conclusive for the human mind that does not rebel against its inborn imperative to seek and know truth concerning God. But if the natural evidence of God's existence is seen only as a logical conclusion from syllogistic reasoning it is as yet like the notation of the score of a great symphony, where indeed the printed notes correctly signify the sounds and sequence of the music, but are unavailing in themselves to manifest the ordered beauty and power of the masterpiece resounding in the ears and heart of the hearer.

As our reason is created to ascend to knowledge of God from the starting point of bodily experience, so also our psychological, emotional, and aesthetic constitution is preconditioned to further that ascent. As all our knowing and willing of good is implicitly knowing God and embracing his will, so all our experiencing of goodness, truth, and beauty—in human love and altruism, in the natural world, in literature, in music and the visual arts—is implicitly joying in the goodness, truth, and beauty of God. In my ninth chapter I offer further reflections on the enigmatic sacredness of this world of matter of which we ourselves are a part.

Chapter 3

The Sources and Content of Natural Theology

All that is good, everything that is perfect, is given us from above; it comes down from the Father of all light; with him there is no such thing as alteration, no shadow of a change.

James 1.17

Created in God's image and called to know and love him, man in search of God discovers certain "ways" of coming to knowledge of him. These are also called "proofs for the existence of God," not in the same sense in which the natural sciences seek demonstration, but rather in the sense of "converging and convincing arguments" which allow us to attain true certainty about the truth. These "ways" of approaching God take their starting point from creation: that is, from the physical world and from the human person.

Catechism of the Catholic Church, §31

Atheistic thinkers, contending that nothing exists except matter and its energies, reject and ridicule the notion that the human mind can have knowledge of a supreme spiritual being by rational reflection on empirical reality. They put forward widely differing theories to explain the origin of the idea of God. According to some, religious notions first arose in remote prehistory from the naïve fears, fantasies, and necessities of primitive man confronted with threatening and inexplicable physical phenomena. They variously conjecture that the origins of religion can be traced back to primitive animism, to totemism, to fetishism, to sun-worship, to ancestor-worship, or to sorcery and magic. They suppose that such notions then evolved into polytheist belief and cult, and that the more sophisticated notion of a "high god" or ultimate divine power developed at a much later stage.[1] They brush aside anthropological research which indicates, on the contrary, that an overarching primal monotheism, the sense of a Great Spirit in and above all things, is general even in those religious cultures that are commonly classified as animistic and polytheistic.[2]

Others put forward reductionist theories of a different kind. While admitting the prevalence of the notion of God in all societies, both primitive and developed, they explain it away either as an illusory projection of basic emotions and an expression of repressed cravings latent in the subconscious mind;[3] or, more subtly, as a defensive attitude acquired through biological evolution, whereby the rational animal became better equipped to survive in a universe that is ultimately irrational and purposeless. Thus Lewis Wolpert, while dismissing religion as prescientific and irrational, nevertheless holds that the natural propensity for religious thinking is an evolved instinct conducive to the survival of the human species, since "a full apprehension of man's condition would drive him insane."[4] An interesting variant of such views was that of Carl Gustav Jung. Although earlier disposed, like his master Freud, to regard belief in God as infantilism and illusion, Jung later moved to positive appraisal of it as psychologically beneficial. He concluded that human beings have "a natural religious function," and that, embedded in what he called the collective unconscious of all humanity, there is a universal "archetype of the God-image" which needs to be made conscious for the mental health of every adult.[5]

I refer to those reductionist theories about the supposed origins of God-awareness and religion only to pass them by. My purpose here is not to spend time in refuting or debating them, but to reflect on the common wisdom of humanity which does find Godward meaning in the reality that we experience. Theoretical atheists are indeed a small minority of the human race. The great majority of men and women have through the ages shown awareness of the "hidden power present in the rhythm of nature and in the events of human life," the Holy towards which their religious aspirations are directed.

The Two Sources of Natural Theology

There are then two sources from which human beings in every age gain rational knowledge of God and of their relation to him: one outward, from contemplation of his created works; the other inward, from reflection of the knowing mind upon itself. In the religious quest of humanity those two sources of natural religion are essentially linked and mutually corroborate one another.

From the first of these sources, the external evidence of the created universe, our reason finds testimony of God as the supreme origin of all things, as the supreme actuality and power by which they are empowered to act, as the supreme exemplar to which they have some far-off similitude, as the supreme designer and sustainer of the cosmic order which binds them together, as the supreme purpose giving purpose to them all, and as the enduring ground of all being and act.

The second of the sources of humanity's natural knowledge of God is the internal evidence of intellectual consciousness in each person. Most insistently, awareness of the moral law within us, steering us towards good and away from evil both as individuals and as members of society, prompts us to acknowledge our origin from and subordination to a sovereign lawgiver who is supremely good, wise, just, merciful, and loving.

With his openness to truth and beauty, his sense of moral goodness, his freedom and the voice of his conscience, with his longings for the infinite and for happiness, man faces the question within himself about God's existence. In all this he discerns signs of his spiritual soul. The soul, the "seed of eternity we bear in ourselves, irreducible to the merely material," can have its origin only in God.[6]

Human reason is able to apprehend not only *that* God is, but at the same time something of *what* he is. It comes to infer his existence by those converging "ways" referred to in the second passage cited at the head of this chapter, which together form one way. "Starting from movement, becoming, contingency, and the world's order and beauty, one can come to a knowledge of God as the origin and end of the universe."[7] In acknowledging God's being, the human mind also attributes to him the transcendental perfections which it recognizes as belonging to universal being as such—goodness, truth, beauty, oneness, purposiveness, causal power. Those transcendental perfections, which are apprehended through our experience of created beings yet which are proper to none of them and imply no necessary limit or imperfection, we affirm as veritable Names of God.

The divine origin of all things is not merely postulated as uncaused cause, as unmoved mover, as ineluctable cosmic order, as remote and impersonal metaphysical principle. From reflection on our own personal consciousness, and especially on our moral conscience, we human beings attain analogical awareness that the author of our being, to whom we are related as persons and to whom our lives must be conformed, is supremely personal and holy. *The Catechism of the Catholic Church* expresses these truths as follows:

All creatures bear a certain resemblance to God, most especially man, created in the image and likeness of God. The manifold perfections of creatures—their truth, their goodness, their beauty—all reflect the infinite perfection of God. From those perfections of his creatures, consequently, we can name God (Wisdom 13.5). Admittedly, in speaking about God like this, our language is using human modes of expression; nevertheless it does truly attain to God himself, though unable to express him in his infinite simplicity.[8]

Indeed, it may be objected, is not all this anthropomorphism—the depiction of God in the *morphe* or likeness of man? Yes, in a sense it is, but only because God has first created man in his own likeness, enabling us to make remote but true inference of his infinite goodness and dignity from the finite goodness and dignity he has given to humanity. It is because human nature is, in an analogical but true sense, theomorphic that we can validly use anthropomorphic concepts and language to refer to God, while negating all that is inapplicable in such usage. The *via negativa,* by which the soul's ascent to God in the life of grace and mystical contemplation must be purified, is already implicit in natural theology. While attributing the perfections and values that we encounter in this world to the ultimate divine reality in the highest degree, the religious wisdom of humankind acknowledges that he is infinitely superior to all that we experience and conceive, that in our concept of him we must negate all the limitations of the mutable created being from which we derive our intimations of him. In the trenchant words of the Fourth Lateran Council, "Whatever similitude is recognized between Creator and creature, there must be recognized still greater dissimilitude."[9]

A Syllabus of Natural Theology

Is it possible to formulate a syllabus of natural theology, as discerned by the perennial wisdom of humanity? A summary of its substantive content may be given by bringing together the main elements already mentioned above.

Human beings find themselves oriented towards what they apprehend as good, true, ethically right, loving, and caring; towards what is unitive, beautiful, purposively ordered, and fulfilling; towards what is life-giving, life-enhancing, and beneficial for the common good. When they encounter those noble qualities in their personal experience of human life they are drawn to respond to them with admiration and reverence, recognizing that those supramaterial perfections have some relation and similitude to the ultimate power who upholds the world, who is both within and beyond it. By predicating those perfections of him supremely, they form some unified, albeit analogical, conception of his nature.

Accordingly, in the religious cultures of humankind the ultimate One from which the manifold world originates is commonly proclaimed to be supremely good, loving, knowing, powerful, purposeful, provident, wise, beneficent, merciful, and just. To him are also applied titles derived from the exercize of authority in human society, which point to the divine exemplar of all authority and providential care: titles such as Lord, Master, Father, Ruler, Lawgiver, and Judge.

Natural religion is everywhere social as well as personal. Human beings, both as individuals and in community, feel a need and a duty to offer corporate cult and obedience to the divine supreme being. They pray to him to aid them in their daily needs, to guard them from adversity, and to deliver them from evil. They fear his just anger at their wrongdoing and seek to propitiate it. They offer thanksgiving for his mercy and bounty. They adore him as provident Lord of all.

Natural religion honors the primary human society, the family, bonded together in kinship, love, and mutual support. Its starting point, marriage, is commonly accorded a sacral character and is ritually celebrated. The interpersonal love and fidelity between spouses, with their care for each other and for their children, is recognized to be in conformity with a universal principle of love and duty, to dishonor which is shameful. The loving providence of God is seen reflected in human parenthood, especially in the self-giving love and care of motherhood.

At all levels of human society natural religion manifests itself in ethical codes of conduct which are held to be binding on all and for which divine sanction is recognized. The unique divine Being, designated by many names, is revered as the source and pattern of justice and moral obligation both for individuals and for communities; as the ultimate good, beauty, and beatitude which is the goal of all human striving and merit; as the author of eternal reward and retribution; as the Holy to whom prayer and worship are directed by word and rite.

Natural religion not only recognizes the permanent relationship between the conscious self and the ultimate divine reality to whom worship and service are due, but also attests a general conviction that the spiritual principle of human life cannot cease to exist at the death of the body. Indeed it senses a congruity in expecting an eventual reunion, in some manner, of soul with body. There is a general perception that this mortal life is a probation and a moral arena, and that other-worldly sanctions will hereafter discriminate between good and evil deserts.

This expectation of immortality is a basic article of natural theology. It is a yearning not merely to continue to exist as we do now, but to reach ultimate consummation of our existence in a heavenly state of felicity. The destined goal beyond this life of probation is commonly conceived as attainment of bliss in the presence of the divine reality, and in the company of those who have lived righteously. With the expectation of after-life survival goes a sense of continuity and solidarity with those who have gone before, especially with ancestors and the beloved dead.

There is a concordant sense in the diverse religious cultures that the evil and wrongdoing in the world, though it runs darkly counter to divine goodness, cannot ultimately prevail over or thwart it. The human mind, forming a natural theology through reflection on the world and on the self, also feels the need for theodicy; that is, it seeks to vindicate sovereign divine goodness and power in the face of the enigma of evil in the world and in human life. In my eleventh chapter I reflect further on the speculations within the belief-systems of the world concerning the problem of evil which ever disquiets the human heart seeking ultimate truth.

Evidently, because of physical and moral impediments, there is not practical opportunity for every human being to explicitate for her or himself an understanding of those truths of natural religion. Many do so individually; the wisdom of humanity does so collectively. The religious truths and values summarized in the above outline, which form the substantive content of natural theology, resonate in the hearts of people in every age and place. Cast in diverse thought-patterns and idioms, they are commonly embraced in the teaching of the various religious cultures of the world. Yet the natural religion of humanity is prone to distortion by human error, passions, and illusions. It stands in need of purification and elevation by God's grace and higher revelation of himself.

These reflections on natural religion lead me on to fuller discussion, first of its expression in the organized religions of the world, then of its relation to the revealed religion of Christ. The first of those themes is the subject of the next chapter; the second is the subject of Chapters 5 and 6.

Chapter 4

Religion and Religions
Differing Therapies for the Human Predicament

Men look to the various religions for an answer to the cryptic riddles of human existence, which today as ever in the past deeply trouble their hearts. What is man? What is the meaning and purpose of our life? What is goodness and what is sin? Whence does suffering arise and to what purpose? What is the way to reach true happiness? What happens at death, and what can be known of judgment and sanctions after death? And finally, what is that ultimate and ineffable mystery which embraces our entire existence, from which we take our origin and towards which our life's course is set?

Second Vatican Council, Nostra aetate, §1

The natural religion of humanity described in the preceding chapter is not just the inner sentiment of the individual—"what a man does with his solitariness," as A. N. Whitehead defined it. Nor are the religions of the world only doctrinal creeds or confessions of belief. They are also ways of life, social groupings and loyalties, codes of conduct, systems of corporate ritual; they are historical continuities, schools of formation for each new generation, repositories of communal values and ideals, shared pathways to spiritual experience, and expressions in art, music, and myth of the common quest for the divine reality.

Human beings find religious meaning and purpose both in their individual and in their social life, whether in primal cultures or in the more developed belief systems which present their message as having universal relevance beyond tribal and regional boundaries. They express that meaning and purpose in communities imbued with a sense of the sacred and of ethical law. Sages, spiritual guides, and wielders of religious authority arise in those communities, elaborating systems of doctrine and observance to respond to the needs of the human condition.

After two millennia of Christian mission the non-Christian religions, springing from and giving diversified social expression to natural religion, still sway the thinking and living of the greater part of the human race, even in this age of increasing secularism and indifference to belief. In our own time the Catholic Church has widened its vision and opened its heart to recognize and reverence the God-given truth and goodness to be found in those religions. In the words of the Second Vatican Council, they "strive in various ways to solace the inquietude of the human heart by proposing paths to follow, consisting of teachings, rules of life, and sacred rites."[1]

In marking out their various paths those belief systems, casting natural religion into many disparate and distinctive molds, mix with it their own interpretations, prescriptions, and innovations. The concepts and language in which they express their creeds often reflect cultural idiosyncrasies and aberrant philosophies. Humanity's intimations of deity can be, and often have been, clouded and degraded. Study of the history of religions provides abundant evidence of the corruption of natural religion by polytheism, superstition, and debased cultic practices. Just as individuals can, culpably or inculpably, deform or obscure their reason's natural awareness of God's presence in creation and of the inward law of conscience, so can communities and cultures do so collectively.

In the preceding chapter I offered a survey of the tenets of natural religion taken in general. In this chapter I turn to consider how that common religious consciousness of humanity is expressed, diversified, and often distorted in the organized religions of the world. There is evidently mutual incompatibility between the various belief systems on many substantial points. Yet their very differences serve to point to a wider backcloth against which the body of basic truths and values of natural religion that is common to them all may be discerned. One may classify under three main aspects the teachings about human existence and universal reality that are offered by them severally:

first, each in its own idiom offers an interpretation of the existential situation in which human beings find themselves, and which is the point of departure for their religious quest;

second, each points to goals towards which their adherents must tend, and attainment of which will bring them eventual fulfilment;

third, each prescribes ways and means by which their adherents are to proceed from the starting situation to the desired goal.

Taking those three aspects as a framework for inquiry, one may accordingly ask what answers each religion would give to the following three questions: *From what* initial situation does the religious quest take its rise? *To what* final attainment—this-worldly, other-worldly, or both—does it lead? *By what* means—human or divine or both—is that attainment to come about?[2] To offer a summary conspectus of the answers of the world's main religious cultures to those three basic questions is the object of the present chapter.

The divinely revealed religion of Christ, ushered in by the preliminary revelation given to the people of the Old Covenant, is essentially different from those belief systems elaborated by human reason. In it alone "the inquietude of the human heart" which those other religions seek to allay finds true solace and surcease. Nevertheless there are similarities between it and them. The three fundamental questions formulated above may also be asked of Christian faith, which responds to them with divinely assured answers. After first presenting a survey of the answers given to those three questions by the other religions of the world, I will then briefly set out, in comparison and contrast, the answers given by Christian revelation.

From What?

Each in its own way, all the world's religions may be said to offer a key to understanding the original situation of human life. Although their teachings about the nature of that original situation are very diverse, all are imbued with the sense of "that ultimate and ineffable mystery which embraces our entire existence," of a universal order and unseen power to which human life and destiny are related. That sense motivates the natural religious quest of humanity. In that quest there is both optimism about reality and sombre awareness of its dark depths. There is joy in present experience and in expectation of future fulfilment; there is also sorrow, fear, and endurance of physical and moral evil. Some creeds, affirming the given human situation as good, stress life acceptance and preservation of the *status quo* rather than the need for deliverance from evil. For instance, traditional Confucianism, Shinto, and some schools of Taoism see religion as essentially recognition and celebration of the fundamental harmony of the cosmos and the right ordering of human society as mirroring the archetypal heavenly order. The very word *kosmos*, used by the ancient Greeks to signify the universe, connotes the concept of its ordered wholeness. Generally, however, the religions of the world recognize the initial situation of human life as a predicament in which all stand in need of remedy or deliverance by recourse to higher spiritual power. Most immediately, that predicament is seen as subjection to the miseries, dangers, and material necessities of everyday living. Yet religious cultures, not excepting the primal religions, commonly offer a deeper analysis. They express a sense of spiritual insufficiency, a sighing for release from present anxiety and sorrow, from spiritual as well as material pollution, from ignorance and mental blindness, and a yearning for a higher development of life or soul.

All who seek to interpret reality and human life must address the problem of evil. In different concepts and language the belief systems of the world recognize that human lives and aspirations are set in an environment in which evil, both physical and moral, is pervasive and threatening. They teach that human beings are prey not only to outward dangers and evils, seen and unseen, but to folly, error, and sinfulness within themselves, inclining them to spiritual ruin. In some sense each religion may be said to claim a soteriological role: that is, each proclaims the need for salvation, and points a way to liberation from evil, ignorance, and woe both for individuals and for society.

In the religious thought systems which arose in and spread from India, the primal predicament in which all living beings are involved is presented as arising from the combination of the three cosmic principles of *dharma*, *karma*, and *samsara* in an all-embracing pattern. *Dharma* is a code of duty and right conduct, inherent in the existence of each soul and in society itself, which binds all according to their condition and governs every detail of their lives, both as individuals passing through the successive stages of life and socially as members of family, caste, and community. *Karma*, the inherent moral quality of deeds and the abiding fruit of deeds, proceeds from an impersonal and necessary law that brings to each soul due requital according to its antecedent merits or demerits. Both the inner bidding of *dharma* and the inexorable law of *karma* operate within the eternal wheel of *samsara*, the transmigration of souls in an unceasing cycle of births and deaths at various levels of existence, whether human or animal, heavenly or infernal.

The level of life at which *samsaric* reincarnation occurs is determined by each one's *karmic* deserts in previous existences. Apportionment of good or ill fortune in each succeeding life-span inevitably corresponds to the quality of the inherent *karma*, good or bad, that perdures in the soul from those preceding deserts resulting from its observance or breach of the dictates of *dharma*.

That pattern of cosmic moral accountancy is acknowledged as a fundamental datum of life by Hindus of all traditions and sects, and also by Jains, Buddhists, Sikhs, and followers of other sapiential traditions of Indian origin. The founding prophet of Sikhism, Guru Nanak, shared the common premise of the universal necessity of those three cosmic principles while preaching a pure monotheism and the omnicausality of God. It would seem to follow (though Guru Nanak did not expressly say so) that he assumed that such necessity, and all that resulted from it, proceeded from the predetermining decree of the Creator.

Buddhist teaching, while also presupposing as certain the eternal laws of *dharma*, *karma*, and *samsara*, concentrates on the fact and dire urgency of the human predicament, without concerning itself with metaphysical discussion of its origin and nature. Gautama Buddha likened one who would spend time on debating such questions to a man pierced by a poisoned arrow who refused to have it drawn out from the wound until he had found out who had shot it, what were his characteristics and lineage, from what kind of bow it was shot, and of what materials the bow and arrow were made. Such a man, instead of obtaining the vital remedy he so urgently needed for his wound, would die from it while seeking answers to his futile questions. In the Buddhist perspective, the human predicament is present existence. It is a state of radical ignorance and misery, of illusion concerning reality, truth, and selfhood; it is a state of unsubstantiality, impermanence, and all-pervasive suffering and sorrow. Those who ask why we are in this state and what constitutes eternal reality, are, according to the Buddha, asking "questions which do not help spiritual progress." What matters is to escape from the predicament.

There is no unanimity among the different schools of Taoism in their metaphysical speculation about ultimate reality. The teaching of the school of Lao-tzu on universal emptiness, non-being, and oneness has independent affinities with Buddhist metaphysical doctrine, especially as elaborated in the mystical teaching of Nagarjuna on experience of the ineffable Void, which is the womb and tomb of the illusory world.

Islam (now reckoned to encompass between a fifth and a quarter of the human race) also sees the predicament of humankind as radical ignorance. From this predicament Muhammad's message brings deliverance, but deliverance in a very different sense from that offered by Buddhist enlightenment. The predicament, according to Muslim teaching, is ignorance of Allah's almighty and all-provident will and of the code for human living that he is believed to command. *Shirk*, the idolatry of pagan religion, belonged to *jahiliyyah*, "the days of ignorance," in which men lived in subjection to frailty, delusion, and folly before the coming of the Qur'anic revelation.

For believing Jews the original setting which gives meaning and purpose to their religious quest is not a grievous predicament but a divine choice and vocation. The starting point for each Jew is the fact of being born a Jew, one of a people set apart by God for a special relationship to himself and for a special destiny. Unfolding in historical experience, the communal situation of the Jewish people has indeed often proved to be a dire predicament, but through all tribulations they hold fast to their conviction that God's revealed blessings and promises to his people remain valid forever, to be eventually fulfilled in an eschatological climax.

In the still surviving and once widely influential Zoroastrian creed, especially as elaborated by the medieval Pahlavi theologians, the setting of human life and world history is seen as a cosmic battle between good and evil, light and darkness, truth and falsehood. The sovereign deity and principle of good, Ahura Mazda, is opposed by a dark coeval principle of evil, Angra Mainyu. The former is lord of the blessed spirits, the Bounteous Immortals, the latter of the demons. The heavenly selves of men freely chose to descend to the material world, which had been contaminated and corrupted by the evil one, in order to engage his forces in decisive combat there. Gnostic, Manichaean, and Catharist belief systems likewise postulated a fundamental dualism of good and evil principles, with matter as the realm of evil. According to their teaching, matter itself is the predicament from which humanity needs escape.

Belief systems both of India and of China have a different conception of cosmic dualism. They conceive it not as a radical enmity between irreconcilable powers, but as a polarity in which opposites are paradoxically reconciled. Evil and good are seen by Hindu monists as two sides of the same coin. Chinese sages see the twin principles of *Yin* and *Yang*, of darkness and light, of conceiving and begetting, of the female and the male, of potency and act, of ceasing to be and coming to be, as two universal principles conjoined in all that exists.

The sombre awareness of ever-present evil can take morbid forms, of which history and anthropology show plentiful examples. Here, too, the religious instinct can be and often has been perverted into superstition, whereby prayerful supplication is supplanted by apotropaic magic. In all ages there are cults which foster obsessive preoccupation with demonic forces. Shamans, sorcerers, and soothsayers offer protection against malign influences and the strokes of pitiless fate. In my eleventh chapter I reflect further on humanity's multiple answers to the ever present problem of evil.

To What?

As well as elaborating their theories of ultimate reality, and of the human situation in particular, the religions of the world provide a solution to the predicament of human existence. Each of them, in its own pattern of thought and language, proclaims goals for life and a liberating end to which the religious quest is directed, to be realized either in time or in eternity, or to be partially achieved in this life and perfected in an after-life. For the individual, each religion offers guidance for progressing from the given life situation to a further perfection and final state. For society as a whole, each declares a corporate purpose, likewise to be progressively realized.

The more immediate objectives of such aspiration are visualized as pertaining to the here and now. Believers look to the satisfaction of present material needs and hopes; to protection from evils, dangers, and polluting influences in everyday life; and to the promotion of right relations between individuals and within the social group. Such desires give motivation to their prayer, worship, and codes of conduct. Withal their religious quest is not limited to simple impetration for present and future welfare and for material boons. They also conceive the goals of human life in less mercenary and more spiritual forms. The religions of the world express yearnings for inner purification and forgiveness of sins; for right development of personality, character, and mental attitudes; for conversion and spiritual rebirth; for living righteously and altruistically in conformity with higher divine law; for growth in knowledge of true reality; for moral and spiritual progress; for attainment of repose and beatitude in a heavenly afterlife (or for meriting a nobler reincarnation); for victory over evil and malign powers; and for final union with the divine reality that the cosmos enshrines.

Thus, to resume what was said in the previous chapter, the goals of the natural religious quest, though directly related to the present life, are not restricted to it. While humanity's religious aspiration is directed to pursuing those goals in the arena of this mortal life, it reaches beyond the pursuit of them here towards attainment of an all-fulfilling goal in some other sphere or state of existence hereafter, often visualized as an eternal haven and heaven of transforming bliss in which there is final justice and reward. That beatifying state is conceived of as eternal joy, both spiritual and even bodily; but beyond all as union with the universal holy reality. Arnold Toynbee summed up mankind's supreme common conviction as follows: "There is a presence in the Universe that is spiritually greater than man himself. Man's goal is to seek communion with the presence behind the phenomena and to seek it with the aim of bringing himself into harmony with this absolute spiritual reality."[3]

Speculation about the numinous power to which the course of human life is directed, and about the goal of union with that power, has taken many subtle forms, some of them strange and aberrant. Intricate systems of metaphysical thought concerning the divine Absolute have been constructed both in East and West. In some Eastern traditions especially, the sense of awe for an all-pervasive supernatural presence, found vividly in primal religion,[4] has been interpreted in the language of pantheist and impersonal monism. In Taoist and Confucian thought, in Buddhism, and especially in Advaita ("non-duality") schools of Hindu Vedanta, the ultimate reality is conceived as a unitary principle of cosmic order and power, beyond personhood and intelligibility, with which the existence of human beings is necessarily conformed but with which they cannot have personal relationship. The goal of the religious quest is rather to attain right perception of and attitude towards that mysterious reality.

In those monistic thought-systems the Absolute has been variously named as all-encompassing *Brahman*, as the Tao or Way of Heaven, as *r'ta* or cosmic order, as eternal Buddha-nature, as all-determining destiny or fate, as the unchanging ground underlying a flawed world of illusion and flux, and as *sunyavada* or the ultimate sacred Void. While the sages of those monist traditions considered it vain to seek to worship or serve that impersonal and inscrutable reality, they taught that human souls could, by ascetical practices and abstractive meditation, attain an ineffable realization of their own identity with it. The Advaitin school of Vedanta held that the soul, by realizing such identity, may attain final *moksha*, liberation from this illusory world of suffering and impermanence. Thereby it may find escape from the weary treadmill of *samsara* and from subjection to the law of *karma*, in order to attain final absorption in that holy mystery. Buddhism can be seen as a development of that same subtle strand of ancient Vedic wisdom.

Such rarefied monist speculations have been influential in some ages and cultures, but they are historic digressions from the enduring theism of mankind. A celebrated verse of the Hindu *Rig-Veda*, which sees the diverse names of the gods in the Aryan pantheon as all designating the selfsame divine reality, can be interpreted both in a pantheist and in a theist sense: "They call it Indra, Mitra, Varuna, Agni, and also heavenly, delightful Garutman: the Real is one, though sages name it variously."[5] In the ancient sacred texts of India, monistic and impersonal terms referring to the one ineffable reality are at times qualified by use of personal and purposive attributes to refer to that reality. Even the Upanishads, the mystical and monistic commentaries on the Vedas dating from around the middle of the first millennium, contain intimations of a monotheism lying beyond both polytheism or pantheist monism. They give an explicit expression of awed reverence for the all-encompassing world spirit, *Brahman*, phrased in theistic and personalized language: "He encircles all things: radiant and bodiless, unharmed and untouched by evil, all-seeing, all-wise, all-present, self-existent, he has made all things well and for ever."[6]

Adherents of Advaita Hindu religion, professing the identity of all souls with the Absolute, may still honor that ineffable reality with reverent ritual. To realize communion with it is to enter into *sat-chit-ananda*; that is, ultimate *Brahman* is not only absolute existence but also absolute consciousness and bliss. Who can say whether a profoundly theist sense of divine being and goodness may not exist within a cultural envelope of monist theory and apparently self-centred psychic techniques? In the *Sanatana Dharma*, "the eternal religion" of the Hindus, such a sense is pervasive.[7]

In Indian personal religion bleak theory yields to living experience. It still remains true that "Hinduism is fundamentally monotheist."[8] Fascinating though they may be to students of religious history and thought, the subtle speculations of the monistic sages, Sankara pre-eminent among them, have not eroded the enduring theistic devotion of the Indian peoples, which has been given profound theological expression by teachers such as Ramanuja, Mahdva, and Ramananda. Popular Mahayana Buddhism likewise seeks a holy and propitious heavenly patron to serve and to supplicate. There is a traditional and rueful maxim: "It is hard to have no one to worship and to invoke."[9] Meditation on an impersonal Absolute or yearning for the extinction of self in Nirvana fails to satisfy or correspond to the deepest religious aspirations of the Buddhist multitudes. Joyless and loveless metaphysical speculations do not provide them with a creed for living and loving. Even when they accept in theory a non-theist religious metaphysic, even through the distorting mists of pantheist and polytheistic beliefs, they obscurely seek God, loving and provident Lord of all and the true object of their worship, prayer, and life's course.

Thus within the multiform religion that has issued from the pulsating heart of India there are two radically different interpretations of the goal of human life. One is the subtle religious philosophy of an élite minority, the other the everyday creed of the worshipping majority. In Advaitin monism the goal is realization, by meditation and ascetical techniques, of the non-duality between *atman*, soul or self, and *Brahman*, the universal reality. In Dvaitin theism, which acknowledges the duality between the individual soul and the supreme deity (worshipped principally in the cult of Vishnu and his avatars, especially Krishna and Rama), the goal is ardent *bhakti*, devotion to and service of the divine Lord, leading to intimate and final communion with him. The latter interpretation is by far the more influential in the religious life of the Indian peoples.

Sages attempt to find common ground between those two creeds by distinguishing subtly between *nirguna Brahman*, divine reality without attributes, and *saguna Brahman*, the same reality with attributes. A somewhat similar divide appears within Buddhist religion between, on the one hand, the austere non-theism of Theravada that, true to the agnosticism of Gautama Buddha himself, affirms ultimate reality (*Dhammakaya*) without personality or form, and, on the other hand, the mitigated theism that is the creed of the far more numerous adherents of Mahayana traditions who worship heavenly divinity under various names and forms.

It has been pointed out that even the dualist belief system of Zoroastrianism, which seems to contradict monotheism, supposes an underlying monotheist interpretation of reality.[10] Presupposed in that creed, with its postulate of two rival spiritual powers, is an implicit theodicy, motivated by desire to vindicate the goodness and justice of the supreme deity in a cosmos in which the wicked undeservedly prosper and the just undeservedly suffer. Those dualists, Zoroastrians of Iran and Parsees of India, seek as their final goal eternal spiritual bliss with Ahura Mazda and the blessed spirits of his heavenly court. Gnostics and other anti-materialist dualists likewise seek supernal salvation in ultimate Spirit and the final release of their own spirit from its imprisonment in matter.

The fundamentally monotheistic religions of the world relate all life's goals to God, who is himself the total goal. Islam, while drawing on the Judaeo-Christian heritage, preaches monotheism in a distinctively imperative mood.[11] It proclaims man's primary purpose as absolute submission to the will of Allah, revealed by his Prophet, Muhammad. Muslims are defined as those who thus submit their will to his. By so doing, they may expect the reward of well-being and prosperity in this life and ultimate bliss in Paradise. Motivation to achieve that purpose is reinforced by fear of condemnatory judgment and hell.

Similar understanding of the divine purpose and of the heavenly objective of human living is expressed in the different dialects of other monotheistic cultures. The ageless religion of the Jewish people is likewise proclaimed in the imperative mood, centred on the will of God. Yet, whereas other main world religions profess their message as applicable to the condition and way of life of every human being and promote its general acceptance, historic Judaism has no missionary aim to convert the other peoples of the world—although, in fact, its influence in the religious history of the world has been immense.

The proximate goal in the religion of Israel, both for the individual and for the community, is faithful obedience to God and to the way of life prescribed by him in the *Torah*. The ultimate and divinely assured goal is conceived by Jewish orthodoxy as the redemption of the world and the establishment of the Kingdom of God, ushered in by the coming of the Messiah. Hope for communal redemption takes precedence over hope for individual redemption. While there is traditional belief in a resurrection in the last days, and in divine sanctions and a heavenly life to come, Jewish religious concern may be said to be directed primarily to this world rather than to the next.[12]

By What?

By what means, human or divine, or both, is the transit to be made from life's initial situation to its due term, according to the teachings of the various belief systems of humanity? All religions, not only those which have wide geographical spread, with developed institutional structures, sacred scriptures, and clearly articulated creeds, but also primal and non-literate religions which are proper to individual tribes and communities, assert universal religious truths and values and necessary connection between right conduct and achievement of the purpose of all human life. Commonly they teach doctrines, prayers, ritual acts, and codes of conduct by which their adherents are guided and enabled to live their lives aright and thereby to tend towards the common goal of liberation, beatitude, and divine union.

Preeminent among the means enjoined by the various religions as leading to the goal of the quest is personal and corporate worship. In their rites of adoration, prayer, and sacrifice, believers express their fourfold intent to adore and praise the deity, to ask his merciful forgiveness for their wrongdoing, to implore his favor and help in their needs, and to give him thanks for the good that he bestows upon them.

Some creeds attribute the attainment of salvation and the ultimate goal wholly to divine action; most acknowledge that the process requires human cooperation with divine empowerment. A picturesque simile used in Eastern religious thought illustrates the difference between those two alternative soteriologies by comparing them with the differing modes in which cats and monkeys safeguard their young. When the mother cat rescues her offspring from danger she seizes it by the scruff of the neck and carries it away, passive in the saving grip of her teeth; but when the mother monkey clasps her offspring with her paw to snatch it from danger, it must cooperate in its rescue by clinging to her as she bears it away to safety. The simile quaintly illustrates the difference between a theology of salvation by divine grace alone and a theology of salvation by divine grace working with and through the good works of human free will.

In common with theistic creeds throughout the world, those of Indian origin generally acknowledge the priority of divine initiative and empowerment in bringing about human salvation and achievement of the final end. Both Hindus who adhere to Dvaitin theist cults and Buddhists who follow Mahayana traditions freely invoke heavenly help. Notable among these Buddhist traditions is the Pure Land sect in China and other Far Eastern lands, who worship Amitabha Buddha and look forward to enjoying an enduring and blissful reward in a heaven of delights. Other Buddhas and Bodhisattvas in the Mahayana pantheon are likewise both invoked and adored as saviors. In contrast, Advaitin Hinduism and Theravada Buddhism attribute enlightenment and ultimate liberation solely to human endeavor. "Be to yourself your own lamp," the Buddha himself enjoined. In the course of history Buddhism has spread widely throughout Asia; but although it claims a universal message for all humanity, it does not in practice pursue a general missionary program to convert all the peoples of the earth to its doctrine and practice.[13]

In the rich variety of belief systems brought forth by Mother India, pursuit of life's goals is everywhere motivated by consciousness of *dharma*, the eternal principle of conscience and conduct governing life, both personal and social. Hindu *bhakti* piety demands *puja*, devoted worship and prayer to deity through ritual observances. The higher way to purification and final *moksha*-liberation is through yogic practices, sacred study, and meditation.

Buddhists are enjoined to follow the Noble Eightfold Path marked out by the Buddha's teaching, which traces the middle way between excessive asceticism and undue self-indulgence, and to have recourse to the *Sangha*, the monastic community, to aid them on that path. In theory at least, all Buddhists embrace the prescribed means and practices leading to the en-

lightenment that dissolves the illusion of human experience and culmi-
nates in Nirvana. Compassion with those who are sunk in *dukkha*—namely,
the radical ignorance and insubstantiality that is the common lot—is
preached as a sovereign virtue. Tibetan Buddhism, an amalgam which includes elements from a more ancient indigenous cult, has some distinctive
religious concepts, aims, and aids for the attainment of enlightenment.

African primal religion, in accordance with which tens of millions of
the human race live their life's course, is, to borrow the words of Dr. J. O.
Awolalu, "a religion that has no written literature, yet it is 'written' everywhere for those who care to see and read. It is largely written in the
people's myths and folktales, in their songs and dances, in their liturgies
and shrines, and in their proverbs and pithy sayings."[14] Dr. Awolalu sum-
marizes as follows the substance of the fundamental belief of the traditional religion of sub-Saharan Africa:

> that this world was brought into being by the Source of all beings, the Supreme
> Being given different names by different ethnic groups in Africa; . . . that the Su-
> preme Being brought into being a number of divinities and spirits to act as his func-
> tionaries in the orderly maintenance of the world; that the Supreme Being, the di-
> vinities, and the ancestors have laid down rules of conduct and guiding principles
> for the benefit of men and women and for the maintenance of peace and concord
> in the community. Africans hold that man is vitally related to and even dependent
> upon Deity and his agents, who watch over human behaviour and can reward and
> punish man as the case may be.

In Islamic teaching the means by which the life purpose and final end of
Muslims is attained is through prophetic revelation of God's will, believed
to be given definitive statement by Muhammad in the Qur'an. They
achieve that end by professing faithfully the divine origin of that message
and of Muhammad's prophethood and by proving their faith through per-
formance of the prescribed works of religion, the Five Pillars of *Din*.

In Jewish religion likewise the way to attain the divinely intended goal is
prescribed obedience both of mind and will; that is, by reverent study of
Torah and *Talmud*, of revelation and its traditional interpretation, and by
faithful observance of the *mitzvoth*, the sacred obligations governing all aspects and details of life. Orthodoxy in belief is important, but of most immediate concern is orthopraxy. The soteriology of Midrashic Judaism is
not predeterminist; while God reveals and commands, he leaves the

achievement of human destiny and redemption to be decided by the free cooperation of the human will.

Those Three Questions Applied to the Christian Revelation

I began this chapter by formulating as a heuristic device the three questions—*From what? To what?* and *By what?*—questions which may be asked of all the belief systems which express the natural religion of humanity, albeit while overlaying it with their own inventions and accretions. I there observed that the same questions could also be asked of, and authentically answered by, the revealed religion of Christianity. The natural religion of human reason is the providentially designed seedbed in which that supernatural revelation is implanted and springs to life. Here in conclusion I summarize the answers that are given by Christian faith to each of those three questions.[15]

From what? What does divine revelation tell us about the initial situation and predicament of humanity? Christian faith testifies that human beings were created by God in his image and likeness and called to live in harmony with him and in conformity with his all-provident will; that their mortal life is a transient probation on which their eternal life depends; that, in this world of matter which is the place of their probation they can discern the vestiges of its Creator; that the created universe is itself in a process of development destined by him; that through humankind's sinfulness, primordial and perennial, all have become estranged from God, turning away from the course divinely intended for them; that thereby the divine image has been obscured in them and their natural nobility has been marred; that they have become subject to the manifold ills resulting from the present human condition and from malign forces of evil, which have a kind of usurped dominion in the sinful world; that accordingly human beings stand in an existential predicament threatening spiritual ruin; and that, as well as being in need of succor from the sufferings, perils, misfortunes, and injustices that beset them in this mortal life, they are also in absolute need of salvation, that is, of remedy for their fundamental spiritual disorder and of reconciliation with God.

Although the likeness of God within human beings has been obscured by sin, Christian faith affirms that it is not effaced, and that they are ever encompassed by his all-holy will and providence. They wrestle with a paradoxical polarity between optimism and pessimism in their perception of their plight. They find themselves alienated creatures, tempted to choose evil and to make gods of themselves, yet at the same time children of God, still bearing the lineaments of their Father, their hearts ever restless until they find rest in him. Emerging from a dark lair deep in a tangled wildwood of animal instincts and passions, they seek a sunlit home in a heavenly realm of spiritual truth and goodness. They can be beasts of prey destroying one another, yet they can also be saints moved to compassion and selfless love for one another, for strangers as well as kin. While they experience this world as a vale of tears, they yet live here in hope for a new society, for a new state of being, in which wrongs will be righted and truth will prevail over falsehood. Prone to evil, they still sense as their source the supreme good who is God and yearn for restoration to communion with him.

Christian faith finds the resolution of those paradoxes and true understanding of the human predicament itself in God himself incarnate in the world of his creation. It is Christ who makes us truly conscious of our predicament and not only liberates us from it but brings us to a final goal beyond humanity's natural yearnings and potentiality.

To what? What, according to the Christian revelation, are the goals of this life and that final end towards which our mortal life is set? For all human beings there is the primary and urgent need for salvation from their aboriginal plight; but their ultimate goal and eternal fulfilment is to be raised up with Christ to share in his divine life. The supernatural destiny conferred on humankind by union with him far excels the natural destiny implicit in their original creation. The promise of it is the central strand in the anchor-rope of Christian hope.

Entwined with the hope for that supreme goal of human existence, everlasting life with God, are several supporting strands, this-worldly goals which Christians seek as means to attaining that ultimate goal but which are also ends in themselves to be realized in this life. We pray, as Jesus taught us, that our Father's will be done on earth as it is in heaven. Both here and there, its fulfilment has absolute holiness and value. Christian faith attests that the primary purpose and goal of our life on earth is to know and love God, to honor and serve him. It bids us to attain that purpose here and now, both as individual persons and as members of families and of communities.

For each individual, the necessary first stage is justification before God, that is, his merciful bestowal of forgiveness of the sin that alienates us from him and restoration to his loving friendship and favor. Thereby we come to live the new life of grace as adoptive children of God and co-heirs with Christ, hallowed by the presence of the indwelling Holy Spirit and transformed in our own spirit by a participation in the divine life. From that inward sanctification grow the fruits of the Spirit in the everyday practice of virtue: namely, the theological virtues of faith, hope, and charity and the moral virtues which we are called to exercise in every aspect of our experience, personal and social.

The grace-life of each individual Christian is not self-enclosed; it is encompassed in the corporate grace-life of Christ's Church, his Mystical Body, through which he continues his mission to sanctify the world. We are to perform our life's primary duty of knowing, loving, and serving God not only privately but publicly, by taking our part in his Church's worship and mission according to our degree and capacity. In and with the Church we are to carry out that duty by active love and compassion for each and all of his children, seeking their spiritual and temporal good, and by right use and care of his good creation.

Revelation of the truths concerning the final realities that lie beyond this life is necessarily expressed in figurative and anthropomorphic language. The Christian map of human existence points surely across the frontier of mortal life to those eschatological mysteries beyond: to divine judgment, both particular and general; to the terrible possibility of eternal self-separation from God in hell; to a purifying preparation, as needs be, for entry into eternal life; and above all to the ineffable consummation that we call heaven.

That attainment of the final perfection of human existence after death, as promised by divine revelation, is, like the attainment of the proximate goals set for this life, both personal and corporate. Heavenly life is personal survival and ultimate salvation, final release from all evils, sufferings, and sorrows, and enjoyment of unending bliss; it is the culmination of all good desires and potentialities; it is reward for all the meritorious deeds of the past mortal life; it elevates to a new manner of existence both the soul and, eventually, the body, which together constitute the unity of human personhood. Infinitely excelling all those supernal boons, and giving reality to them all, heaven is the beatifying union with the triune God himself.

This divine consummation is through and with Christ the incarnate Word who, by entering into our human nature, has made it possible for us to share in his divine nature. Through him and with him the blessed in heaven attain the final fruition of their life's end and purpose. United with him in the divine embrace, they share personal fellowship with him in his glorified humanity, with his blessed mother Mary, Queen of Heaven, with the angels and community of saints who are the Church in glory, and with all who were dear to them on earth.

Not only the Church and each of its members but all creation shares that ultimate goal and promise of final consummation, summed up by the Second Vatican Council as follows:

The Church will receive her perfection only in the glory of heaven, when will come the time of the renewal of all things. At that time, together with the human race, the universe itself, which is so closely related to man and which attains its destiny through him, will be perfectly re-established in Christ.[16]

By what? By what means are the life goals and ultimate end of human existence to be achieved? In a Christian context, the question must be re-phrased—*By whom?*—and the answer of Christian faith is: *By Jesus Christ*, the one savior and one mediator between God and men, the eternal Word of God who has come into this world and taken our nature to dwell with us forever. Unlike the religious philosophies of the East which see existent reality as in a cyclical state of eternal return, without beginning or end, Christianity sees it as in linear progression towards a foredestined term and consummation:

God's revelation enters into time and into recorded history. In the Christian faith time has fundamental importance. History marks out, as it were, a pathway for the People of God, which they must follow to the end. The Eternal steps into time, the All lies hidden in the part, God takes on a human face.[17]

Entering into this world of matter and into human history, the eternal Son of God has, by his incarnation, life, and teaching, revealed God and his will for us. By his passion, death, and resurrection Christ has delivered us from evil and spiritual ruin, and raised us to share in his own divinity and to ever-lasting life with him. By that saving work he has accomplished once for all the universal and objective salvation of humankind. Through his sacra-mental Church, ever celebrating his Eucharistic Mystery, the power of his redemptive work is operative in every age and place. From the universal baptismal font of his grace, spiritual healing and sanctification is bestowed on all who receive that grace with faith and love, and freely collaborate with it in their lives of Christian virtue.

�֎

In several respects the tenets of the non-Christian religions of the world have clear similarities with the revealed doctrines of the Christian faith, briefly summarized above, on these fundamental questions concerning the ultimate meaning and purpose of human life and the means by which human beings are to attain that purpose. Those points of similarity relate to concepts that are common to most of the non-Christian religions, drawn from the common fount of natural religion, as distinct from the idiosyncratic tenets of particular credal systems.

From the viewpoint of Catholic theology, that similarity is not surprising. As well as the higher mysteries of Christian faith that are above the reach of human reason, there are also included in the content of Christian revelation truths that are not above its reach and which are common also to natural religion, as St. Thomas Aquinas observed in a passage alluded to by the First Vatican Council: "It was also necessary for man to be instructed by divine revelation concerning those things pertaining to God that can be investigated by human reason."[18] In my next two chapters I dwell further on the relation between revealed and natural theology and on the fulfilment by divine revelation of the natural religion of human reason and experience.

Chapter 5

The Relation between Natural and Revealed Knowledge of God

So Paul, standing in the middle of the Areopagus, said: "Men of Athens, I perceive that in every way you are very religious. For as I passed along, and observed the objects of your worship, I found also an altar with this inscription, 'To an unknown god.' What therefore you worship as unknown, this I proclaim to you. The God who made the world and everything in it, being Lord of heaven and earth, does not live in shrines made by man, nor is he served by human hands, as though he needed anything, since he himself gives to all men life and breath and everything. And he made, from one, every nation of men to live on all the face of the earth, having determined allotted periods and the boundaries of their habitation, to seek God, trying to reach out towards him and find him. Yet he is not far from each one of us, for 'in him we live and move and have our being'; as even some of your poets have said, 'For we are indeed his offspring.'"

Acts of the Apostles 17.22–28

Faith clearly presupposes that human speech, with its universal ambit, can signify—albeit analogically, none the less truly—divine and transcendent reality. Were it not so, it would follow that the word of God, which remains divine though contained in human language, could signify nothing about God.

Pope John Paul II, Fides et ratio, *§84*

The two manners in which God draws us to know him, by natural reason and by faith, are coordinated in his all-encompassing plan of love to bring us to himself and are unified in the Christian life of grace. In what sense are those two modes of knowing God "necessarily interconnected"? With what justification can it be said, as I said earlier, that the full revelation of God in Christ *presupposes, transforms,* and *fulfils* the natural cognizance of God that the human mind draws from the created world? Four mutually complementary reasons may be given for saying so:

first, the natural religion of human reason, based on the evidences of God in the world of our experience, provides the very concepts and language necessary for communication of the divine revelation received by faith;

second, natural religion serves as a providential preparation for the eventual preaching of the Gospel of Christ and as a powerful apologetic suasion for its acceptance;

third, in the life of divine grace the truths and virtues of natural religion are purified and elevated by the theological virtues of faith and love and are taken up into the higher knowledge, understanding, and wisdom that are the supernatural gifts of the Holy Spirit;

fourth, in the light of the Christian Church's deepening understanding of the mystery of God's universal salvific will, I argue the theological conclusion that the natural religion of humanity provides an entry point and channel for bestowal of the saving grace of Christ on that majority of human beings who, inculpably, do not come to know and worship him as Lord and so remain strangers to the Church through which he dispenses that grace.

These four propositions, which are interconnected, call for scrutiny in turn. The first three are discussed in this chapter; the fourth will be the subject of the two following chapters.

Natural Religion as Receptive Matrix of Revelation

The first of the four propositions set out above has been denied by Protestant divines, notably by Karl Barth, who continue the tradition of Reformation fideism and who deny that there can be veritable knowledge of theological truth by natural reason. Yet on closer consideration the validity of such knowledge can be seen to be undeniable—as another Evangelical divine, Emil Brunner, argued against Barth in a celebrated controversy.[1]

Our natural capacity to know of God from the created world and to express that knowledge in human language is indeed an essential prerequisite to knowing and testifying to him by faith. As the *Catechism of the Catholic Church* expresses it simply, "Without this capacity, man would not be able to welcome God's revelation."[2] The natural religion of human reason indeed provides the cognitional matrix within which is set the higher revelation that brings communion with God through Christ. It provides the necessary means, conceptual and linguistic, to express and communicate that higher truth. To reject natural theology and the patterns of religious thought and language that comprise it, as do those who assert that human reason by its own power can utter no relevant truth about God and our relation to him, is a futile attempt to saw off the branch upon which all theologians must sit.

In my second chapter I reflected on the truth that our intellect is attuned by its very nature to grasp the analogy between the created being that it experiences and the creative Being from whom all things ceaselessly receive their existence, and that natural theology formulates its concepts concerning God by extrapolating the higher perfections discerned in this universe and affirming their existence in infinite measure in their one all-perfect Source. Revealed theology is formulated in continuity with that same process; it depends on those selfsame analogical concepts as means to express the divine message. As our reason is the necessary instrument for receiving and responding to God's gift of faith, so our language is the necessary instrument for expressing his gift of revelation and for transmitting it to others. The divine condescension in thus clothing heavenly truth in earth-based words is likened by the Second Vatican Council to the *kenosis* of the divine Word in becoming incarnate in human nature:

So in sacred Scripture, without any abasement of divine truth and holiness, there is manifested the wonderful "condescension" of eternal Wisdom, "in order that we may learn the loving-kindness of God, and how, in his providential concern for the capacity of our nature, he has so signally adapted his message to it." For the words of God, as expressed by human tongues, have become assimilated to human language, just as the Word of the eternal Father, when he took to himself the flesh of human weakness, became like human beings.[3]

Divine revelation does not bestow upon human nature new powers of conceptualizing and reasoning, or new laws of semantic usage. Revealed truth can be made meaningful to human beings only if it is expressed in ideas and words that are in continuity with the antecedent structure of human thought and language, which is our sole medium for receiving and conveying truth about spiritual and divine reality. In order to express the higher revelation of God and his will for humankind, the inspired writers of both Old and New Testaments necessarily used that pre-existing conceptual language of natural theology which is the common patrimony of humankind. While the New Testament draws upon the religious concepts and language of the Old, both inspired Scriptures speak of God and express his higher revelation of himself and of his will for humankind in the universal religious language that derives from humanity's rational awareness of divine reality and law as reflected in this created world. Jesus Christ himself spoke his divine message to humankind in that language. As well as the inspired text of the Bible, the articles of the Christian creeds and all the dogmas of the Church are written in it.

In the divine revelation through Christ, the language derived from the concepts of natural religion is employed to express both truths concerning God that are above our reason's reach and those that are within it. It was such language that Jesus spoke to reveal the divine secrets, undiscoverable by natural reason, of God's trinitarian life, of his own divinity, of his abiding presence in his Church, of man's supernatural destiny, and of the sacramental economy of grace. He also used it to restate with new power and clarity the general religious aspirations and moral law that are attested by human reason. The sublime prayer to the Father that he taught his disciples, to be the daily and distinctive devotion of all Christians, contains no doctrine or terminology specific to the Christian revelation but is phrased in the universal religious language of humanity.

In *Fides et ratio* Pope John Paul II dwells with new emphasis on this fundamental fact that Christian dogmatic theology, in order to expound "the universal meaning of the mystery of the one and triune God and of the economy of salvation," necessarily relies on universally communicable concepts and conclusions formulated by the philosophy of right reason. Were there no such natural ability of human beings to apprehend truth about divine reality and to express it in human language, the Pope states in the striking words cited at the head of this chapter, "it would follow that the word of God, which remains divine though contained in human language, can signify nothing about God." It would thus be impossible for theology to speak truly "about God, about the interpersonal relations within the Trinity, about God's act in creating the world, about the relationship between God and man, about Christ's identity as true God and true man." The same impossibility, the Pope also attests, would also apply to the formulation of the divinely revealed precepts for living the Christian life.[4]

In brief, the first of the four reasons outlined above may be recapitulated as follows. The human intellect attains its natural intimations of divine reality in a unique manner. By virtue of its innate power to abstract higher meaning from its sense-based experience of this material universe, it is able to attain some true awareness of transcendent divine Being, some likeness of whose nature and law is mysteriously reflected in the very structure and activity of his creation. The religious and theological language that humankind uses to express that awareness was in use before the coming of the Judeo-Christian revelation; its origin is in human rationality itself. In the fulness of time that conceptual language was adopted and elevated to be the medium of the higher, supernatural communication of God to humankind through Jesus Christ.

Natural Religion as Pedagogy and Preparation for the Gospel

I turn to the second of the four manners in which natural theology may be said to be antecedent and ancillary to revealed theology. Not only does it provide the necessary conceptual substrate and linguistic vehicle for divine revelation, but, more specifically, those intimations of the creative presence of God which the human mind draws from experience of this world are seen in the light of Christian faith as a *praeparatio evangelica*, a providential means by which minds were prepared for the spread of the unique Gospel message through the worldwide mission of Christ's Church.

The Incarnation took place at a particular point in human history, prepared for by a preliminary revelation to the chosen people with whom God entered into covenant. The religious culture of the Jews, which was itself conditioned by the wider human culture in which it was set, formed the first seedbed of the Christian Gospel. Yet providential preparation for the mission of Christ and his Church, and for its outward expansion beyond the bounds of the land and nation of Israel, was also made through a pattern of religious, historical, and cultural factors which served to widen the seedbed for the propagation of the Gospel in the gentile world and to provide strong apologetic argument for its acceptance.

Central among those enabling factors was the natural quest for God in all human societies which arises from rationality itself. To that common religious awareness, ceaselessly springing up in the human heart even amidst the weeds of superstition and false cults, the Christian missionaries, when preaching the message of Christ, appealed from the beginning, and throughout the centuries, to peoples for whom the prophecies of the Jewish Scriptures had no authority. The first and greatest of Christian missionaries, Paul of Tarsus, made appeal to those universal foretidings of the Gospel in the words cited at the head of this chapter, addressed to the Athenians in the Areopagus. Echoing his words, the Second Vatican Council taught that the natural search of humanity for God, though insufficient in itself, has a preliminary role in preparing minds for explicit acceptance of the Gospel message that proclaims the salvation of the human race through the mission of the Son of God into the world. That universal salvific plan, the Council declared, cannot be brought into effect simply

> . . . by those endeavors, religious though they may be, by which, in many different ways, men seek God, "trying to reach out towards him or find him—though he is not far from each one of us" (Acts 17.27); for those endeavors need to be enlightened and purified. Nevertheless they may serve, in accordance with the loving purpose of divine providence, as a pedagogy leading to the true God, even as a preparation for the Gospel.[5]

Is that pedagogy and preparation fruitless where it does not result in explicit acceptance of the Gospel and conversion to faith in Christ? Does the mission of the Church remain without effect in the case of those—the majority of the human race—who remain in lifelong and inculpable ignorance of the truths of Christian faith? The theological development (discussed more fully in the two following chapters) of the Church's belief concerning the salvation of non-Christians, which came to fruition in the Second Vatican Council, has led to deeper understanding of the great commission given by the risen Christ to his Apostles (Matthew 28.19–20). His primary and ever urgent command to his missionary Church was to seek to make all the peoples of the earth his disciples, to baptize them in the name of the triune God, and to show them the way to the eternal life he had promised. But implicit in his parting commission to his Church was a mandate to speak of God and of the meaning of human life and society to those also who still remain strangers to his life-giving message and who are not visibly gathered into his Church during their mortal life.

It was in the light of "deeper penetration into the mystery of the Church" that the Second Vatican Council, at the beginning of its *Pastoral Constitution on the Church in the Modern World*, acknowledged its obligation "to address not only the children of the Church and all who call upon the name of Christ, but also all human beings." It interpreted the Church's universal mission as calling it "to enter into dialogue with the whole human family" about fundamental questions that confront all humanity—"pressing questions about present world development, about the place and role of man in the universe, about the meaning of his endeavor, individual and collective, and finally about the ultimate purpose of all things and of human beings."[6]

How can there be meaningful dialogue between the Catholic Church and the non-Christian majority of the human family—dialogue about divinely sanctioned morality in human society and common stewardship of the earth, about religious duty and destiny, and about the ultimate purpose of all—when the non-Christian members of that family do not acknowledge the validity of the dogmatic language in which the Church proclaims her religious interpretation of reality? The answer to this question is that there *is* a common medium for such discourse. It is the ageless and universally current language that the Church and the non-Christian world share in common, the language of natural religion based on the innate power of the human mind to draw knowledge of divine reality from experience of the created world. The *Catechism of the Catholic Church*[7] puts this in a nutshell:

In defending the ability of human reason to know God, the Church is expressing her confidence in the possibility of speaking about him to all men and with all men, and therefore of dialogue with other religions, with philosophy and science, as well as with unbelievers and atheists.

I recapitulate the second of my four reasons. Humankind's natural affirmation of God can be seen to have a vital ancillary function as a precursor of the Gospel and a support for Christian missionary apologetic, preparing minds to receive the full and explicit divine revelation brought by Jesus, the

incarnate Word of God. It also makes possible the Church's mission to proclaim divine goodness to those who live and die without explicit knowledge
of that revelation and to cooperate with them for the spiritual and temporal welfare of the whole human family. Unbeknownst to those non-
Christian multitudes, the Church, which thus speaks to them outwardly of
the purpose and conduct of human life is, in God's loving plan for the salvation of all his children, the sacramental means by which his grace is in a
hidden manner operative to bestow upon them the gift of eternal life. In
the two following chapters I return to further reflection on this deep theological truth, seen in new and clearer light in our own age.

Natural Religion Contained and Elevated in the Life of Grace

The third of the three reasons indicated above, arguing the necessary relation of natural to revealed theology, refers to the continuity in the Christian life of grace between natural knowledge of and obedience to God and
the supernatural elevation of that knowledge and obedience in the faith
and life of the believer. Through the grace of the indwelling Holy Spirit,
the acknowledgment and service of God by natural reason is corrected,
perfected, and integrated with the higher truths of divine revelation in the
totality of the life of faith.

The contribution of natural to revealed religion is, then, not confined to
providing the necessary conceptual language and context in which to express the divine message and to prepare for its wider acceptance. The
whole truth-content of authentic natural theology, comprising those substantive religious truths and values summarized above (in Chapter 3), is
also contained in the higher truth-content of revelation. This was taught by
the First Vatican Council when it included in the category of revealed
truths "those things pertaining to divine reality that are not beyond the
reach of human reason," but which are also directly revealed by God "in
order that they can be known easily, with firm certainty and with no admixture of error."[8]

Thus what is *per se* knowable by reason concerning the existence, action, and attributes of God, and concerning the relation of creatures to
him, is confirmed, clarified, and given new supernatural finality by revelation, grace, and faith. The believer accepts those naturally knowable religious truths and values as certain not simply because the power of human

intellect shows them to be so, but also, in the higher order of faith and grace, on the authority of God directly revealing those truths about himself. So there is no inconsistency in the Church's doctrine that we both believe in God by faith and at the same time can know of his existence and attributes by reason. There is no incongruity between, on the one hand, the first article of Christian faith professed in the Nicene Creed, "I *believe* in one God, the Father almighty, maker of heaven and earth, of all things visible and invisible" and, on the other, the dogmatic definition of the First Vatican Council: "God, the beginning and end of all things, can be *certainly known by the natural light of human reason.*"

The natural outreach of the mind to God by the light of reason does not become otiose in the life of grace, but is therein supernaturally elevated by the theological virtue of faith and progressively perfected by what are called "the intellectual gifts of the Holy Spirit"—namely, the higher knowledge, understanding, and wisdom, which, enriched by grace, give abiding awareness of the Godwardness of all things and which illumine the mystical path to God.[9]

Conversely, the rational knowledge of truth concerning God, still retaining in the life of grace its natural immediacy for the human mind, can avail to strengthen the faithful resolve of believers when, not seeing but believing, they are called to confess higher truths concerning God that are above the reach of their natural reason. Those central dogmas of Christian revelation could never be discovered or verified by unaided reason, but are apprehended only by the obedience of faith. Natural theology can give no prior knowledge of God in Trinity nor of God incarnate in human nature, but only knowledge of God in his unity and of his attributes mirrored in his creation. Our intellect necessarily finds obscurity in the revealed truths of faith which are above its natural scope. Because of that obscurity and of human frailty, faith may meet difficulty and temptation to doubt. At such times, the rational assurance we have of God's existence, attributes, and moral law, an assurance that retains its experiential force in the life of grace, can be a potent support for the faith that is also called to embrace those higher truths of God that lie beyond the reach of reason.

The third of my four reasons, then, can be recapitulated as follows. Natural religion not only provides the conceptual and linguistic envelope for revealed religion and a providential pathway for Christ's mission, but in the life of grace and by the higher light of revelation it is divinely ratified and supernaturalized to become within us the heavenly wisdom of the Holy Spirit. The life of divine grace is not simply knowing truth about God and his action in the world; we are "to grow into Christ by showing forth the truth in love" (Ephesians 4.15). Just as our rational knowledge of God is subsumed and elevated in the gift of faith, so the exercise of all the natural virtues to which we are consciously oriented by the prompting of natural conscience is likewise supernaturally elevated in the Christian life of grace.

Chapter 6

Natural Religion in the Divine Plan of Salvation

The Church is entrusted with the duty of making manifest the mystery of God, who is the ultimate end of man; in so doing, she opens to man the meaning of his own existence, the innermost truth about himself. Truly she knows that only God, whom she serves, can satisfy the deepest longings of the human heart, which the delights of the world can never fulfil. She knows too that man, ever stirred by the Spirit of God, can never be wholly indifferent to religious questionings . . . Only God, who created man in his own image and who redeemed him, can give the ultimate answer to those questionings; and that answer he gives through revelation in Christ his Son, who became man.

Vatican II, Gaudium et spes, §41

Those also can attain eternal salvation who, with no fault on their part, do not know the Gospel of Christ or his Church, yet who seek God with a sincere heart and, aided by grace, strive by their deeds to do his will as they know it through the dictates of conscience. Nor does divine Providence deny the helps necessary for salvation to those who, inculpably, have not yet arrived at an explicit knowledge of God, and who strive—not without grace—to live rightly.

Vatican II, Lumen gentium, §16

It remains to discuss the last of the four propositions put forward at the beginning of the previous chapter concerning the relationship of natural religion to the Christian revelation. What theological justification can be

given for the assertion made there that the Church's deepening understanding of the mystery of God's universal salvific will enables us to recognize that the natural religion of humanity provides an entry point and
channel for bestowal of the saving grace of Christ on that majority of
human beings who, inculpably, do not come to know and worship him as
Lord and remain strangers to his Church through which he dispenses that
grace? Unfamiliar though such a proposition may appear to some, it finds
support in theological insights and perspectives that have come into clearer
focus in the Catholic Church in recent times, especially through the teachings of the Second Vatican Council and of the papal magisterium. This
newly clarified teaching of the Church on the salvation of non-Christians
and on the value of their religious communities, beliefs, and rites, is directly relevant to discussion of the relation between natural and revealed
religion.

In the light of that teaching, we may realize more clearly that the knowledge of divine reality derived by reason from the evidences of creation and
from conscience, to which all human beings who seek truth and live rightly
are attuned, is linked in God's mysterious plan of love with his salvific will
to offer all human beings the higher communion with himself that is mediated through Jesus Christ, the divine Word through and for whom all
things were made (Colossians 1.16). Only in those whose minds are culpably darkened, to whom St. Paul refers in the primary scriptural assertion of
natural theology contained in the first chapter of his Epistle to the Romans, does the innate power of human reason to know of God remain un-
graced and spiritually sterile. For, while there is no inherent necessity in
human nature to be raised by supernatural grace to a higher participation
in divine being, there is a natural receptivity for that gift (what in traditional
theological parlance is called a *potentia oboedientialis*, the power to obey the
divine call).

In the passage of *Lumen gentium* cited at the head of this chapter Vatican
II teaches that those who are without explicit knowledge of the Christian
revelation—or even of God himself—yet who live their lives in sincerity of
heart and obedience to the natural dictates of their conscience can reach
him and attain eternal salvation. Even unknowingly, they are searching for
and are welcomed by him who is ultimate truth and goodness, and who is
the meaning and end of human life. Several other passages in the conciliar

decrees likewise indicate that for all such seekers the path to God and salvation lies through the natural religion that springs from right reason and obedience to conscience. In so teaching, the Council is careful to repeat that such Godward exercise of natural reason is "aided by grace"; that the salutary practice of virtue according to natural conscience is "not without grace"; and that all grace and salvation comes from Christ, whose saving work is sacramentally perpetuated through his Church.

I preface fuller discussion of this question by amplifying the sense in which I am here using the term "natural religion." In previous pages it has frequently been used as a synonym for "natural theology," that is, to refer primarily to the mind's intellectual affirmation of divine reality through reflection on the created world and on the inner voice of conscience. However, the natural religion of humanity which serves as entry point for divine saving grace is not simply intellectual awareness. For nature to be informed by grace there is required a reactive response—that is, obedience to the inward imperative that bids every human being to acknowledge the divine reality by submission, adoration, love, and service. Such acknowledgment of God's sovereignty and law, to which human beings are oriented by nature and which is perfected by grace, is expressed not only in their concepts and words but in their deeds and life. Nor is this natural religion only an activity of individuals in isolation from their fellow men. It is expressed in their social as well as individual life, in worship and right conduct, and above all in love of neighbor, that natural sacrament of the love of God.

In so using the term "natural religion" I do not suppose that the capacity of human beings to know, love, and serve God is exercised, or can be exercised, in some other sphere of human existence outside that of God's all-provident grace. I recall here, with new emphasis, what was said on that subject in my first chapter. Catholic theology now realizes more clearly that there is in the present order no such other sphere, no neutral form of religion that is unrelated to the supernatural destiny of the whole human race and to the divine economy of grace and salvation through Jesus Christ. All Godward religion is, explicitly or implicitly, related to the incarnate divine Word through whom all things were made, the true light who enlightens all human beings, the sole mediator between God and humankind. While all men and women have the naturally inborn potentiality to orient their minds and wills to God, whenever they actually do so they are, albeit unknowingly, energized and ennobled by the supernatural grace of Christ.

It remains true, nevertheless, that even within that all-embracing sphere of grace there is a difference in kind between, on the one hand, the cognizance of God and his law that human beings can acquire from his created works by the light of their natural reason and, on the other, the higher supernatural knowledge and law that they receive from the revelation of Christ by the light of faith.

Earlier Stages in the Unfolding of the Doctrine of Salvation

To explore the theme indicated by the title of this chapter, one must look back at the earlier stages in the unfolding of the Christian doctrine of salvation.[1] This survey serves to emphasize how truly remarkable has been the development in recent times of theological understanding in this field, culminating in the new doctrinal synthesis achieved by the Second Vatican Council.

St. Peter, confessing Christ crucified and risen, said to the rulers and elders in Jerusalem after Pentecost, "There is salvation in no one else, for there is no other name under heaven given to men by which we must be saved" (Acts 4.12). That the revelation and saving work of Christ is all-sufficient, unique, and absolutely necessary for human salvation has been central in Christian belief since the beginning. It was to bring that salvation to the whole human race through his Church that the risen Christ gave to his Apostles his great commission to make all nations his disciples (Matthew 28.18–20). The scriptural assurance, "God our saviour desires all men to be saved and to come to the knowledge of the truth" (I Timothy 2.4), was cited in earlier centuries to stress the urgency of the Church's mission to evangelize and baptize all the peoples of the earth. It was not taken to imply that there could be a way to eternal life even for those not converted to Christianity.

The belief in Christ's Church as the one ark of salvation, which came to be expressed in the traditional dogmatic axiom, *"Extra Ecclesiam nulla salus,"* which is translated, "No salvation outside the Church," has powerfully motivated the Christian missionary endeavor throughout the past two millennia. The origin of that dogmatic axiom, equivalently found in the teaching of many Fathers both of East and West, is traced to a letter of

St. Cyprian of Carthage in the third century. The doctrine was solemnly defined by the Fourth Lateran Council in 1215: "There is one universal Church of the faithful, outside which no one at all is saved."[2] The Lateran definition has been echoed in several other authoritative documents of the Church.[3]

Thus for much of the history of the Church the revealed doctrine concerning human salvation has been commonly interpreted in an exclusive sense as meaning that salvation could be attained only by Christians who were incorporated into the Catholic Church by baptism and explicitly professed the true faith. It was usually assumed that all others were necessarily outside the way of salvation because of their lack of right belief and the saving grace of Christ which is mediated to humankind only through his sacramental Church. The same pessimistic assumption was made not only about the eternal destiny of non-Christians but also about that of other Christians outside the Catholic fold. In his bull *Unam sanctam* of the year 1302, Pope Boniface VIII asserted that it was "absolutely necessary for salvation for every human creature to be subject to the Roman Pontiff."[4] A notorious instance of extremist interpretation of the axiom, "no salvation outside the Church," is to be found in a decree of the Council of Florence in the year 1442, which contained the following intransigent assertion:

The Holy Roman Church . . . firmly believes, professes, and proclaims that none of those who are outside the Catholic Church—neither pagans, nor Jews, nor heretics, nor schismatics—can become sharers in eternal life. Unless they are gathered within its fold before the end of their life, they will go into the fire prepared for the devil and his angels.[5]

The exclusivist outlook so starkly expressed in those statements (which can now be seen clearly to lack the essential notes of a dogmatic definition by the Church) has been progressively modified and eventually superseded by deeper theological understanding of what has been revealed concerning God's universal salvific will. In the process, the seemingly uncompromising rigor of the traditional axiom, *"extra Ecclesiam nulla salus,"* has undergone a remarkable reinterpretation.

Sources for the later development of a more inclusive theology of human salvation can be found in patristic writings from the second century onwards: for instance, in the writings of Justin Martyr (whose reference to "seeds of the Word" sown broadcast among all humankind is twice echoed by Vatican II), of Clement of Alexandria, of Origen, of St. John Chrysostom, and even in some statements by St. Augustine, who otherwise took a deeply pessimistic view on the possibility of grace and salvation for those outside the visible Church. Medieval theologians prepared the way for deeper doctrinal penetration. Even the greatest of them, St. Thomas Aquinas, while holding that those inculpably ignorant of revealed truth would not be condemned by divine justice, did not challenge, but seemed rather to echo, the prevailing assumption that the Christian faith had been sufficiently promulgated in the world and that therefore those who rejected it could not be inculpable.

In some passages of the writings of Aquinas, however, one can find glimpses of a wider horizon. In one very far-reaching theological speculation, the implications of which were not to become apparent and influential until long afterwards, he affirmed that by an interior prompting of grace all human beings are offered, at the dawn of moral and religious awareness in their reason and conscience, an opportunity for decisive self-orientation to the divine good for which they are made. If they respond aright, they will receive the grace of first justification and of faith leading to eternal life.[6]

St. Thomas also considered the hypothetical case of an infant abandoned in a remote wilderness who, surviving by some means, might come to the use of reason deprived of all contact with and indoctrination by humankind. How, he asked, could such a one be said to have the opportunity of receiving Christian faith and saving grace? His answer was that if the castaway used his natural powers rightly, choosing what is good and avoiding what is evil, "God would either reveal to him, by an inner inspiraton, what must be believed, or would send a preacher to him, as he sent Peter to Cornelius."[7] (I find that a similar case with a similar solution from an Islamic perspective had been put forward earlier in an allegorical novel by a Spanish Muslim thinker, Ibn-Tufayel or Alfayel.)

In the sixteenth and seventeenth centuries the discovery of hitherto unknown lands in the Americas and elsewhere around the globe brought heightened realization that there existed great multitudes of souls blamelessly ignorant of the Christian revelation. That realization led to further advances in Catholic theology towards a more optimistic understanding of the possibility of salvation for non-Christians. Significant contributions to

such understanding were made by the Dominican theologians of Sala-
manca, notably De Vitoria, Cano, and Soto; also, in a remarkable manner,
by Albert Pigge of Louvain;[8] and by the post-Tridentine Jesuits Bellarmine,
Suarez, and De Lugo.[9]

Pigge's contribution to this debate is of particular interest. He argued
that the multitudes living since time immemorial in the newly discovered
lands, to whom the Gospel had never been promulgated, could be in the
same situation as the gentile centurion Cornelius who had already been
pleasing to God before hearing any tidings of the Gospel. He further speculated boldly that erroneous belief and even denial of the Christian faith
could be blameless in sincere Muslims who kept the natural law divinely
written in their hearts. They might, Pigge further suggested, find a path to
the saving faith and grace of Christ by their knowledge and reverence of
God as creator and rewarder, thus implicitly embracing his salvific plan
which is explicitly revealed in Christ.

The theology of the Protestant Reformers was uncompromisingly exclusivist. Calvinist divines saw lack of Christian faith among the newly discovered pagan peoples as indicating that they and all their forebears were
among the reprobate irrevocably predestined by divine decree to eternal
damnation. The ultra-Augustinian rigor of the Reformers was paralleled
within the Catholic Church by that of the Jansenists in the Low Countries
and in France. The latter, reacting particularly against the inclusivist teaching of the Jesuit theologians of the Roman College, insisted on severe interpretation of the dogmatic axiom *"extra Ecclesiam nulla salus."* Their views
were censured by doctrinal statements of the Holy See, which stated in a
general sense that divine grace, sufficient for salvation, is granted to those
outside the Church.[10] As yet, however, there was no explicit statement by
the magisterium that any could be saved who remained until death outside
the Church.

Further debate was stimulated in the age of the Enlightenment by deist
and free-thinking objections to the Christian theology of salvation. It was
during the nineteenth and twentieth centuries that the pace of the development of a more inclusivist theology quickened appreciably. While continuing to confess unswervingly that the sole path to God is that revealed
through the unique mediator and savior Jesus Christ, a path that is followed
with explicit intent only by believing members of his Church, Catholic

theology came eventually to recognize and profess that the same sole path may also be implicitly sought and found not only by members of Christian churches and ecclesial communities separated from the one Catholic Church but also by adherents of non-Christian religions—and indeed by all human beings, even those apparently alienated from all religion. I cite below relevant Church documents which show what importance this newly clarified teaching attributes to natural religion, elevated by grace, in the divine salvific design.

Fruition of the Long Process of Doctrinal Clarification

The first express acknowledgment by the Church's magisterium that a way to eternal life lies open to those living and dying outside the fold of the Church came in the middle years of the nineteenth century, during the pontificate of Pope Pius IX. The principle that inculpable ignorance of revealed truth certainly excuses them from guilt in the eyes of God, which had been briefly enuntiated by that pope in an allocution in the year 1854 (*Singulari quadam*), was given fuller theological explanation in his encyclical letter *Quanto moerore conficiamur*, addressed to the bishops of Italy in 1863.[11] While reprobating "indifferentist" theories that would deny the unique primacy of Christ's revelation and would attribute like salvific value to all religions, and while also reiterating as Catholic dogma that any who contumaciously separated themselves from the unity of the Church could not be saved, Pius IX declared, as "a known truth":

> Those who labor under invincible ignorance concerning our most holy religion, yet who live morally and righteously, duly observing the natural law and its precepts inscribed by God in the hearts of all and ready to do his will, can attain eternal life with the aid of divine light and grace. For God, who fully sees, weighs, and knows the minds, hearts, thoughts, and ways of all, would certainly not, in his supreme goodness and clemency, permit any to be punished by eternal torments who were guiltless of willed fault.

In that first explicit declaration by the Church's magisterium that a way to salvation and eternal life lies open to those traditionally called "infidels," Pius IX specifically indicated that this path, made viable by divine light and grace, lies through observance of the natural law and its precepts in submissiveness to God's will.

In the course of the twentieth century, especially during the pontificate of Pius XII, theological understanding of the relation of all human beings to the Church of Christ deepened appreciably. In his encyclical *Mystici Corporis* of 1943, Pope Pius taught that those not actually incorporated in the Church may be related to it "by a certain unrecognized desire and resolve."[12] The meaning of that phrase was further elucidated in a further declaration of the Holy See, the "Boston Letter" of 1949,[13] in which it was made clear that intent to embrace God's will (an intent which implicitly includes readiness to enter his Church) can, empowered by divine grace, avail to the attainment of eternal life by those invincibly ignorant of the way of salvation revealed by Christ.

That long development of doctrine came to full fruition in the teaching of the Second Vatican Council (1962–1965). There it was still more expressly stated that saving and transforming grace, brought to humankind by the life, death, and resurrection of Christ and perpetually dispensed through his Church, is operative for the salvation of all human beings, including those who are and remain outside the visible community of the Church; and that God-given truths and values are to be found in non-Christian religions. "All peoples are one community," the Council taught; "all have the same ultimate end, God, whose providence, loving-kindness and plan of salvation extend to all."[14] The words of the dogmatic constitution *Lumen gentium* cited at the head of this chapter state the Church's final recognition that the way to divine saving grace and to eternal life lies open not only to those within the visible fold of Christ's Church but to all human beings.

Thus the age-old and sternly exclusivist interpretation of the Christian doctrine of salvation has been finally discredited as a historic misinterpretation. Statements such as those of Pope Boniface VIII and of the Council of Florence, cited above, have in past times been mistakenly supposed to be dogmatic definitions of the Church. They did not present the Church's perennial faith, being based merely on culturally conditioned and transient assumptions.[15] The dogmatic axiom *Extra Ecclesiam nulla salus* has now come to be interpreted in a positive rather than negative sense as meaning that all salvation, including that of non-Christians, lies within the ambit of the Church as universal instrument of Christ's saving work and grace. In this wider interpretation, the axiom is inclusive rather than exclusive. There is in truth no salvation apart from the Church because, in the words of Vatican

II's *Dogmatic Constitution on the Church,* "Christ constituted his Body which is the Church as the universal sacrament of salvation." The Council reiterates the latter phrase in several places.[16] It teaches moreover that in God's salvific plan every human being is related to the Church:

To this Catholic unity of the People of God, which prefigures and promotes universal peace, all are called. Belonging to it or related to it in different ways are the Catholic faithful, all who believe in Christ, and indeed all human beings, who are all called to salvation by the grace of God.[17]

Ratification of this universalist teaching on salvation may be seen as the most momentous of all the achievements of the Second Vatican Council. A theologian who contributed much to its work, Karl Rahner, expressed his judgment that what he called "the optimism concerning salvation" of Vatican II "marked a far more decisive phase in the development of the Church's conscious awareness of her faith than, for instance, the doctrine of collegiality in the Church, the relationship between Scripture and tradition, the acceptance of the new exegesis, etc."[18]—major themes which were also clarified at the Council.

Two Essential Aspects of the Revealed Way of Salvation

The teaching of Vatican II on the salvation of non-Christians must be interpreted in the light of the totality of revealed truth concerning the manner in which God brings human beings to reconciliation and union with himself. Catholic theology perceives two essential aspects of the process by which those who have the use of reason receive the grace of justification leading to salvation. One is subjective, relating to necessary predispositions in the person to be saved; the other is objective, relating to the divinely ordained means by which she or he comes to salvation and eternal life. Subjectively, each must in some way receive knowledge of the truth concerning God who saves through Christ and must personally respond to God's initiative through obedient faith and love. Objectively, the Christiform grace by which each is saved is, in the divine salvific plan, necessarily mediated through the sacramental Church, which is "made by Christ his instrument for the redemption of all," as Vatican II repeatedly testifies.

Since the sources of revelation, the Scriptural teachings authoritatively interpreted by the Church, show both those two elements, subjective and

72 Natural Religion in the Divine Plan

objective, to be essential requisites in the divinely established economy of salvation, they must in some manner be present and operative whenever a human being is justified before God and inwardly transformed by his sanctifying grace.

Yet one may well ask: how can those two elements, both absolutely necessary for each person to attain eternal life, be present and operative for the salvation of those who adhere to non-Christian religions and ideologies? They may have virtually no knowledge of, or may even explicitly reject, the revelation of Christ. How can they be said to have faith in him or to love him when they do not acknowledge him as Lord? They have no contact with his sacramental Church, "the universal instrument of salvation," nor access to the sacraments of Baptism and Holy Eucharist—the grace of which, Scripture and Church doctrine proclaim, is necessary for eternal life. How is it, then, that the Church can declare that the way to salvation lies open to them?

Answer to those questions is to be found through theological reflection on the place of natural religion in God's design for bestowing eternal life upon his children. Corresponding to each of those two essential aspects of the divinely willed economy of salvation there may be discerned analogues in natural religion which, elevated to a supernatural finality, avail as entry points for the saving grace of Christ into the life of each of those countless men and women who outwardly appear far from him.

To consider the first essential aspect, the subjective, it may be seen from the doctrinal statements of the Church summarized above that the acknowledgment by human reason of God's existence, providence, and law can serve, for every human being inculpably heedless of Christ's revelation, as a gateway to the gift of supernatural and saving faith. Certainly, inspired Scripture and the Church's doctrine teach that faith in Christ the Savior is requisite for salvation. However, in the deeper understanding of that doctrine by the Church, which is the divinely guided interpreter of inspired Scripture, explicit faith in Christ the Savior is not required from all, but implicit faith may suffice.[19]

The essentially sufficient truth-content of saving faith is seen to be that stated in Hebrews 11.6: "It is impossible to please God without faith, since anyone who comes to him must believe that he exists and rewards those who try to find him." All who so believe in God—namely, as supreme Lord, provider, and rewarder—equivalently assent to the truth of the whole economy of salvation accomplished by God through the incarnate Son. By confessing their faith in his sovereignty, justice, and merciful providence, they are implicitly embracing in their comprehensive act of faith all that his loving plan entails, including above all the redemption of the human race wrought by Christ. Nor even, in this theological perspective, is it necessary that one who is saved by such implicit faith in Christ should have an explicitly formulated theological concept of God as creator, lawgiver, and rewarder. The faithful outreach of the mind and heart to ultimate goodness, purpose, and righteousness may provide the equivalent of that faith-concept.

As well as responding to his loving initiative by faith, either explicit or at least implicit, those who receive justification by God's grace must also respond to him by loving obedience. In one blamelessly ignorant of Christ's revelation, that response of the will may be equivalently given by right living and loving according to the dictates of natural conscience, unknowingly elevated by grace, as the documents of the Church cited above attest.

What of the second essential aspect in the revealed economy of salvation, namely, the objectively necessary instrumentality of Christ's sacramental Church in mediating his redemptive work to humankind? As the Word became incarnate and brought salvation to all humanity by his action in this world, so too it is his will to transmit his saving power to all through his Church, in which he continues to be sacramentally present in this world. But how can those who are beyond the bounds of his visible Church be linked to its sacramental life? The sources of revelation assure us that they are so linked but do not provide us with a clear explanation of *how* they are linked. As the Second Vatican Council teaches, "Since Christ died for all, and since the ultimate vocation of mankind is in fact one, and divine, we must believe that the Holy Spirit offers to all the possibility of sharing, in a manner known to God, in the Paschal Mystery."[20]

While the manner of that sharing is mysterious, lack of knowledge of it does not bar the non-Christian multitudes of humankind from receiving Christ's grace of redemption and eternal life. In God's loving design to give access to salvation and eternal beatitude to all his children, just as it is not necessary that all those who are saved by Christ should have explicit knowledge of him and his saving work, so also it is not necessary that they should have awareness of their sharing in the Paschal Mystery of salvation through the sacramental medium of his Church. In the next chapter I indicate further reasons for concluding that the vital though unrecognized link with Christ's Church is provided for non-Christians within their own religious communities through the practice and institutions of natural religion, given salvific finality by divine grace.

In this wider understanding of the theology of salvation, the divinely established necessity of the grace bestowed through the sacraments of Baptism and Eucharist is no whit diminished. It is certainly the belief of the Church since its beginning, based on the solemn words of Our Lord in the Gospel, that no one comes to his gift of eternal life save through the grace conferred by the sacraments of baptismal regeneration and of eucharistic union with himself. In the course of time, however, the Church came to recognize that a *votum sacramenti*, that is, an efficacious desire to receive those sacraments of salvation is held acceptable in the heavenly reckoning as equivalent to actual reception of them.[21] It is now likewise recognized that, in those who are blamelessly ignorant of the Christian dispensation, the desire to submit themselves to God, the ultimate truth and good, and to conform to all that he wills includes implicitly such an efficacious *votum* to receive those two primary sacraments of salvation and so opens the way to conferral of their grace.

❄

Such then, are the theological reasons for concluding that, in the divine salvific design, the natural religion of humankind serves as the providential means whereby Christ's saving grace and light, transmitted through his sacramental Church, is available to every human person, even though he or she be seemingly separated from the Christian fold.

Catholic theology now recognizes that all non-Christians are individually related to the Church of Christ. Are there also theological reasons for supposing that the religions to which they belong have a corporate relation to the Church? In the divine economy of salvation, do those religions collectively serve as channels of grace? Does not the respect which the Second Vatican Council expresses for them imply as much? On these questions I offer further reflections in the following chapter.

Chapter 7

Are Non-Christian Religions Channels of Revelation and Salvation?

The Catholic Church rejects nothing that is true and holy in those religions. She holds in sincere esteem those ways of life and conduct, those precepts and doctrines which, though differing in many respects from what she herself holds and teaches, nevertheless often reflect a ray of that truth which enlightens all men. Yet she proclaims, and is in duty bound to proclaim unceasingly, Christ who is "the way, the truth and the life" (John 1.6). In him, in whom God reconciles all things to himself, men find the fulness of religious life.

Vatican II, Nostra aetate, §2

Missionary activity . . . is the realization in the world and in its history of the plan of God . . . It makes present Christ, the author of salvation. It purges of evil associations and restores to Christ their source whatever elements of truth and grace that are found to exist—through a secret presence of God, as it were—among the peoples of the earth . . . So whatever there is of good found sown in the heart and mind of man, or in the particular rites and cultures of the peoples, is not only preserved but is healed, elevated, and fulfilled, to the glory of God, to the confusion of the devil, and to the eternal beatitude of man.

Vatican II, Ad gentes, §9

Christian theology has come to recognize clearly that the sphere of divine salvific grace is not limited to the visible bounds of Christendom, but is coterminous with human experience. It honors the non-Christian religious cultures in which the lives of the majority of the human race are set. Within those communities multitudes of God's children come to acknowledge the evidences of him in the visible world and in themselves and are led to order their lives aright according to the innate law of conscience. Therein they seek and find clearer knowledge of God's holy will, guided by pious parents and by wise and upright teachers. Although the forms and institutions of human religion can be and often are corrupted by error and evil, the religious quest for God, instilled in human nature by its Creator and corporately expressed in those religious traditions, has a sacred character demanding reverent respect.

The Second Vatican Council expressed esteem for the non-Christian religions of the world in a manner unprecedented in the previous teaching of the Church. It testified that they "preserve in their traditions precious elements of religion and humanity."[1] In the testimonies cited at the head of this chapter it averred that they often reflect rays of divine light, and that there are present in them elements of truth, grace, and holiness, which have Christ as their source.[2] It also exhorted the faithful to engage in "dialogue and collaboration with followers of other religions and, while bearing witness to Christian faith and life, to recognize, preserve, and foster the spiritual and moral good found among them, and also their social and cultural values."[3] It urged Christians living among non-Christian peoples to "make themselves familiar with their national and religious traditions" and "to uncover with gladness and respect those seeds of the Word that lie hidden among them," in order "to learn, through sincere and patient dialogue, what riches God in his generosity has distributed among the nations."[4]

Pope Paul VI likewise reminded the Christian faithful of the rich spiritual heritage of those age-old religious traditions of humankind:

The Church respects and esteems those non-Christian religions because they are the living expressions of the soul of vast groups of people. They carry within them the echo of thousands of years of searching for God, a quest which is incomplete but often made with great sincerity and righteousness of heart. They possess an impressive patrimony of deeply religious texts. They have taught generations of people how to pray.[5]

Thus the Catholic Church has now embraced what is often called "the wider ecumenism." This term reflects the understanding of the Greek word *oikoumene*, from which the term "ecumenism" is derived, not simply in its specifically Christian usage to denote all Christendom, but in the more general sense of the word as referring to "the whole inhabited earth." Vatican II's teaching, especially in its *Constitution on the Church in the Modern World (Lumen gentium)*, manifests that universal concern.

For better or sometimes for worse, the peoples and regions of the earth are being linked ever more closely in mutual interaction. Global forces, political, social, economic, scientific, and cultural, are reshaping our world in a new common mold. The communications revolution has brought a new immediacy in international relations and in awareness of the lives of other peoples. Even at the level of secular solidarity there is a new sense of the oneness of the human family, of our common responsibility for the essential needs and rights of human beings in all lands, of shared anxiety about our common perils, and of determination to work together for the future of the human family. The post-conciliar Church sees all this as the context for the wider ecumenism of interreligious dialogue and cooperation, to which it is committed.

The inclusivist teaching of the Church's magisterium on the eternal destiny of non-Christians and on the truths and values to be found in their religions is of course essentially different from the pluralist theory of those who proclaim a "Copernican Revolution" in perception of the relation of the various world religions to the divine Absolute and with one another. The implication of the metaphorical use of that expression is that each of the existing world religions, Christianity among them, is, so to speak, in independent orbit around that divine Absolute, and that the Christian religion therefore has no unique centrality or primacy.[6] Evidently such a theory, which may be called theocentric but not also Christocentric, is incompatible with fundamental Christian belief in Jesus Christ as the one divine redeemer and sole mediator between God and man.

In the light of the new appraisal by the Church of the truths and values contained in non-Christian religions, Catholic theologians reflect anew on the manner in which those religions are included in God's plan for bringing salvation and eternal life through Christ to all his children. We recall Vatican II's testimony that "God, in ways known to himself, can lead those who are inculpably ignorant of the Gospel to that faith without which it is impossible to please him (Hebrews 11.6)."[7] So the question arises: may not one of those hidden ways by which they can be led to faith and salvation be through the beliefs and sacred observances of the religious communities to which they belong?

The inward orientation of individual members of those religions to ultimate truth and right is outwardly expressed by their words and deeds and by their collective participation in the worship, devotions, and codes of conduct of their communities. Their inculpable adhesion to tenets and practices that are not compatible with the truths of Christian revelation does not nullify their comprehensive affirmation of divine being and goodness, an affirmation, which, elevated by grace, implicitly becomes salvific faith leading to eternal life. Cannot the religions to which they belong, it is now asked, be therefore recognized as channels and organs of salvation for their adherents?

"Quasi-ecclesial elements" in Non-Christian Religions?

Pursuing that line of inquiry, one asks whether an analogy may not legitimately be drawn between the wider interreligious ecumenism and intra-Christian ecumenism, that is, between, on the one hand, the status and value of the non-Christian religions affirmed by the Second Vatican Council and, on the other, the dignity and role that the Council recognized as belonging to the Christian "churches and ecclesial communities" separated from Catholic communion. In several testimonies the Council reverently acknowledged that Christ's sanctifying power is operative within those churches and communities, mysteriously linking them with his universal Church, notwithstanding any defects there may be in communion, doctrine, and discipline. May not a similar quasi-ecclesial link be postulated in the case of those non-Christian religious systems? Serious arguments are put forward to support a positive answer to that question. Just as there has been a development in Catholic theological understanding of the ecclesial dignity of other Christian communities of faith, it is urged, may not a similar development be made in appraisal of the God-given dignity of non-Christian communities of faith?

In its *Constitution on the Church*,[8] the Council firmly proclaimed the dogmatic truth that "the sole Church, which in the Creed we profess to be one, holy, catholic and apostolic" is that which "subsists in the Catholic Church governed by the successor of Peter and by the bishops in communion with him." Nevertheless it went straight on to testify that in the Christian communities outside the visible bounds of the one true Church "may be found many elements of sanctification and truth which, since they are gifts belonging to the Church of Christ, give impulse towards Catholic unity." It further testified:

The Church recognizes as joined to herself in many respects those who, baptized and honored with the Christian name, do not however profess the integral faith nor preserve unity of communion with the successor of Peter . . . In some real way they are conjoined in the Holy Spirit, who works with sanctifying power in them also, through his gifts and graces.[9]

In its Decree on Ecumenism Vatican II indicated more explicitly which are the elements of sanctification and truth to be found in the separated Christian churches and communities:

Of the elements and endowments by which the Church is built up and given life, some—indeed the greater number and the most significant of them—can exist outside the visible boundaries of the Catholic Church: the written word of God; the life of grace; faith, hope, and charity; the other inward gifts of the Holy Spirit, as well as visible elements. All of these, which come from Christ and lead back to him, belong by right to the one Church of Christ.

Hence it follows, the Council avowed, that

those separated churches and communities have by no means been deprived of significance and value in the mystery of salvation; for the Spirit of Christ does not decline to use them as means of salvation, which derive their efficacy from the very fulness of grace and truth with which the Catholic Church is endowed.[10]

It is with these doctrinal developments in mind that the question is now asked: can those principles of Christian ecumenism stated by Vatican II have application still more widely "outside the visible boundaries of the Catholic Church"? May not at least some of the ecclesial elements that the Council recognized to be present and operative in the separated Christian churches and communities be also present and operative, in a hidden manner, in the non-Christian religious communities to which the greater number of human beings belong? We recall the Council's testimony that within those other Christian bodies are "many elements of sanctification and truth" properly belonging to Christ's Church and "inward gifts of the Holy Spirit." We compare this with its assonant testimony that "elements of truth and grace," having Christ as their source, are present in non-Christian religions. May it not therefore be argued, from the affinity of phrasing in those conciliar pronouncements, that the precious elements acknowledged to exist in non-Christian religions are there accorded a dignity and efficacy akin to that of the similarly designated elements acknowledged to exist in Christian ecclesial communities separated from the Catholic Church? May it not be said that, in the former religious societies as well as in the latter, such supernatural elements mysteriously link them with the divine Redeemer and his Church, thus enabling those non-Christian religions to serve, albeit unknowingly, as conduits for his saving power?

Vatican II recognized that there is at least one religion other than Christianity that constitutes a community of saving faith, and in which believers collectively find a supernatural path to eternal life: namely, the religion of the Jews. The Council expressed reverent esteem for their religion as divinely instituted. "Pondering deeply on the mystery of the Church," it recalled "the spiritual bond by which the People of the New Testament are joined with the descendants of Abraham," sharing together "so great a common spiritual patrimony." Although, it declared, the greater number of the Jews at the time of Christ did not accept the Gospel, and indeed many opposed it, the Jewish people as a whole are not to be held culpable for rejecting Christ; they remain "most dear to God," who "does not repent of his gifts and vocation" to them.[11] It follows from this conciliar teaching that Jews seeking God's will have access to divine truth and eternal life not simply by the individual path of natural religion elevated by grace, but on account of the special revelation and covenant, attested in Holy Scripture, which was given to them collectively and irrevocably in God's sovereign plan of salvation.

Is Judaism unique among non-Christian religions in possessing this God-given dignity as a faith-community of revelation and grace? Can Catholic teaching allow that there may be other non-Christian faith-communities likewise collectively serving as pathways to eternal life for their adherents? While giving special honor to the Jews and their religion, Vatican II further stated in Lumen gentium[12] that "the plan of salvation also embraces [others] who acknowledge the Creator, in the first place the Muslims, who adore with us the one merciful God who will judge men on the last day." Likewise in Nostra aetate[13] the Council said of the Muslim believers:

They adore the one God, living and subsistent, merciful and omnipotent, who has spoken to men. They endeavor to submit themselves to his hidden decrees with all their heart, as Abraham, with whom Islamic faith freely aligns itself, submitted himself to God. Though not acknowledging Jesus as God, they venerate him as a prophet, and honor his virginal mother Mary, sometimes indeed devoutly invoking her.

May it then be said that the "Islamic faith" referred to by the Council unites Muslims in a sacred community, which, in a hidden manner, efficaciously mediates the salvation brought by Christ? The Qur'an reflects both Jewish and Christian influences and contains many references to persons and themes spoken of in the inspired Scriptures of the Old and New Testaments. As long ago as the seventeenth century Juan De Lugo made the bold speculation, singular indeed at that time, that the faith of Muslims might be appraised as direct assent to supernatural revelation, brought to them externally by tradition originating from the Christian Church.

If any Turks and Muslims were invincibly in error about Christ and his divinity . . . there is no reason why they could not have a true supernatural faith about God as the supernatural rewarder, since their belief about God is not based on arguments drawn from the natural creation, but they have this belief from tradition; and this tradition derives from the Church of the faithful and has come down to them, even though it is mixed with the errors of their sect.[14]

In putting forward that speculative suggestion De Lugo was concerned to interpret scriptural texts such as St. Paul's words in his Epistle to the Romans (10.14): "How are they to believe in him of whom they have never heard? And how are they to hear without a preacher?" Later theologians found themselves progressively freer to adopt the wider view, outlined in the preceding chapter and now confirmed by Church teaching, according to which the natural knowledge of God by human reason, supernaturally elevated by grace, may present the essential truth-content for an act of justifying faith, not only for Muslims but for all people of good will. By such faith those who adore God as revealer and merciful Lord of all and who seek to submit to his will in all things implicitly embrace the essential content of saving faith as stated in the Epistle to the Hebrews 11.6: "Without faith it is impossible to please God. For whoever would draw near to God must believe that he exists and that he rewards those who seek him."

While honoring the unique destiny and dignity of the Jewish people in the divine plan for the human race, and while speaking of the Muslims with special respect, Vatican II also expressed "sincere esteem" for adherents of other religions, to whom it referred more generally as "those who in shadows and images seek the unknown God," yet from whom "God is not distant."[15] Of those other religions, only two are explicitly mentioned in the conciliar documents: Hinduism, in which seekers "have recourse to God in confidence and love," and Buddhism, which "proposes a way of life by which men may with confidence and trust attain a state of perfect liberation and reach supreme illumination, either through their own efforts or with the aid of divine help."[16]

Surrogate Organs of Revelation and Salvation?

Since the time of Vatican II there has been much theological speculation about the implications and possible further development of the Council's teaching on the truths and values contained in non-Christian religions. Some authors do indeed propose the opinion that those religions, not only Judaism but also Islam and the other faiths of humankind, may in God's salvific plan be corporate channels for conveying supernatural revelation and salvific grace to the non-Christian multitudes of humankind.[17] Put forward within the limits of Catholic orthodoxy, such an opinion is essentially different from the pluralist theory, which supposes that each of the world's religions is an independent and alternative source of divine revelation and grace, and which thus contradicts belief in the uniqueness of Christianity as the all-sufficient and all-encompassing manifestation of God's purpose for humanity.

In considering the question whether the other religions of the world may have such a corporate salvific role, one must recognize that, while all of them manifest humankind's natural and universal yearning for the divine reality, they are very different in character. To some of them, such as Hinduism, Buddhism, Taoism, and primal religions, it is inappropriate to attribute a corporate institutional unity, whether in organization, beliefs, or observances. Different, too, from the traditional religions of the world are the new religious movements that have attracted to their ranks so many eager seekers in recent times.

One may distinguish two different senses in which the non-Christian religions are said to be communities of salvation. In the first sense, the proposition is interpreted to mean that, in the divine plan for humanity, those religions providentially serve as the communal environment in which the natural religious orientation of their adherents comes to supernatural fruition under the hidden but universal sway of the redeeming grace of Christ, mediated through his Church, "the universal sacrament of salvation." In the second sense, which is more questionable theologically, the proposition is interpreted to mean that the non-Christian religions serve, each in its own pattern of creed and cult, as divinely sanctioned pathways of revelation and salvation in their own right, parallel to—yet independent of—that of Christianity, leading their adherents to the ultimate union of all believers in the eschatological Kingdom of God, towards which all religions converge.

The difference between those two interpretations is not merely terminological but substantial. It must be recognized that the second interpretation is not supported by what the Church's magisterium explicitly teaches about the mediation of Christ's salvation; and that the first interpretation clearly accords with that teaching.

Governing all theological speculation on these issues is the fundamental Christian belief that God has given the human race one supernatural and definitive revelation of himself, one destiny, and one all-sufficient way to reach it. That way is solely through the incarnation, life, teaching, example, piacular death, and resurrection of the divine redeemer, Jesus Christ, who ever continues his saving and sanctifying work for all humankind through his presence in his Mystical Body, the Church. The revelation divinely given to the People of the Old Covenant was not a different revelation from that of Christ, but precursory to and fulfilled by it.

According to Catholic teaching, it is the saving truth and power that originates from that sole divine source, Christ, and that is perpetually channelled to all humanity through his Church that gives salutary value to the faith and ministry of Christian churches and ecclesial communities separated from the fulness of Catholic unity. It is consonant with the same teaching to affirm that, in the divine providential plan, the non-Christian religions provide the setting in which their adherents receive the saving grace of Christ mediated to all through his Church. But that teaching does not warrant the assertion that those religions provide independent pathways to salvation in their own right, possessing alternative divinely inspired scriptures, revelations, and means of mediating God's grace.

It is relevant here to recall again the doctrinal development by which, during the past century and a half, it has come to be explicitly taught by the Church that salvation is attainable by those who live and die outside its visible bounds. The documents of the Church's magisterium in which that teaching is unfolded uniformly proclaim the uniqueness and all-sufficiency of the revelation and saving work of Christ, sacramentally operative through his Church in all ages. They testify, certainly, that "seeds of the Word" are to be found sown broadcast in humanity and do not deny that non-Christian religions may provide the context in which divine saving grace is bestowed upon their members. However, those doctrinal sources not only provide no support for the theory that those religions are corporate and authentic channels of salvation in their own divinely bestowed right, but they indicate positively that for adherents of non-Christian religions (with the possible exception of those who may, directly or indirectly, derive knowledge of God and his will from Judaeo-Christian sources), it is observance of the natural religion of human reason and conscience, elevated by grace, that provides the path by which they are linked with Christ, the sole Savior. It is relevant to recall the coherent and progressive testimony of those doctrinal statements.

Deepening of Doctrinal Understanding

When, for the first time in its history, the Church's magisterium declared that those who remain strangers to the Christian religion can nevertheless be saved and granted eternal life, it was natural religion, elevated by divine grace, that was indicated to be the providential path leading to such fulfilment. In the passage in his encyclical *Quanto moerore conficiamur,* cited in the previous chapter, Pope Pius IX declared that with the aid of grace they can attain eternal life, provided that they "live morally and righteously, duly observing the natural law and its precepts inscribed in the hearts of all by God and ready to do his will." The same path to supernatural life through observance of natural religion and law, elevated by supernatural grace, was likewise indicated in the teaching of Pope Pius XII and reiterated with explicit clarity in the doctrinal decrees of the Second Vatican Council—as in the passage from *Lumen gentium* cited at the head of Chapter 6 and in several other passages.

Although Vatican II considerably developed the Catholic understanding of the dignity and worth of the non-Christian religions, recognizing the elements of God-given truth and goodness that they contain, it did not attribute to them any divinely instituted revelatory and salvific function as surrogates of Christ's Church. Nor do the relevant statements of the papal magisterium made since the time of the Council attribute to them any such function.[18] While further extolling the truths, goodness, and spiritual values to be found in those religious cultures and belief-systems, the papal statements do not countenance the view—but rather expressly exclude it—that they have in their own right a divinely instituted function to mediate, each in its own fashion, supernatural revelation and salvific grace to humanity.

In an address to the faithful in Rome in the year 1966 Pope Paul VI spoke as follows of those other religions:

> They are attempts, efforts, endeavors. They are arms stretched towards heaven, to which they seek to arrive; but they are not a response to the act by which God has come to meet man. This act is Christianity, Catholic life.[19]

Nine years later Paul VI repeated and reinforced that judgment in his apostolic exhortation *Evangelii nuntiandi*, addressed to the whole Catholic world. There he referred to the non-Christian faiths as "natural religious expressions most worthy of esteem," but emphatically contrasted them with the religion of Jesus, which, he said, "effectively establishes with God an authentic and living relationship, which the other religions do not succeed in doing, even though they have, as it were, their arms stretched towards heaven."[20]

The teaching of Pope John Paul II relating to the divine plan for the salvation of non-Christians lays special emphasis on the active presence of the Holy Spirit in each person. This emphasis is present in his three encyclicals *Redemptor hominis* (1979), *Dominum et vivificantem* (1986), and *Redemptoris missio* (1991). "The Church's relationship with other religions," he said in the latter document, "is dictated by a twofold respect: respect for man in his quest for answers to the deepest questions of his life, and respect for the action of the Spirit in man."[21] He did not see salvation for those who do not consciously encounter Christ and his Church as being effected by some parallel and quasi-ecclesial mediatory function on the part of the religious communities to which they belong, but by that hidden presence and action of the Holy Spirit within each individual by grace:

For such people salvation in Christ is accessible by virtue of a grace which, while having a mysterious relation with the Church, does not make them formally part of the Church but enlightens them in a way which is accommodated to their spiritual and material situation. This grace comes from Christ; it is the result of his sacrifice and is communicated by the Holy Spirit. It enables each person to attain salvation through his or her free cooperation.[22]

The "spiritual and material situation" referred to here comprises the religious and social environment in which the non-Christian peoples of the earth live their lives. The gift of Christ's saving grace bestowed upon them is, the Pope says, "accommodated" to that situation. Such grace, bringing them to eternal life through a mysterious orientation to and vital relation with Christ's Church, the universal sacrament of salvation, is indeed not unrelated to the religious cultures in which they come to know and serve the ultimate divine reality. While non-Christian religions are not corporate organs of supernatural revelation and salvation and do not have an ecclesial role in mediating God's revelation and saving grace, their teachings, observances, and communal life may providentially serve for their adherents as salutary "mediations" in a general sense. That is, they collectively safeguard and proclaim the truths and values of natural religion which are elevated and supernaturalized by Christiform grace.[23]

In like manner so-called "secular mediations" too (e.g., love of neighbor, upright living, willed orientation to truth and goodness, pursuit of noble humanistic values and of the common good) may providentially serve as means to open the way to grace and eternal life through Christ for those who do not profess any religion and even do not explicitly acknowledge God. The avowal by Vatican II and the papal magisterium that such a path to salvation lies open even to those accounted as "non-believers" is relevant to discussion of our present question. Since they, though adhering to no religious tradition, can reach eternal life through their grace-aided testimony to truth and goodness and through their practice of natural virtue, the same may be said of those who are adherents of non-Christian religions, without any need to postulate a salvific function proper to each of the religious cultures to which they belong. Concerning such general and extra-ecclesial mediation of salutary grace, Pope John Paul II spoke as follows: "Although participated forms of mediation of different kinds and degrees are not excluded, they acquire meaning and value only from Christ's own mediation, and they cannot be understood to be parallel or complementary to his."[24]Thus, according to the newly clarified teaching of the Church, the spiritual truths and values that non-Christian religious communities contain and transmit to their adherents are not drawn from any new divine revelation or mission proper to those religions themselves, but from the God-given source, open to all, of natural theology, as the Pope observes in his encyclical *Fides et ratio*:[25] "Inasmuch as those cultures attest the spiritual values of ancient traditions, they point—implicitly but no less truly—to God manifesting himself in nature." Humanity's natural quest for God is pursued "through shadows and images," as the *Catechism of the Catholic Church*, first issued in 1994, reverently attests:

The Church's bond with non-Catholic religions is in the first place the common origin and end of the human race. The Catholic Church recognizes in other religions the search—among shadows and images—for the God who is unknown yet near, since he gives life and breath and all things and wishes all men to be saved.[26]

A Challenge Both to Ecclesiocentrism and to Christocentrism

Given the purpose and perspective of this book, as stated in my introductory chapter, I digress only rarely to discuss the controversial opinions of individual authors. In discussion of the theme of this chapter one such longer digression seems needful, in order to take account of a challenging theological study which was first published in 1997 and has since aroused considerable interest. It is the work of Fr. Jacques Dupuis, S.J., *Toward a Christian Theology of Religious Pluralism*.[27] Some debatable opinions expressed in it evidently have direct relevance to major themes discussed in this chapter and elsewhere in my pages. Critical appraisal of the renowned author's book provides opportunity and stimulus for deeper exploration of those themes.

Dupuis's book has been justly acclaimed for its comprehensive survey of the vast range of historical developments and theological teachings and controversies relating to the Christian assessment of non-Christian religions through the centuries. That historical survey is contained in Part I of his work, concerning which the publishers confidently claim that it "is so comprehensive that it will remain the definitive historical analysis of the question for many years to come."

Part II of the work, however, is of a notably different character, and seems less likely to win general acclaim and agreement. In it the author offers a "synthetic and thematic" study, which includes a critical discussion of established theological positions concerning religious pluralism. Convinced that a further development—indeed a corrective reappraisal—of those positions is possible and desirable, he seeks in that second part of his book to promote such a process by a dialectic contribution of his own, which he sets out in a complex theological essay.

In presenting his thesis he draws on other recent and innovative writings on the subject, by both Catholic and non-Catholic authors, elements from which he incorporates in his own synthesis. He also draws on his own long experience of teaching theology in a non-Christian cultural environment and on his specialist knowledge of Indian religious thought. He considers that there is an imbalance in current theological assessment within the Church of the place and value of non-Christian religions in the divine economy of salvation, an imbalance which should be corrected by recourse to Asian, and particularly Indian, perspectives. His total argument (which is intricate and in some places of uncertain coherence) cannot be adequately conveyed in a brief summary, but some points crucial to the issues discussed earlier in this chapter call for particular comment here.

Dupuis adopts the standpoint of a higher critic of recent doctrinal documents of the teaching Church, especially the statements of the Second Vatican Council and of the post-conciliar papal magisterium relating to non-Christian religions.[28] While conceding that Vatican II's pronouncements on that question, though primarily "pragmatic," were "not devoid of doctrinal significance," he repeatedly deplores the "limitations" that he discerns in the conciliar documents. The special target of his criticism of the Council is what he describes as the "strongly ecclesiocentric perspective of its doctrine in general and of *Nostra aetate* in particular." Indeed, he sees in its unduly Church-centered perspective "the probable reason for its limitations and silences" in its teaching about the place and value of other religions. His disagreement with what he sees as the Council's blinkered ecclesiocentrism necessarily leads him to discount its often repeated insistence on the role of the Church as "the universal sacrament of salvation."

He also considers that the teaching of Paul VI and John Paul II suffers from the same defects. He especially regrets the lack of openness of those pontiffs to the more liberal theories that he advocates, theories that assert the God-given role and dignity of the non-Christian religions as being in their own right "legitimate paths of salvation for their members," distinct from the path of the Christian Church. He finds particular fault with John Paul II's encyclical *Redemptoris missio*, which he judges to suffer, like the documents of Vatican II, from the defects of what he repeatedly describes as a "narrow ecclesiocentric perspective." While critical of the "shortcomings" and "limitations" of those recent documents of the magisterium, he is nevertheless alert to detect phrases within them which might be construed as favorable to the opinions that he approves.[29]

Dupuis discusses the question, raised by some authors in recent years, whether the plurality of religions, ever persisting in human history,[30] is *"de facto* or *de jure,"* that is, whether such plurality is to be reckoned as an imperfection in humanity's conformity to the divine salvific plan, to be deplored and progressively remedied, or whether it is to be assessed positively, as witness both "to the superabundant generosity with which God has manifested himself to humankind in manifold ways," and to the value of humanity's "pluriform response" to God. He favors the latter alternative,[31] seeing each such diverse response as having its own validity. He cites with approval a testimony from an Indian source that in theological dialogue between differing religions there is built up a community of understanding in which "differences become complementarities and divergences are changed into pointers to communion."[32]

He weighs the value of various "paradigms" or "models" that are proposed as patterns of inquiry in present-day debate on the theology of religious pluralism. Leaving aside the model of "ecclesiocentrism," which he criticizes as too narrow, he includes among the relevant heuristic models those of "Christocentrism," "theocentrism," "soteriocentrism," "reality-centrism," and "regnocentrism." While he regards those "isms" as complementary, it is to the perspective of regnocentrism that he attributes primacy, as being the most inclusive model and a universally applicable "key of interpretation." He describes it as

the Kingdom-centred model—transcending a narrow Church-centred perspective—which in turn makes it possible to visualize how Christianity and the other religious traditions share together in God's Reign, which they are called upon to build together unto its eschatological fulness.[33]

The case put forward in his thirteenth chapter, he claims, "shows that a reg-nocentric perspective, correctly understood, offers a broader horizon for a theology of religious pluralism than can be offered by an ecclesiocentric perspective, often narrowly conceived in the past."[34] In the same vein he writes elsewhere,

The Church has no monopoly on the Reign of God. The members of the other re-ligious traditions, who perceive the call of God through their own traditions, share truly—even without being formally aware of it—in the Reign of God present in his-tory, of which they are members in their own right.

Those who propose such a notion of regnocentrism as an all-inclusive paradigm to describe the universal religion of humankind and to indicate the ultimate goal towards which all the religions of the world are leading their members by distinct and self-sufficient paths add to it a corollary. That is, it is further concluded that, for members of non-Christian religions jour-neying to that Kingdom, which subsumes and transcends all religions, it is at no stage necessary to have a salvific bond with Christ's Church, whether in history or in the final *eschaton*. Indeed, the survival of an eschatological Church is questioned. Dupuis appraises positively the opinion of some au-thors who conclude that the Church "is provisional by nature and that it is due to disappear when the fulness of the Kingdom is achieved, since, as a sacramental reality, it was subordinated to the Kingdom." This way of thinking, he explains, "can show how the followers of other religious tradi-tions who have belonged to the Kingdom of God in history without being members of the Church, can at the end of time share in the fulness of the Kingdom without having to be linked at the last stage to an eschatological Church."[35] One may compare this viewpoint with traditional doctrine con-cerning the Church in the glory of heaven, recalled by Vatican II in its refer-ence to "the Church endowed with heavenly riches" in indivisible continu-ity with the Church on earth.[36]

While duly attesting "the fulness of revelation in Jesus Christ," Dupuis adds a qualification: "Nevertheless, this revelation is not absolute. It re-mains relative." He writes positively of "different and complementary" rev-elations. He makes passing reference to divine revelation mediated by the prophet Muhammad. He reverentially explains a sense in which the sacred writings of non-Christian religious traditions may be acknowledged to be divinely inspired scriptures, citing the nuanced conclusion of a group of Indian Christian theologians that, for the members of those traditions, those writings are "God-given means leading them to their ultimate destiny."[37]

When referring to the non-Christian religions as "legitimate paths to salvation for their members," the author is careful to avow that those paths are "necessarily in relation to the mystery of Christ." He writes also of "the reciprocal relation that exists between the path that is in Jesus Christ and the various paths to salvation proposed by the religious traditions to their members." But it seems clear that he conceives that relation as one of divinely coordinated parallelism, not as one of necessary dependence of those other paths on the uniquely salvific path of Jesus Christ, made available to all humankind through his Church. It is the latter doctrine that is expressed in the documents of the Church's magisterium cited earlier in this chapter.

As well as discounting any such necessary relation of non-Christian religions and of their members to the Church, Dupuis's thesis has another and still more problematic aspect. It is his discussion of their relation to Jesus Christ himself. From statements in his book it appears that, in reassessing the various "interpretative keys" proposed for deeper theological understanding of religious pluralism, not only must the narrow paradigm of ecclesiocentrism be replaced by the universalist paradigm of regnocentrism, but the traditional paradigm of Christocentrism itself must be reappraised and redefined.

He remarks at the beginning of his study that from the year 1970 onwards, "traditional Christocentrism, which had so far provided the backbone for a theology of religions, was now being submitted to serious questioning in Christian circles."[38] What, one may ask, has motivated this questioning? There is no doubt that the apparent intransigence of traditional Christocentric doctrine can be a stumbling block to mutual agreement in interreligious dialogue between Christians and non-Christians—as I myself have observed when taking part in many such colloquies. Spokesmen for non-Christian religions may object that it is unacceptable or even offensive to them to be told, in the famous phrase of Karl Rahner, that they are really "anonymous Christians," and that Christ and his Church provide the sole efficacious means by which all peoples, themselves included, can reach eternal life. To remove that stumbling block, or at least to soften its harsh edges, is clearly the irenic intent of those "sensitive authors in Christian circles" to whom Dupuis refers, who are now seriously questioning traditional Christocentrism. It appears that he himself approves their revisionary enterprise. With them, he criticizes as outmoded "the fulfilment theory," according to which the other religions are precursory to and find their true meaning only in the revealed religion of Jesus Christ, the sole Savior and Mediator between God and man.

True, Dupuis faithfully attests the unique significance of the Incarnation: "The historical event of God's becoming flesh marks the deepest and most decisive engagement of God with humankind; it establishes with it a bond of union that can never be severed." Yet he goes on to qualify this testimony with the following reservation: "But this event is, of necessity and irremediably, marked by the particularity of every historical happening." He then asserts:

Truth and grace found elsewhere must not be reduced to "seeds" or "stepping stones" simply to be nurtured or used and then superseded in Christian revelation. They represent additional and autonomous benefits. More divine truth and grace are found operative in the entire history of God's dealings with humankind than are available simply in the Christian tradition.[39]

Those whom he describes as "recent authors sensitive to the demands of an open-ended theology of religious pluralism" seek a conceptual model according to which the "historical particularity" of Jesus Christ can be integrated into a more universal divine plan. Dupuis writes with special approval of such a model which has been proposed in recent years. It is described as a "Trinitarian and Spirit-Christology," which, he says, "allowed a deeper appreciation and more positive evaluation of religious founders and traditions outside Christianity."

This newly proposed "key of interpretation," it is claimed, makes it possible to widen the meaning of the term "Christology." As well as denoting the life and work of Jesus of Nazareth, the divine Word incarnate and founder of the Christian religion in history, the term may also be taken to refer, as Dupuis explains, to "the universal active presence of the divine Word and his Spirit, as a source of enlightenment and inspiration of religious founders and the traditions which have sprung from their experience."[40] It is argued that this "Word/Spirit presence," transcending historical particularity, can be called a "Christ-presence" in all the world's religions, making it possible for each of them to serve in its own right as an organ of salvation and eternal life.

Dupuis's Christological reflections can be seen to have affinities with the notion of the extra-historical "Unknown Christ of Hinduism," developed in a celebrated book by Raimun Pannikar bearing that title,[41] and with the similar speculations of other authors. It would seem that those thinkers (ancient and modern) who have spoken of a distinction between the historical Jesus Christ of Nazareth and "the cosmic Christ," transcending historical and cultural particularity, confuse such a postulated distinction with the duality affirmed by Christian faith between the divine nature and the human nature of the one Person of Jesus Christ. That faith confesses Jesus of Nazareth to be the Son of God made man, and to be the way, the truth, and the life for all human beings in all religious cultures. No attempted application of the theological principle of *communicatio idiomatum* can validate a theory of a pluriform salvific act in history of the transcendent "Word/Spirit" distinct from the uniquely salvific act of the incarnate Word who is Jesus the Nazarene. No theoretical explanation of the salvation of humanity can accord with Christian orthodoxy if it bypasses the humanity of that Word incarnate. Critical dissent from this new-fashioned soteriology seems imperative, "lest the cross of Christ be emptied of its power" (1 Corinthians 1.17).

By extending and altering the meaning of the term "Christology," those authors seek to retain the term "Christocentrism" when propounding their theory of parallel and independent roles of the different religions in the economy of salvation. In traditional Christocentric perspective, all that God does and continues to do through history to bring to himself those who belong to the non-Christian religions is seen as essentially relational to the mystery of his unique self-disclosure in Jesus Christ. Contrariwise, the new perspective, Dupuis explains, "has led to viewing the mystery of God's self-disclosure in Jesus Christ as essentially relational to what God has done and continues to do through history, from beginning to end."[42] In other words, those other religions are no longer seen to be essentially relational to Christianity in the divine plan of salvation, but both they and Christianity are seen to be essentially and independently relational to a wider and more comprehensive divine plan.

It is evident that the principles that I have assumed as basic in this discussion of "the theology of religious pluralism," and that I see as indicating the necessary parameters within which all Catholic theological discussion of this question must be set, differ radically from the presuppositions of Dupuis and of the other writers who have in recent years put forward revisionist opinions similar to his. Central among the basic principles assumed here is faithful adherence to the authoritative interpretation given by the Church's magisterium to the scriptural truths on which Christology, soteriology, ecclesiology, and indeed all dogmatic theology is based.

Others too have made criticisms of obscure aspects of Fr. Dupuis's speculative thesis, and a discreet call came from an authoritative quarter for clearer explanation of its meaning.[43] While recognizing that in his reverent search for fuller light he expresses his questionable speculations in the subjunctive mood, I have felt constrained to express dissent from those problematic aspects of his thesis, and to indicate my reasons for concluding that it cannot be regarded as pointing the way to an authentic development in Catholic understanding of the place and role of non-Christian religions in God's salvific plan for humanity.

❄

I end this chapter by reflecting once again that natural religion, while common to all peoples, exists nowhere in the world in a pure state or as a recognizable entity. Its God-given light is refracted, obscured, and often distorted by the medium of the human institutions in which it is visible. Expressed in diverse forms in the many religious systems of the world, natural religion is, in the existing condition of humanity, fallible and flawed. As is all human experience, the profession and practice of human religion is affected by the dark counter-mystery of sin and iniquity. It can at times be radically perverted and can present a face of demonic evil. While natural religion is a pervasive reality throughout human history and society, pointing to humanity's need to know and serve God, it also points to its own need to be purified and transformed by the higher self-revelation of God. In the words of Vatican II cited above, the "elements of truth and grace found existing among the peoples of the earth" must be "purged of evil associations and restored to Christ their source."

Whatever is true and good in human experience, both individual and social, can be ennobled by supernatural grace to avail towards everlasting life.

In the mystery of divine love, the People of God who visibly form Christ's Church on earth are invisibly joined in a community of salvation with the other peoples of the earth who, inculpably, do not accept Christ, yet are all alike embraced by his universal love and redemptive grace. Reverently contemplating that mystery, Christians rejoice in the Gospel treasure they themselves have received in their life of explicit faith and sacramental grace within the bosom of the Church, through which Jesus Christ communicates his saving power to all humanity. They also find, in the good and holy lives of countless members of non-Christian religions, examples to be followed and mirrors reflecting that hidden presence of Jesus Christ, the God-man who died upon the cross for all. They may therefore thankfully and humbly rejoice that he, the Lord who invites all alike to the heavenly wedding feast, welcomes with equal love those who here are not yet recognized, and who do not yet recognize themselves, as his own.

Chapter 8

"THE ONE WHO IS"

This name, THE ONE WHO IS, is the most proper name of God, for three reasons. First, because of what it denotes: for it does not signify any particular form, but existence itself. Wherefore, since to exist is God's essential nature, which is true of no other, it is clear that this, out of all other names, is most properly applied to God . . . Second, for its universality. By the use of any other name there is limitation to one particular mode of substantial reality; but this name does not delimit any particular mode of existing—rather it encompasses all modes without distinction, and thus it refers to the boundless ocean of reality. Third, because of what it connotes: because it implies existence [esse] entirely in the present tense; and this is most proper to God, whose existence is beyond any limits of past or future.

St. Thomas Aquinas, Summa theologiae, I.13.11

The revelation of the ineffable name, "THE ONE WHO IS" contains the truth that God alone IS. It was in that sense that the Greek Septuagint translation of the Hebrew scriptures, which was followed by the Church's tradition, understood the meaning of the divine name [YAHWEH]: God is the fulness of Being and of every perfection, without beginning and without end. While all creatures receive what they are and have from him, he alone is his very Being, and he is of himself everything that he is.

Catechism of the Catholic Church, § 213

The central theme of this book is the relation of created beings to divine Being in the light of faith and reason. To meditate upon that fundamental theme of all religion is not mere metaphysical speculation. In experiential realization of the sacredness of being, saints and sages find in all ages a path to spiritual wisdom and loving service of God. That path is not reserved for a favored few but is open for all Godfaring humanity to follow.

In earlier pages I spoke of the significance of the Names of God in the languages of humankind and observed that many of the terms used in Christian theology to designate God are also deeply rooted and freely used in other religious cultures: titles such as Father, Lord, Creator, Ruler, Judge; and adjectival attributes proclaiming him as supremely good, wise, provident, merciful, loving, just, powerful. Sharing in common the rational cognizance of God and of his law, Christians and non-Christians alike name and praise him in the common language of natural theology, spoken with equivalent meaning in the multiple dialects of human speech. It is that shared conceptual language that makes it possible for us to join together in meaningful interreligious dialogue and understanding with those of other faiths and cultures.

Out of all the terms and titles by which human beings designate God, one may be singled out that is unique yet omnivalent, one in which people of all faiths and cultures can find profound meaning. Aquinas testifies to it in the passage cited above: "This name, THE ONE WHO IS, is the most proper name of God." That same sacred name, in Hebrew, YAHWEH, can be found written both in the Bible and in the book of nature. Christian and Jewish believers read in their Scriptures of its revelation to Moses on Mount Horeb (Exodus 3.13–15). It may also be known to all men and women from the natural religion of humankind. Its characters are inscribed not only as a sacred tetragram in the Holy Scripture but also as a cryptic hierogram in the structure of the holy creation, to be deciphered by those who reverently seek its meaning.

In this chapter, which develops the preliminary outline of the theme introduced in the latter part of my second chapter, I draw upon a paper I presented to an interfaith symposium held at Assisi some years ago. The object of that colloquy was to discuss and compare the ways in which the various religions of the world designate and conceive of the ultimate divine reality. For the title of my contribution (which was later published in India),[1] I took the opening words of the passage cited at the head of this chapter from the *Summa theologiae* of Aquinas. Presenting here the argument put forward in that paper, in revised and much augmented form, I reproduce its first five paragraphs within quotation marks as a reminder that the text originated as a discourse addressed to fellow seekers of many faiths. I began as follows:

"It is good that believers belonging to the different religions of the world should reflect together on the ways in which we attempt to name the One who is above all denomination. We ask how, in each of our religious traditions, we refer to the transcendent Absolute in whom we find universal meaning and towards whom all of us, in our different ways, orientate our lives. We seek to compare those diverse names for the divine, and to penetrate beyond the words to what they signify. Let us explore together the possibilities of finding equivalence between the various names and forms of language that we use in our diverse traditions to refer to that supreme reality. Like all of you who join in this interreligious meeting of minds and hearts, I seek to learn from other believers how their sense of religious ultimacy is expressed and interpreted.

"My own patterns of thought and religious language have been shaped within the Christian tradition, in its Catholic form. Nevertheless, I submit that the theological insights which I offer here are not restricted to the thought-forms of that tradition, but accord with the religious intuitions of the whole human family. In this multifaith gathering I will not expound at length the meaning of the specifically Christian terms for denoting the supreme divine reality. There is the distinctive Christian dogma that proclaims our belief in the Trinity of Father, Son, and Holy Spirit, one God, not three gods. There are as well the Christological doctrines concerning God the Son, the eternal Logos, the divine Word who became incarnate in human nature as Jesus of Nazareth in order to reconcile the world to God and to raise human beings even to share in his own divine life. We know well that these Trinitarian and Christological tenets present special difficulty in dialogue with believers belonging to the other monotheistic religions, especially Judaism and Islam. In the perspectives of Eastern (especially Hindu) religion they are less of a stumbling-block, and may even provide scope for comparative interreligious discussion.

"Those central dogmas excepted, Christianity nevertheless shares with other religions a wealth of theological and devotional names and expressions by which to address and adore the Lord of all and to proclaim his sovereign holiness and law. So, for example, when Muslims devoutly recite the

Beautiful Names of Allah their litany of praise is in unison with the prayers and praises by which Christians in their own idiom honor God the almighty, beneficent, and merciful Lord of all. This category of theistic titles and attributes common to different religions offers a most fruitful field for comparative discussion between Christians and those of other faiths. It is within this field that I situate the theme of my contribution to our present colloquy.

"Of the many hallowed terms and titles by which the theistic piety of humankind acclaims God, I do not here single out for discussion any particular divine attribute or quality. There is, I submit, one all-encompassing way of apprehending and denoting the supreme divine reality which, while deeply influential in Christian theological contemplation, is not dependent on specifically Christian dogmatic premises but provides a common ground of contemplation and discourse for adherents of all religions. It has in fact been followed throughout the ages not only by the sages of the Christian tradition but also by those of the other faith-cultures.

"That way may be called the way of religious ontology—a rather daunting term used to refer to the human mind's grasp of *being*, our living experience of existent reality in all its amplitude. As theology means wisdom relating to God, so ontology means wisdom relating to *being*, existent reality. In the natural religion of the human race the two merge into a unitary wisdom which may be called (even more dauntingly!) ontotheology, the theology of being. St. Thomas Aquinas, most renowned of Catholic theologians, found in the concept of 'THE ONE WHO IS,'[2] of absolute existence, 'the most proper name of God.' His words are cited in the title of this discourse. What can be the meaning and justification of such an assertion?"

With that exordium I invited my brothers and sisters of many faiths present at that colloquium in Assisi to enter into meditative reflection and dialogue on the meaning and mystery of Being. I pursue that reflection more fully here. The reader will naturally understand that the wider discussion of specific themes of Christian dogmatic theology which is presented here was not included in my address to that interfaith gathering.

Probing the Ultimate Meaning of Being

What is our everyday notion of *being*? Can we explain the meaning of the verb "to be," the most basic and universal constituent of all human language? Logically and grammatically, it has many nuances of usage;[3] but how can being itself be defined? Is the concept of being a mere logical abstraction, the most generic and formless distillation of all our thoughts, as linguistic philosophers would have it? What could such a seemingly abstract and empty concept have to do with the idea of God?

No, our awareness of being—of what is, of reality itself—is not the impoverished ultimate residue of all our thoughts, but the universally rich matrix of them all. We may indeed formulate a generic concept and a name to refer to being, but our grasp of it precedes all conceptualizing. It is the foundation of our rational consciousness, the first evidence which is the fount of all other evidence, the *a priori* apprehension of the real which validates all our reasoning. Implicitly it embraces universal reality as knowable by our minds. As the epistemological first principle, being is necessarily indefinable and inexplicable. All definition of an object is by combination of previously known concepts in order to situate it within an existing fabric of knowledge. But to define or explain being by such a process is impossible, for there is nothing antecedent to it in our knowledge.

This primordial awareness of being gives us simple and immediate certainty of the interrelatedness of all beings in one coherent fabric of reality and of the universal validity of the innate principles or laws of mind that condition the exercise of our reason. By subsequent introspection we may consciously reflect on the awesome power we have to judge truly according to those first principles of reasoning. We may give names to the latter, such as the principle of contradiction and the principle of causality or sufficient reason, and explicitly invoke them in logical argument. But, like the basic awareness of being itself which it manifests, the power of our intellect by which we apply those reasoning principles to all reality is not itself a logical premise; it precedes, makes possible, and verifies all our ratiocination.

It is traditional to refer to God as "the Supreme Being," a phrase worn trite by familiar usage. What is to be understood by "Being" in this phrase? Is it just that we use the word "beings" as a generic term applying to all persons and things, and we simply mean that God is the greatest being of them all? The objection to such a statement, piously intended though it may be, is that it puts God in a category together with his creatures. If he were one of a kind, albeit the greatest, he would not be God. Created being is not something additional to divine Being, but is wholly contingent on and incommensurate with the infinite plenitude of God's creative Being.

The notion of being that we humans draw from our experience of the created world may be predicated of God, but not in an univocal sense. Our manner of predicating being of God, referred to as "the analogy of being," is unique in our mental processes. We experience all reality as permeated with intelligible meaning. Life is a search for the meaning of being, and ultimately for the holy mystery of Being, for God, THE ONE WHO IS. He is the source and fulness of existent being and actuality.

This truth, expressed by St. Thomas Aquinas in the passage cited from his *Summa theologiae* at the head of this chapter, had been affirmed by St. Augustine nearly a millennium earlier in a limpid phrase: "I should say that God is no other than existent being itself" (*"Deus nihil aliud dicam esse nisi idipsum esse"*).[4] In the Eastern Church the same insight was expressed with forceful clarity by St. John Damascene in the following testimony, which St. Thomas Aquinas explicitly recalled five centuries later in the passage cited above:

Most appropriate of all the names that are attributed to God is ὁ ὤν, THE ONE WHO IS; as he himself replied to Moses on the mountain, saying, "Tell the sons of Israel, THE ONE WHO IS has sent me." All-encompassing, he possesses within himself the totality of being (ὅλον τὸ εἶναι) as in a measureless and limitless ocean of reality.[5]

Ontotheology was the common wisdom of the Christian doctors and schools. At the dawn of the golden age of medieval scholastic theology and philosophy, St. Anselm, prophet of the primacy of love in the understanding of faith, likewise gave witness to the wisdom that contemplates God as the supereminent Being above and beyond all being conceivable by the human intellect. Together with St. Thomas Aquinas and St. Albert the Great, St. Bonaventure used the same ontological terminology to express the meaning of the divinely revealed name: "He is very Being itself, most certain, which cannot be thought of as not being."[6] Whatever their differences on other disputed questions, the scholastic theologians and metaphysicians were at one in recognizing that the truth of the divine name revealed to Moses is the same truth that is the deepest discovery of the human intellect. No less than the Augustinian, Victorine, Dominican, and earlier Franciscan doctors, Duns Scotus attributed ultimate ontological significance to Exodus 3.14: "Revealing to [Moses] your ever-blessed name, you replied, 'I AM WHO AM.' Wherefore you are true Being, perfect Being [*esse verum, esse perfectum*]."[7]

When those Fathers, saints, and theologians of the Christian Church proclaimed that the highest expression of the nature of God was to acknowledge him as *idipsum esse*, very Being and the source of all derived being, did they hold that to be a truth supernaturally disclosed by divine revelation or a truth naturally discoverable by the human intellect? They held it to be both.

Their confession of God as sovereign and all-encompassing Being was scripturally based on the text of Exodus 3.13–14, as St. John Damascene testified in the passage cited. In that Exodus text it is related that, speaking to Moses on Mount Horeb, God revealed his identity and the name by which he should be designated. Moses asked of him, "If I come to the people of Israel and say to them, 'The God of your fathers has sent me to you,' and they ask me, 'What is his name?' what shall I say to them?" The divine reply, according to the literal rendering of the Hebrew words traditionally used in the Western Church, was, "I AM WHO AM." He said, "Thus shalt thou say to the children of Israel, 'He Who Is has sent me to you.'"[8] The definitive revelation of the holy name (in the original Hebrew, written as the sacred tetragram, YHWH, later vocalized as "YAHWEH") is further emphasized in the following verse: "This is my name for ever, and this is my memorial unto all generations."

In the Greek Septuagint version of the Old Testament, completed in the second century BC and used by the Christian Church from its beginning, the Hebrew phrase, *'ehyeh 'asher 'ehyeh*, literally translated above as "I AM WHO AM," was rendered as ἐγώ εἰμι ὁ ὤν, "I am the existing one"—that is, using the Greek present participle of the verb "to be" to express the meaning of the predicate. Although some critics would loftily discount as quaint and anachronistic the idea that the Hebrew phrases of Exodus 3.13–15 could be meant to express an ontological statement about ultimate reality, Catholic exegetes continue to interpret the inspired text as patient of that deeper sense.

On the meaning of the Hebrew word YAHWEH, declared in Exodus 3.15 to be the divine name forever, the editors of the *Jerusalem Bible* first note that this archaic form of the verb "to be" has been taken by some scholars to be a causative form of the verb, signifying, "he causes to be," "he brings into existence." But, they point out, "it is much more probably a form of the present indicative, meaning 'he is.'" They go on to comment as follows on the disputed interpretation of the Hebrew phrase 'ehyeh 'asher 'ehyeh, which was the opening phrase of God's reply when Moses asked to be told the divine name:

Speaking of himself, God can only use the first person: I am. The Hebrew can be translated literally: "I am what I am," which would mean that God does not wish to reveal his name; but in fact God is here giving his name, according to the Se- mitic way of thinking, ought in some degree to define him. But the Hebrew can also be translated literally as "I am who am," and by the rules of Hebrew syntax, this corresponds to "I am who is," "I am the one who exists," and this is how the translators of the Septuagint understood it: *ego eimi ho on*. God is the only truly ex- isting being. This means that he is transcendent and remains a mystery for man, but also that he acts in the history of his people and in human history, which he guides towards an end. In essence, this passage contains the developments to be given by subsequent revelation (Revelation 1.8: "who was, who is and is to come").[9]

That meaning of the sacred name YAHWEH was implicitly attested in the solemn declaration of Jesus Christ to his hostile hearers: "Before Abraham came to be, I AM" (John 8.58). Because of their understanding of that meaning they took up stones to strike him down as guilty of blasphemy.

The contemplation of God as THE ONE WHO IS by the Fathers and theolo- gians of the Church, while based on the scriptural revelation, also harmon- ized with neo-Platonist mystical philosophy, especially the writings of Plot- inus, which St. Augustine had studied deeply. In the light of their Christian faith they corrected, purified, and deepened that flawed recondite lore.[10] The influence of neo-Platonism is also apparent in the writings of some Muslim and Jewish thinkers of the Middle Ages. Despite its inadequacy, the Platonist vision of eternal divine being and goodness, seen reflected and re- fracted in the world of matter and change, has been an enduring expression of the natural theology of humankind and of the ceaseless yearning of the soul for ultimate divine reality.

The Philosophy and Theology of Esse

While the Fathers and theologians took it as evident that the Exodus text signified the primary truth of THE ONE WHO IS, their understanding of God as *ipsum esse per se subsistens*, self-subsistent absolute Being, has its own inner coherence and rational validation, which is independent of their exegesis of the Exodus text. Aquinas was awed by the direct revelation in Holy Scripture of what he called *"haec sublima veritas"*—"this sublime truth." From the divine self-disclosure on Mount Horeb, he concluded, "it follows that the essence or nature of God is divine act-of-being itself, *ipsum divinum esse*." At the same time he recognized that the same sublime truth is also certainly known by the reflection of the mind, which rises to God from the knowledge of created being, and that it is the supreme discovery of human reason. St. Thomas expresses his profound reflections on ultimate reality and on the relationship of created being to creative Being in dispassionately metaphysical language that may seem disconcertingly impersonal and dry. His manner of theologizing is markedly different from that of St. Augustine, who in his *Confessions* pours out his deepest spiritual experience and emotions in loving prayer and adoration addressed directly to God. Yet both testify to the same truth in the same Spirit.[11]

In honoring the sacred name of THE ONE WHO IS, Aquinas affirms God as infinite actuality, limited by no essential form or particular mode of being as are all his creatures. Making explicit a profound metaphysical insight (expressed six centuries previously by Boethius in his condensed maxim, "*Diversum est esse et id quod est*"), he reflects that in all created beings a real distinction may be discerned between *essentia* and *esse*, between essence and existence. Our intellect is fashioned to know both the nature of things, *what* they are, which it learns by conceptual reasoning and, more immediately, *that* they are, which it apprehends by an intuitive grasp of existential reality. In the supreme creative reality from whom they proceed, however, there can be no such duality between essence and existence. God's essential nature is to exist.[12]

To speak of "existence" as a noun is to run the risk of conceptualizing and reifying it. The actuality of existent being defies any attempt to enclose it in a concept or to define it as a thing. To signify the present actuality of existent being in a dynamic sense, scholastic Latin uses the infinitive of the verb "to be," *esse*, thus distinguishing it from *essentia*, a term which has a circumscribed and static connotation, referring to the specific nature and qualities of beings. In this discussion I follow that use of the Latin infinitive-noun, *esse*, to point to that indefinable aspect of "being-in-act."

The same usage is followed by Pope John Paul II in his encyclical *Fides et ratio*.[13] There he emphasizes the central importance for Christian theology of what he refers to as "the efficacious and dynamic philosophy of *esse*." As an equivalent expression, he also refers to "*philosophia essendi*," so using the (non-classical) Latin gerund of the verb "to be" to emphasize that dynamic sense of "being." In Chapter 14 I will return to further discussion of the significance of his adoption of such terminology, unprecedented in the documents of the Church's magisterium.

It is the human experience of *esse*, existent being, that validates the ascent of the mind to God by the ladder of created things. In earlier pages I dwelt on the reflected evidences of God that human reason finds in the form, harmony, beauty, causal potency, purposive order, and holy law that we encounter in our experience of this world. Those created perfections form a many-faceted mirror of the unitary divine perfection. They are formal aspects of the seamless fabric of reality, which we distinguish in our conceptual thought and on which we base rational arguments to demonstrate the existence and attributes of God. Permeating and empowering all those complementary ways by which the mind mounts to God is its basic awareness of dependent *esse*, the very existence of creatures, which universally manifests the creative act of THE ONE WHO IS.

The relationship of the contingent *esse* of creatures to the plenitude of divine *esse* is shrouded in deep mystery beyond our comprehension. Though we experience our own existence and that of the world around us, *esse* ever remains opaque to our understanding. By scientific inquiry our minds can arrive at a more or less accurate understanding of the nature and essential characteristics of created beings, but no human science can explain how they or we exist, nor can the human mind comprehend existence itself. We directly experience and mentally apprehend existent being and in so doing are drawn to awe and reverence for the necessarily existent Being on whom the existence of all contingent beings depends. To exist is, for a creature, to stand out from nothingness by God's creative fiat, to be actuated and energized by receptive participation in the infinite act and energy of the divine source of all being who is *idipsum esse*, very Being.

The Ontological Intuition

We come to the exercise of rational consciousness already possessed of the capacity to apprehend created being in all its limitless multiplicity and in its unity. The universal apprehension of the *esse* of things and of their present actuality is implicit in that consciousness. While explicit awareness that all the beings we apprehend are derived from transcendent, creative

Being is not given to us *a priori* by an innate concept, we can, however, attain
that awareness inferentially in the course of our lived experience of reality.

The ontological intuition itself, the mind's immediate grasp of being,
can be referred to only indirectly in conceptual language. As a personally
lived experience it is incommunicable, yet intensely real. Not only have
saints, spiritual masters, philosophers, and poets testified to it throughout
the ages, but countless men and women without historical fame also share
the same experience, which is by no means rare. For Everyman there are
times when the multiplicity and superficiality of things, the motley and
clamor of life's market place, fade into the background of consciousness,
and a penetrating sense of the actuality and sacredness of universal being
coming from its transcendent source strikes home.

The ontological intuition may come in diverse places, times, and
circumstances.[14] To some it comes as a sudden transforming apprehension
of the existent world that is *there*; in an instant all reality may be descried in
a grain of sand. The intellect's intuition of being can be quickened by our
rational emotions and affections, whether by the wonder that is evoked in
us by the elemental power of Nature, by the splendor of a starscape in the
night sky, by the beauty of great music, or by the self-sacrificing love of a
mother caring for her child. To many the ontological experience comes as
slow and silent dawning of deeper enlightenment as they reflect on the
Godward meaning and mystery of things and on their knowing selves.
They need no book learning to find that secret wisdom, humbly and word-
lessly, in prayerful contemplation. The grasp of God-like being may bring a
glow of lasting peace in the soul, or it may come as a transient shaft of beatifying light which at its passing leaves the soul in desolate longing for its return. In his *Confessions*, soliloquizing before God, St. Augustine recalls one
such moment of blissful enlightenment when his mind "in the flash of a
trembling glance attained to that which is. At that moment I saw your 'invisible nature understood by the things that are made.'" But, he lamented,
"I did not possess the strength to keep my vision fixed." So it passed, leaving him "only a loving memory and desire."[15]

On the ladder of being-awareness that leads to God there are many
lower rungs as well as those mounted by the great saints, mystics, and
seers. At those lower stages one may already gain an experiential awareness
of the interrelatedness of all beings and of the mysterious unity of all

being. It is a ladder that may be climbed with or without effort or direct intent. Some recognize an inner urge to make that ascent. "By continued reflection," wrote Fernand Van Steenberghen, "we must try to bring home to
ourselves the extraordinary and unique power which is implied in our capacity to know the real, or being, and our capacity to say 'that is.'"[16]

In different patterns of word and thought, the religious and philosophical systems of humankind give common testimony to the ontological experience, the awareness of the sacred mystery of being which brings a
sense of cosmic wholeness and holiness. Hindu seers may witness to it in
their heartfelt prayer to be led from the unreal to the real. It may lie at the
silent centre of the enlightenment by which Buddhist sages seek freedom
from the illusory world of fleeting phenomena—whether in timeless and
self-negating meditation or in the sudden irruption of *satori* in Zen. It is
alive in Jewish contemplation of *En Sof*, the Infinite, and of *Shekinah*, the divine immanence in the world. Muslim mystics affirm it in meditation upon
Al-Haqq, the Real. For the community of Islam at *salat* it may come in the
rhythmic adoration of Allah and total submission of self-will to his all-holy
and all-enacting will. It is evoked by the ecstatic *dhikr* of Sufi devotees. It
underlies the deep reverence of Jains for all life and their meditative quest
for the divinizing state of *arhat/mukti*. It is present in the bliss of Sikhs real-
ising *sahaj*, the non-separation of creatures from Creator; and in the piety
of Zoroastrians hymning the light of Ahura Mazda glowing in all that is
good. In ageless Chinese religion it motivates reverence of the all-
pervading *Tao*. It is sensed by the followers of primal religions living close to
Nature, reverencing the sacredness of the earth and all that it brings forth.

Even some who have no formulated religious convictions are yet fascinated by the stark fact and mystery of existence. So Ludwig Wittgenstein,
who has fame as a radically anti-metaphysical philosopher, mused at times
in strange wonder "that there should be anything rather than nothing." His
wonderment was expressed in incidental reflections that seem to belong to
a sphere of thought far removed from his positivist philosophy. "It is not
how things are in this world that is mystical, but *that* it exists," he said. "For
me the facts are unimportant. But what they mean when they say that 'the
world is there' lies close to my heart."[17]

For not a few speculative thinkers ontological awareness is a disconcerting challenge, even a decisive arena for choice for or against God. We may

compare, for instance, the differing reactions of three twentieth-century existentialist philosophers: Martin Heidegger, John Paul Sartre, and Karl Jaspers.

In the face of the insistent mystery of *Dasein*—"being-there-ness," sheer existence—Heidegger, like Kierkegaard and others, felt both wonder and *Angst*, anxious dread. In his massive work, *Being and Time*,[18] he wrestled through hundreds of pages with his dark inklings of the riddle of being, seeking to rescue the quest for authentic existence from what he saw as the aridity of traditional metaphysics. He ended his volume with an enigmatic admission that he had left still unaddressed and unresolved the fundamental question of "the interpretation of being." In his apparently secular and esoteric gospel of authentic existence some have discerned a radically religious concern, even a search for a "non-objectifying" theology.[19]

A different reaction was that of Sartre, atheist philosopher of being, who felt moved by the challenge of existence not to anxious dread but to nausea. His major work, *L'Être et le Néant*, revealed a love-hate attitude to the mystery of existent being—both fascination with its actuality and depths and at the same time repugnance from what he saw as its unacceptable implications. It has been aptly observed that "Sartre's whole interpretation of existence postulates the pursuit of God."[20] His response to the ontological enigma was to dismiss the human craving for relation to transcendent Being as an everlasting illusion. He felt an inverted missionary zeal to contradict and annul the idea of God that seems, he admitted, to surge up from reflection on being. In reaction, he conceived being as essentially flawed, in a state of dissociation and disintegration; in its dark depths he found ultimate absurdity.[21] While he recognized that existent being, *l'Être*, seems inevitably to present to the mind a reflection of God, he rejected it as a pseudo-image of a *Dieu manqué*, a meaningless and mocking non-God. Sartre's antisophical philosophy of being was autobiographical.

Karl Jaspers, my third chosen witness from the thought-world of secular existentialism, was also profoundly preoccupied with the challenge that *Existenz* presents to the human spirit, and with what he saw as the problematic question of how our experience of being, which seems to point to transcendent Being, can be meaningful. He acknowledged that the philosopher of *Existenz* "may well wish for a real direct presence of transcendence," even for "a real relationship to God in prayer." Nevertheless, be-

cause Jaspers supposed that transcendent deity must be in principle unknowable and ineffable for the human spirit, he saw no path open to the
seeker after ultimate reality but that of agnostic silence and inexpressible
yearning:

> If the boundary [of transcendence] were to be crossed, the necessary consequence
> would be to keep absolute silence. For any attempt at expression of it would at once
> make the deity into an object. Whatever had been experienced would become un-
> true in communicating it. Only in mystery is the hiddenness of God inviolate. Yet in
> the silence of its inwardness the soul will not, by fanatical denial of the possibility
> [of relationship with God], exclude itself from it.[22]

Elsewhere Jaspers spoke of the paradoxical self-negation of mind
needed before the seeker can take the ultimate stride to affirm transcendent *Existenz*. "It is thinkable," he wrote, "that the unthinkable exists."[23]
Missing from his philosophical theorizing was the concept of the analogy
of being, for want of which he remained agnostic about the power of the
human mind to be cognizant of divine being. He too was influenced by
Nietzsche, Kierkegaard, and the long legacy of Protestant fideism. Yet Jaspers still witnesses, though in a different idiom, to the same challenging ontological experience that was the wellspring of the long tradition of natural theology, of which St. Thomas Aquinas is the greatest exponent.

All created causation proceeds from the infinite creative Cause. All finite
being and act, including all that we do and all that is done to us, proceeds
from infinite divine being and act. At every instant and in every event of our
lives the holy will of God is declared and mediated to us by "the sacrament
of the present moment." Echoing that pregnant phrase of Jean-Pierre de
Caussade,[24] I offered to my companions at the Assisi colloquy this closing
reflection on the practical realization of the theology of being in the daily
living of our life:

> In the universe of nature, in all finite being, there is a primal revelation of infinite
> Being; and the universal actuality of the being that we experience is a primal sacra-
> ment mediating to the human race his holy purpose.

In that interreligious colloquy I invited my fellow-seekers of many faiths
to see the theology of being, the Godward experience of universal reality,
as "not simply a refinement of Western thought, but as pertaining to the

common spiritual patrimony of the human race," and to recognize that "the ontological intuition lies at the heart not only of Christian, Jewish, and Islamic meditation on God, but even of Buddhist, Hindu, Taoist, Sikh, Jain, Zoroastrian, and indeed all religious meditation on ultimate sacred reality." I ended by asking them, "In this common ascent from beings to Being is there not a path that all religions and believers may travel together?"

A number of my hearers responded to that question, then and in later conversation and correspondence. To our mutual joy, they testified that they did know that path, and that the same fundamental truth that I was trying to express in the language of my own religious culture was deeply present, albeit expressed in other language, in their own diverse traditions—and in their hearts. Such testimonies were given not only by Muslims and by a Jewish scholar, but also by Hindus, by a Sikh, and even by a Buddhist. A Zoroastrian *yasna* was cited: "Changeless art thou, Ahura Mazda, the same now and for ever. Thou art supernal Being moving all, yet moved by none." I learned of the ancient compendium of the Jain religion, the *Tattvartha Sutra*—"That Which Is."

Theological and metaphysical discourse on the divine mystery of being may seem to be mere arcane lore expressed in dauntingly technical language. It becomes authentic wisdom when it proceeds from and evokes loving self-submission to the omnipresent divine Creator and Lord who is that mystery. We can truly know him only when we orientate ourselves to him personally in mind and heart and living deed. Awareness of the God in whom we live and move and have our being is not esoteric philosophy but a simple and prayerful state of mind and will giving motivation to our every act.

I return to the theme of ontotheology in my fourteenth chapter, where I discuss the interactive relationship between "the philosophy of being" and the theology of Christian revelation. There I dwell further on the necessary connection between the two, which has been affirmed by Pope John Paul II in *Fides et ratio* to be of central importance for the faith that seeks understanding.

Chapter 9

Created Matter
Seedbed of Spirit, Shrine of Divinity

By the very nature of creation, the material universe is endowed with its own stability, truth and excellence, its own order and laws . . . Methodical research in all branches of knowledge, provided it is carried on in a truly scientific manner and in accordance with moral norms, can never conflict with faith, because the things of the world and the things of faith derive from the same God. It can be said, indeed, that one who humbly and perseveringly applies himself to investigating the secrets of nature is being led, even unknowingly, by the hand of God, who, holding all things in existence, causes them to be what they are.

Second Vatican Council, Gaudium et spes, §36

The question of the origins of the world and of man has been the object of many scientific studies which have greatly enriched our knowledge relating to the age and dimensions of the universe, to the development of life forms, and to the emergence of man. These discoveries move us to extol still more the greatness of the Creator, to give thanks to him for all his works, and for the understanding and science that he bestows upon those scholars and researchers. The great interest aroused by these studies is strongly stimulated by a question of another order, which goes beyond the proper domain of the natural sciences. It is not only a question of knowing when and how the universe arose physically, or when man appeared, but rather of discovering the meaning of such origin.

Catechism of the Catholic Church, §§ 283–84

Matter is our natural habitat. It is what is most immediately real to each of us. Although the immaterial spirit which animates our material body will not share its eventual decay and dissolution, it is essentially conjoined with this body in every vital activity at every moment of its mortal life. Our very rationality, which sets us apart from and in a higher plane of existence than all other animals, depends for its exercise on our bodily processes and on the data of the senses from which our intellect abstracts conceptual meaning. Sense-perception of material reality is the necessary precondition for even the highest reach of our natural reason, the attainment of knowledge of God himself. While bodily factors beyond our control—disease, injury, or senescence—cannot separate us from God's mercy and love, they can restrict and do eventually bring to a close the conscious outreach of our mind and will to him in this mortal life.

Rooted in matter by our very nature, we human beings are nevertheless ambivalent in our attitude towards it. We sense a rivalry between the two elements, spiritual and corporeal, which are united in our own personhood. Though powerfully swayed by natural desire for bodily satisfactions, we are also moved by a natural inclination to seek higher spiritual goals and values. From the inner voice of conscience, and in the light of both natural and revealed religion, we apprehend that material good must be subordinate to spiritual good; that the goods of this world are not our ultimate true good; and that by inordinate pursuit of sensory satisfactions we inflict harm upon ourselves and upon others, turning good to evil.

Very diverse theories have been proposed about the enigma of matter. At one extreme, Gnostic dualism supposes that matter is fundamentally evil, and views the material world as a prison from which spirit must be liberated. At the other extreme is the materialist dogma, which rejects all notions of spirit as illusion and asserts that there is ultimately no other reality than matter and its energies, ruled by the blind determinism of chance. If this, claimed by some to be "the scientific worldview," were true, the conclusion would necessarily follow that our rational consciousness itself is a by-product of that random flux of brute matter and its forces. Likewise illusory and ultimately meaningless would be our awareness of personal and permanent identity, our experience of free will, our sense of right and wrong, our ability to distinguish true from false, our search for values, beauty, and purpose in life. Such a nihilist and corrosive creed was starkly and defiantly proclaimed by the tormented agnostic Bertrand Russell: "Brief and powerless is man's life. On him and all his race the slow sure doom falls pitiless and dark. Blind to good and evil, reckless of destruction, omnipotent matter rolls on its relentless way."[1]

The Judeo-Christian vision of the material universe is essentially one of God-centred optimism. "And God saw everything that he had made, and, behold, it was very good" (Genesis 1.31). Scripture teaches that the created world is lovable because God its maker loves it:

> You ordered all things by measure, number and weight. You love all that exists, you hold nothing of what you have made in abhorrence; for if you had hated it you would not have formed it. And how, had you not willed it, could a thing endure, how be conserved if not called forth by you? How would anything have endured, if you had not willed it? You spare all things because all things are yours, Lord, lover of life, you whose imperishable spirit is in all. *(Wisdom 11.20, 24–26)*

True wisdom apprehends the material universe not as the ultimate reality, nor as merely data for scientific research and exploitation, nor as cosmic illusion, nor as a sinister thicket of evil from which entrapped spirit must escape, but as the meeting place of humanity with God. For the soul that seeks him, the world of matter is a garden of divine promise through which those who seek find the way to him. Although at times, with our perception dulled by toil, care, and self-love, we may feel alienated from that Eden and hear only faintly the far-away sound of the Lord God walking in his garden in the cool of the day, we can still live in constant hope and yearning to meet and greet him as we journey onward towards him through the mists:

> Since, tho' he is under the world's splendour and wonder,
> His mystery must be instressed, stressed;
> For I greet him the days I meet him
> and bless when I understand.[2]

To the faith that seeks understanding, matter matters profoundly. As the handiwork of the Creator, bearing his impress and pointing us to its divine origin, the material creation has the fundamental sacredness of all being. Matter is the seedbed in which the spiritual soul of each human person springs to life and grows to maturity. It is the stuff of this mortal body that is informed by immortal spirit and that is destined to be raised up and reunited with the soul in eternal life in a manner beyond all our imagining. Matter is the pathway through which we journey to God and the setting in which we serve and meet him. From matter are molded the good gifts that his providence presents to us for our sustenance and enjoyment in our earthly wayfaring. Above all, matter is sacred because in it God the Son has become incarnate: "The Word was made flesh and came to dwell among us" (John 1.14). The assumption of human nature by God himself, a divine mystery beyond the reach of self-vaunting reason but freely revealed to humble faith, is the supreme consecration of matter. The enfleshment of the divine Logos has opened to us new knowledge of God; it has also shown us new meaning in this world of matter. "He is the image of the invisible God, the first-born of all creation. All things were created through him and unto him. He is before all, and in him all things hold together" (Colossians 1.15–17). This material world is not only the reflection of God's transcendent being, goodness, and glory, not only the realm that he rules from above in power and wisdom, but it has become his very home. He has entered it to dwell in human body and soul. Humankind has become his own kin; a woman has become his own Mother.

Christian faith, confessing Jesus Christ to be both God and man, adores him both in his eternal Godhead and in his human body, which was conceived by the power of the Holy Spirit and born of the Blessed Virgin Mary, which is now risen and glorious in heaven, and which remains also truly present in this material world under the sacramental veils of the Eucharist. The presence at the heart of this universe of the Person who is both God and man reveals to us in new light the relationship of all creation to the omnipotent Creator. We see all created being as newly wrought and newly consecrated because in the human life of that divine Person the seemingly unbridgeable gulf between the infinite and the finite has been bridged. By becoming embodied in the world the eternal Son has transformed it. Through him not only all humanity but also all corporeal reality is ennobled. By entering into time he has given a new destiny to all that moves in time. Through him will come that final transmutation of all matter presaged in the New Testament, the consummation for which "the whole creation waits with eager longing," when there will be "a new heaven and a new earth."[3]

Matter, Science, and Religion

In our own age the human race has made momentous scientific discoveries relating both to the origins and composition of the material universe and to the evolution and genetic structure of living organisms. In a brief span of years—no longer than two human lifetimes—secrets of matter and of life hitherto unknown to humanity throughout all ages have been laid open. The ability of the human intellect to probe those secrets is itself one of the greatest wonders of the created world. We realize that God's all-provident will intended that his rational creatures should thus attain eventual understanding of the origins, basic structures, and energies of the material creation of which they are a part.

In the sphere of astrophysical cosmology, scientists have found cogent evidence to conclude that this universe of matter, vast beyond imagining, had a moment of absolute beginning. We listen wonderingly while they tell us of "Big Bang"; of a moment in which this material cosmos with all its potentialities originated, starting from a zero point at which there was neither mass nor energy; of an initial phase of primal and cataclysmic indeterminacy; of immediately subsequent emergence of the structures, forces, and order of matter; and of the ensuing spatial expansion and diversification of this universe that has been continuing ever since.

In the biological sphere, science has shown convincingly that organic life, eventually arising in this speck of the universe that is the planet Earth, evolved through countless ages from primitive structures to ever more diversified, complex, and well-adapted forms; and that the emergence of human life was in continuity with that evolutionary process. At the present time life-scientists are proceeding to unfold the secrets of the genetic constitution and programming of the human body and of all living organisms, leading to a new understanding of their hereditary characteristics and functioning. The river of DNA, they are convinced, sprang from a single source, from which all living species, humankind included, are derived. This scientific consensus has been summarized as follows: "The genetic code is in fact literally identical in all animals, plants and bacteria that have ever been looked at. All earthly living things are certainly descended from a single ancestor. Nobody would dispute that."[4]

One may muse on the strange parallelism between those two very different areas of discovery; between those two beginnings, cosmological and biological, detected by modern science. There is the zero point of matter and energy from which this material universe began and there is the zero point of the origin of life on this planet. Astrophysical science has heard the echo of Big Bang and has traced out its consequences. It continues to speculate on that moment and on the mathematical and physical puzzles relating to it. But it cannot explain or probe behind the occurrence of that primordial event in which, it concludes, this universe of matter with its order and energies began. Biophysical science has found that all existing genes on this planet are in one same line of descent from one primal living organism; but it is powerless to explain the origin of life itself, still less the origin of rationality which makes the species of *homo sapiens* essentially different from and unique among all other living species.

Facts firmly established by empirical science cannot be in contradiction with the revealed truths that we know from divine revelation. Truth is one wherever it is found, proceeding from one divine source, as John Paul II reiterates:

It is one and the same God who creates and validates our faculty of understanding and our reasoning about the intelligibility and rational coherence of the natural order of things, upon which scientists confidently rely, and who reveals himself as the Father of our Lord Jesus Christ.[5]

There are, however, different levels in our perception of truth. The deeper questions arising from the facts discovered by science cannot be answered by scientific research alone. In the words of the Church's *Catechism* cited above, "It is not only a question of knowing when and how the universe arose physically, or when man appeared, but rather of discovering the meaning of such origin." The investigative scientist has no prerogative in that search for ultimate meaning; it is the common concern of all thinking men and women.

There are many scientists who find in personal reflection on the material universe evidence of God's existence and creative power. In so doing they pass beyond the premises and methods of the natural sciences and express their conviction in the language of common sense, philosophy, and theology. Contrariwise, there are unbelieving scientists who adopt an atheistic and purely materialistic interpretation of the data of the universe and strive zealously to persuade others to accept it. They too are making assertions about fundamental reality and causal origins that go beyond the methods and premises of empirical science—albeit while distancing themselves from the common sense of humanity.

How do those scientific discoveries of natural science relating to the origins of the material universe and of life relate to the truths concerning the creation of the world and of man that we learn from scriptural revelation? The account now given by the natural sciences of the genesis of the universe and of life is indeed different in kind from that given in the Book of Genesis and in the Church's teaching, but it is not in conflict with it. While science is concerned with empirical investigation of the physical data and with proposing conclusions that best explain those data, inspired Scripture uses symbolic language to convey the deepest truth about the created world and man's place in it. Theological understanding of that language has developed and deepened in recent times.

Resolution of a Needless Quarrel

In the Darwinian age, too-literalist interpretation of the first three chapters of the Book of Genesis led biblical exegetes into a needless quarrel with biologists. The essential truth revealed in the scriptural accounts of the origin of the world and of man is that all things exist and act by the creative and provident will of God; that there was an absolute beginning of this universe, of which we are a part; that, according to the divine creative plan, an initial inchoate state was followed by subsequent ordering of the universe and the advent of life; that human beings are unique among all creatures inasmuch as they are immortal spirit embodied in matter, made in the image and likeness of God with a unique dignity and destiny; that all things and all happenings are subject to God's providence and are continuously dependent upon his almighty power; and that moral evil derives from the disobedience of rational creatures to his will.

Those essential truths of revelation are not, and cannot be, disproved by the facts discovered by modern science. Rather, while the recent findings of astrophysical cosmology, tracing the origin of this universe back to a moment which was the starting point of its systematization and expansion, cannot prove the revealed doctrine of *creatio ex nihilo*, they are evidently compatible with it. They also discredit the materialist and necessitarian theories, both ancient and modern, which supposed that this universe has existed eternally, unoriginated and perduring eternally in space and time.

Likewise biological science does not contradict the essential truths about the origin of humankind revealed in Scripture when it shows that the advent of *homo sapiens* was integrated in the same evolutionary sequence, influenced by natural selection, by which all life-forms developed and diversified; and that the bodily structure and processes of human beings are genetically programmed in the same manner as those of other living organisms. But here too empirical science can neither detect nor disprove the unique spiritual dignity and purpose of human nature.

When discussing biological evolution in a theological context, one must also observe the remarkable change that has come about during the past century in the attitude of the Christian Church towards the findings of science on that question. There has been progressive abandonment of the doubts that had earlier been expressed as to whether the conclusions reached by scientists concerning the emergence of human life within a common pattern of biological evolution were compatible with the scriptural revelation concerning the creation of the world and in particular concerning the special creation of man in the image and likeness of God. Those doubts have now been laid to rest. The study of the origins of life, and of human life in particular, is seen no longer as merely a field of dispute between believers and secularist scientists or as a problem to be faced by Christian apologists, but as a subject for reverent theological reflection.

Catholic theology is penetrating still more profoundly into the mystery of the divine creative and salvific plan for the human race, and in so doing reflects anew on the manner in which the material universe was prepared to become the shrine and altar of the incarnate Word of God. In the second of the two passages quoted at the head of this chapter, the *Catechism of the Catholic Church* acknowledges that "many scientific studies have splendidly enriched our knowledge relating to the development of life forms and to the emergence of man." In the first passage quoted there, the Second Vatican Council declared that "one who humbly and perseveringly applies himself to investigating the secrets of nature is being led, even unknowingly, by the hand of God." May one not, with due respect, confess also that the hand of God is leading his Church to fuller knowledge of his creative plan by means of the diligence and talent of those scientists who perseveringly apply themselves to investigating the secrets of nature?

Chapter 10

Theology and Teleology
Divine Design and Created Order

The created universe has its own goodness and proper perfection, but it did not spring
forth completely developed from the hands of the Creator. It was created "in statu
viae," in a state of wayfaring toward an ultimate perfection yet to be attained, to
which God has destined it. The dispositions by which God guides his creation towards
this perfection we call divine providence . . . God bestows on creatures not only their
existence, but also the dignity of action proper to themselves, of being causes and
principles in mutual interaction, and thus of cooperating in the accomplishment of
his design.

Catechism of the Catholic Church, §§ 302, 306

The human mind seeks to know causes; it asks what things are, how
they come to be so, and what they are for. It is this natural drive of our intellect that gives impetus both to scientific research and, at a deeper level,
to the quest for the ultimate meaning of the universe and of human life.
Causation as such cannot be an object of empirical investigation. The natural sciences rightly profess to deal only with physical phenomena and their
observable interconnections. Positivist philosophers of science, following
in the footsteps of David Hume, assert that causality is not a physical reality but a mere statistical concept that it is fruitless to discuss further. However, in order to make sense and use of the empirical data and to conduct

further investigations into the structure and properties of matter, all scientists—even those who dismiss causality as a mere conceptual figment—have to presuppose it in practice as a universal principle governing all physical phenomena. In so doing they are at one with the common sense of the human race.

Our questing intellect finds in secondary causes intimation of the First Cause from whom all causation derives. Our meditation on the reality of things leads us to affirm God as he who is the transcendent exemplary cause of their form and beauty; as he who is the efficient cause of their being and activity; as he who is the purposive cause of their end-seeking. In that threefold affirmation of divine causality, three pathways to the rational knowledge of God converge in one. They correspond to the three aspects of causal origin called in traditional philosophical terminology "formal," "efficient," and "final" causality. It can be said, analogically, that God in creating is the formal, efficient, and final cause of all things. In the mind's natural quest for that divine origin of all, it is the third of those three pathways, traditionally called the way of final causality, otherwise "the argument from design," that has for many seekers chief attraction and cogency.

"Prior among all the causes is the final cause," says Aquinas.[1] The reason he gives for this statement is that final causality is necessarily presupposed by both formal and efficient causality, giving purposive origination both to the nature of the effect to be caused and to the activity of the causal agent. Since the usage of the term "final causality" is no longer widely current in the sense intended, I use as a substitute for it in this discussion the specific word "teleology," which, though not more widely current than the former term, can be freed from the ambiguity of that term. The word "teleology," applied to the created universe, is here taken to signify the principle of operative purpose discernible within it: in other words, the intrinsic tendency that is in natural agents to act in a manner that furthers the achievement of *telos* or goal. Like the equivalent English word "end" and the Latin word *finis*, the Greek word *telos* means both a purpose to be pursued and a terminal point or perfection attained. It is the first of those senses that the word "teleology" reflects.

Without need for philosophical explanation of what teleology means, the common sense of humanity knows its reality in the dynamic order present in the world of matter and in the mind itself. The human mind finds evidences of that purposeful order in the laws of nature and the laws of thought; in the structural properties, energies, and mathematical harmonies of inorganic matter; in those wonders of cosmogony that science progressively reveals; in the evolution of life in all its myriad forms; in the directional thrust of all living organisms to develop, survive, and procreate. Most immediately, there is the experiential evidence of teleology in the intellect reflecting on design and purpose within itself. In so doing it realizes its own pre-established harmony with the purposive order that pervades the universe. In differing patterns of thought and language, the religious cultures of humanity recognize such teleology in the world of our experience. From experiential awareness of the dynamic end-seeking everywhere manifest in nature, they rise by inference to the higher purpose and power who is its source.

Counter-Argument against the Argument from Design

The theological argument from design, based on that recognition of physical law and purposiveness in the natural world, is singled out as a special target for attack by atheistic philosophers of science. They maintain that the coherent structures and regularities in the material universe that, especially in the biological realm, seem to betoken intelligent ordering, are not to be interpreted as proceeding from a purposeful origin, but as first arising from the random play of chance and then stabilized through subsequent conditioning by extrinsic factors. They brush aside as of no consequence the conclusions of other philosophers of science who calculate that the mathematical probability of the random concurrence of the physical preconditions necessary for the existence of life is so exponentially remote as to be scientifically negligible. They ridicule the further inference that is drawn from that utter improbability: namely, the presence of a non-random directional factor underlying the physical processes that eventually led to actuation of those necessary preconditions for the eventual appearance of human life—a factor that has been called "the Anthropic Principle."

Opponents of the theistic argument, which, in all ages, is based on the design and purposiveness apparent in organic life, currently find an eloquent spokesman in Richard Dawkins. He and his fellow "neo-Darwinists" proclaim with assurance that the first origin of life and all its subsequent developments, including the highest attainments of the human intellect, can be explained as consequences following from a single chance configuration that once arose from the random interaction of material particles and energies in aimless flux. Dawkins states his reductionist creed as follows:

> When the ricochets of atomic billiards chance to put together an object that has a certain, seemingly innocent, property, something momentous happens in the universe. That property is an ability to self-replicate; that is, the object is able to use the surrounding materials to make exact copies of itself, including replicas of such minor flaws in copying as may occasionally arise. What will follow from this singular occurrence, anywhere in the universe, is Darwinian selection and hence the baroque extravaganza that, on this planet, we call life.[2]

Starting from that dogmatic and arational premise[3]—namely, that the mysterious "ability to self-replicate" originated from a single chance collision of particles occurring fortuitously in the purposeless game of the blind and witless billiards player, brute matter—Dawkins proceeds in all his widely acclaimed books to tell "the story of the repercussions that can ensue when the phenomenon of replicators is injected into the hitherto humble game of atomic billiards."[4]

Dawkins and those who proceed from the same non-scientific first premise further posit that the extraordinary property of self-replication, once randomly acquired by the primeval living cell, was somehow transmitted as a permanent quality to descendent forms of self-replicating matter. From then onwards, they maintain, the whole course of biological evolution and the apparent thrust of living matter to reach ever higher forms can be sufficiently explained by natural selection, whereby those life-forms possessing fortuitous characteristics which give them advantage in their environment survive and prosper, while others decline and perish. Thus emerge, it is asserted, the regularities and advantageous properties of organisms that the human mind naturally but mistakenly takes to be signs of prior design. Those apparently purposive patterns in living species, we are told, are not to be taken as signs of intelligent design but are merely deceptively "designoid"[5] in appearance, giving "an almost perfect illusion of design."

In his prolific writings on the subject, Dawkins ardently pursues his missionary objective of countering the common conviction that there is purposeful direction in the natural development and activity of life-forms.

He replaces the notion of design with that of "utility function." He uses that expression to state what he considers to be the ultimate explanatory principle of life in all its forms: "The true utility function of life, that which is being maximized in the natural world," he asserts, "is DNA survival."[6] "But," he goes straight on to explain, "DNA is not floating free; it is locked up in living bodies and it has to make the most of the levers of powers at its disposal."

Thus, for Dawkins and for those who share his views, all living organisms, human beings included, are by-products of a purposeless process, organic machines gradually evolved to greater complexity by random mutations and natural selection to serve as robotic containers for DNA. The ultimate "utility function" served by that blind process is furtherance of the survival and advantage of an entity which Dawkins asserts to be the permanent subject and beneficiary of all biological self-replication and development. That fundamental unit of evolutionary change and of success in the struggle for survival, he concludes, is neither the species nor the individual organism (as other philosophizing scientists variously suppose), but what he famously calls "the Selfish Gene." Or rather, as appears from his fuller explanations, it is not really the matter of the gene, which is ephemerally transient. He identifies, as the ultimate subject and beneficiary of the whole purposeless process of life, simply and solely the genetic programming code which is borne by sections of DNA strings and perpetually transmitted to succeeding generations of genes. Even that code is not necessarily permanent, since it can be modified by mutations.

Despite their resolute opposition to any notion of intrinsic purposiveness in the development and survival of life-forms, the neo-Darwinists find it virtually impossible in practice to avoid using the language of teleological direction and end-seeking when referring to the remarkably proactive tendencies observable in all life-forms. They appear indeed to attribute to "the Selfish Gene" a bizarrely isolated autoteleology.[7] In a later development of Dawkinsian doctrine,[8] belief in the absolute autarky of each selfish gene has been somewhat modified by the further explanation that through natural selection it has also become "a Selfish cooperator" with others of its ilk, finding mutual advantage in joint association. Thus "the whole gene pool of a species," taken collectively, is now asserted to be the performer and beneficiary of the robotic and aimless dance of material particles which is supposed to explain the progress of organic life and to constitute its ultimate utility function.

Intrinsic Teleology and Extrinsic Conditioning

To show that extrinsic conditioning factors are operative in the processes of biological evolution does not disprove the presence of intrinsic teleology within those processes. Both intrinsic and extrinsic factors must be inferred, the latter subordinate to the former and both coordinated within the all-embracing design of the transcendent Creator.

Clearly, the organized development of the material cosmos was the necessary precondition and setting for biological evolution. Clearly, too, natural selection, sifting vital characteristics that have value for survival and well-being from those that have not, is a major factor shaping the survival and further development of organic life-forms. The cumulative effect of accidental mutations is likewise a modifying element in the occurrence of evolution and of variation within species. However, significant though those external factors undoubtedly are, they cannot alone suffice to explain the intrinsic dynamism of life-forms and their advance to higher planes of organization and activity.

There is much that cannot be satisfactorily explained by the theory which accounts for the evolution and subsequent diversification of living organisms as resulting purely from those extrinsic factors. In the first place, it cannot account for the emergence and purposeful dynamism of life itself. It cannot provide an explanation of the proactive tendencies within living organisms to pursue activities that give them no present advantage but that promote future good for themselves and their offspring. It cannot explain the holistic purposefulness of life-forms: for instance, the multivalent potentiality of the originating cells of the embryo (each of them with identical DNA), which, as they subsequently multiply and diversify, serve to form different organs and tissues with different functions, yet are all coordinated by a unifying principle which correlates all parts and functions of the organism to serve the whole.[9]

So too, the theory that evolution results wholly from the environmental conditioning of natural selection, coupled with fortuitous mutations, cannot explain the development within species of those behavior patterns that have an altruistic character and can be seen to go counter to the immediate advantage of individuals, to the advantage of others, present and future. It cannot explain the inherent tendencies in organic life that proactively promote survival and advantage not only for individuals and their young but, more widely, for their species. Above all, it cannot explain the mystery and marvel of the emergence and exercise of human rational consciousness. Conscience, with its innate bidding to altruism and ethical conduct, contradicts the preposterous theory that human beings are evolved as mere "survival machines for selfish genes," with the sole and pointless utility function of promoting the permanence of the DNA coding that those genes temporarily contain.

There are intricate organic structures that throughout the process of their evolution, during immense spans of time, would have had no interim advantage but rather the reverse, and which would have given superior survival value and utility function only when they became functional at the end of that long preparatory process. Only intrinsic teleology governing that process can account for its continuance and consolidation. Moreover, in the evolutionary evidence there appear discontinuities and "quantum leap" developments that cannot be sufficiently explained by the supposition that evolution is a gradually continuous process whereby chance mutations eventually become stabilized simply because of their superior survival value. Rather, natural selection operates within a universal life-system that is intrinsically teleological and that thus evidences its origin from an intelligent and purposeful source.

It is further objected against the theological argument from design that in the evolutionary processes, and in the genetic programming of species and individual organisms, there is manifest evidence of defects, failures, and wastage on an vast scale, which therefore contradicts the hypothesis of a wisely provident and omnicompetent divine designer. The proponents of that objection are tilting naïvely at a notion of creation that makes no distinction between, on the one hand, the primary teleology that is in the transcendent will of the Creator and, on the other, the secondary teleology that his creative fiat imparts to created causes in a world destined (as we know from revelation) to proceed from a state of becoming and imperfection to an eventual state of completion and perfection.

The veritable argument for God's existence drawn from consideration of the design and order inherent in creation does not depend on the naïve supposition that divine purposive causality is on the same plane and of the same character as the purposive causality of secondary agents; that is, that God is, as it were, busily at work within the created system, endeavoring to devise (though with only partial success) natural mechanisms and procedures of flawless craftsmanship and design. Such a naïve notion was assumed by Charles Darwin to be necessarily implied by the doctrine of divine creation. He wrote, in a passage that Dawkins, who shares the same crude conception of the argument from design, quotes with relish: "I cannot persuade myself that a beneficent and omnipotent God would have designedly created the Ichneumonidae with the express intention of their feeding within the living bodies of Caterpillars."[10]

The counter-arguments with which neo-Darwinists continue to ridicule the theological argument from design thus suffer from the fallacy that traditional logic calls *ignoratio elenchi*, namely, lack of comprehension of what they are contradicting. The argument from design, properly understood, does not suppose that God is involved in the evolving processes of matter as a superior physical force guiding other physical forces, nor that he must necessarily design the most aesthetically perfect universe out of all possible universes. There is a necessary distinction to be made between transcendent divine teleology and the secondary created teleology discernible both in biological evolution and in the activity of living organisms. Created order is contingent and flexible. The existence of an intrinsic principle of teleology in the biological sphere and in individual organisms is not disproved by occurrences and developments that we perceive as falling short of aesthetically perfect order. In the following chapter I reflect further on the light that is shed by revealed truth and by right reason on the riddle of physical evil and disorder in the created world.

To avoid confusion in philosophical debate on purposiveness in the universe of nature, one might therefore adopt, as a synonym for the phrase, "the argument from design," the more explanatory if unfamiliar alternative, "the argument from teleology." Moreover, when considering the necessary distinction between the transcendent teleology of the Creator and the secondary teleology intrinsic to his creation, the analogy of being must again govern our understanding and our concepts. Just as the concept of being cannot be predicated univocally of God and of creatures, neither can the concepts of causality and teleology which are essential aspects of being. As the finite goodness, causality, and beauty that we discern in created beings reflects from afar the infinite goodness, causality, and beauty of the divine Being, so too the finite order and teleology discernible in the created universe gives us intimation of its origin from the infinitely intelligent and purposeful Creator. So it is by the ladder of the analogy of being that the human intellect rises, from its recognition of created purposiveness within finite reality, to affirmation of the creative purposiveness of the infinite divine reality from which it originates.

Teleology within the Universe of Non-Living Matter

We distinguish three boundaries within the natural world: the first, between non-living matter and living organisms; the second, between sentient and non-sentient organisms; and the third, between human beings and all other animals. Intrinsic teleology is apparent in different modes and grades within all those different realms. While it is most immediately discernible in living matter, it also governs the inanimate world, where necessary consequences follow from the universal sway of the laws of mathematics and physics intrinsic to the whole cosmos.

While there are cogent objections which invalidate it, the theory which postulates that biological evolution and diversification proceed wholly by random interactions, leading through natural selection to the survival of the more advantageous configurations of living matter, does at least present a specious coherence. However, in the sphere of cosmogony no theory of natural selection can be adduced to explain how the forces and structures of matter itself developed after the moment of "Big Bang"— how, within an instant of time, a universal and perduring order of mathematical and physical regularity emerged from matter's initial state of formless indeterminacy.

The scientific postulate of a sphere of indeterminacy in matter, whether in its initial emergence from its zero point or at the quantum level of its existing sub-atomic structure, does not conflict with recognition of physical law and teleological order in the material world. Even in that quantum sphere of apparent physical indeterminacy, science can apply the mathematical laws of statistical probability to make valid conclusions relevant to the more accessible sphere where physical law clearly prevails. Science perceives the physical order of the macrocosmic sphere as issuing from a microcosmic sphere where fixed regularities cannot be discerned. We can realize that both discernible regularity and order in the macrocosm and apparent absence of it at the quantum level of unpredictability are coordinated in the total teleology of the created order, which originates from the transcendent purpose of the infinitely wise and provident Creator.

Thus apparent lack of order in the cosmological sphere at the quantum level does not contradict the argument from design—just as, in the biological sphere, similar considerations enable us to realize that what we see as the limitations, frustrations, and even aberrations in evolution and in the processes of organic life, which atheist critics allege as objections to the theist argument from design, do not disprove the truth of primary divine purpose in the created world. All things and events are subservient to the creative and all-embracing design of God, which is reflected in, but which infinitely transcends, the teleological pattern that we discern within created things.

In fine, although empirical science as such cannot detect teleology (or indeed any causality), unprejudiced reason discerns, not only in the data brought to light by cosmological and biological science but in everyday experience, evidence of universal order and higher design in the world of matter.

The frontiers of human understanding of the structures and processes of the material world are still being ever further extended by the tireless work of talented scientists. The extraordinary advances that the cosmological and biological sciences have achieved in the modern age arouse in our minds fascinated admiration and wonder. Yet reflection on the metaphysical implications of those scientific findings relating to the origins of the universe and of life remains a mere intellectual exercise if it does not lead, by grace, to the true wisdom of humble acknowledgment and adoration of the Creator, who is the transcendent origin and final end of the purposeful order manifest in his material creation and in ourselves.

Chapter 11

The Dark Mystery of Evil

The world we live in often seems very far from the one promised to us by faith. Our experiences of evil and suffering, injustice and death, seem to contradict the Good News; they can shake our faith and become a temptation against it . . .

We believe that God created the world according to his wisdom. It is not the product of any necessity whatever, nor of blind fate or chance . . . Because creation comes forth from God's goodness, it shares in that goodness—"and God saw that it was good, very good"; for God willed creation as a gift addressed to man, an inheritance destined for him and entrusted to him . . .

If God the almighty Father, the Creator of the ordered and good world, cares for all his creatures, why does evil exist? To this question, as pressing as it is unavoidable and as painful as it is mysterious, no facile answer will suffice . . . Why did God not create a world so perfect that no evil could exist in it? With infinite power, God could always create something better . . .

Catechism of the Catholic Church, §§ 164, 295, 299, 309–10

At the outset of these meditative musings I spoke of the bewilderment I feel, in common with Everyman, at finding in this world of divinely ordered and redeemed reality strange cosmic riddles and, worse, a sinister zone of darkness that seemingly negates divine light. We joyfully sense God's presence, goodness, and beauty suffused throughout the universe of his making, but we also encounter here multiple evil, physical and moral, disfiguring and countervailing his good creation. Our mind is lifted to him by its recognition of purposive design in the fabric and dynamism of the cosmos, evidences that point to the designer of all; yet with perplexed disquiet we also sense that discordant counterpoint of physical disorder and moral evil clashing with the God-given harmony that resounds in the external world and in our minds.

Despite the omnipresent evidences of intrinsic teleology and divine design in the material world, we also sense there dark depths where not order and benevolent will but chaos and the play of blind chance seem to prevail. Matter itself seems to be the seat of random forces that are incalculable, anarchic, and destructive. In the biosphere, as well as wondrous organic structure and function, there is disease, malfunction, and seemingly prodigal waste of life-forms. Nature, red in tooth and claw, ceaselessly inflicts suffering and violent death on sentient creatures, the survival of species depending on that internecine carnage. Our human sensibilities are disconcerted by the welter of natural disorders that seem to mar the fair face of creation.

At the summit of that material creation, in the lives of rational creatures everywhere and in every age, countless ills oppress the human heart: bodily disease and deformity; hunger and misery; natural calamities and dangers; fear, suffering, and grief. Through it all, and worst of all, is the endless evil of man's inhumanity to man. The laments of Job are echoed throughout all ages. Human life is beset with moral iniquity and social inequity, with no apparent correlation between merits and good fortune. The joyous optimism that sees this created world as a garden lit by the sun of divine goodness and beauty is clouded by somber experience of it as also a darksome vale of tears that narrows at the farther end to become the dread valley of the shadow of death. "There is weeping in all things, and mortality weighs upon the mind of man."[1]

In the world's religious cultures we find, as well as lament for natural calamities and for the ills and sins of humankind, also fearful inklings of anti-God evil that is other than human, of demonic influences assailing this created world and human life. Often there is a superstitious preoccupation with evil spirits and the occult that perverts true religion. Yet scriptural revelation itself tells of the existence and agency of a malign power hostile to all good and warns believers that life directed to God demands readiness to stand steadfast in spiritual warfare against latent forces of evil.[2] The Second

Vatican Council starkly attests, "The whole of man's history has been the story of dour combat with the powers of evil, stretching, so our Lord tells us, from the very dawn of history until the last day."[3] The Church's *Catechism* comments, "It is a great mystery that providence should permit diabolical activity."[4]

It is by use of the ladder of the analogy of being that theology, both natural and revealed, makes meaningful attribution to almighty God of our highest concepts of wisdom, loving providence, justice, and holy purpose. We infer that the noble perfections that we honor in human beings, who are endowed with intellect and will after his own image and likeness, must exist in unitary perfection and infinite measure in their divine archetype. Natural knowledge of this primary truth is confirmed and perfected by divine revelation and faith. Yet, confronted with omnipresent and enduring evil in the world created by God, the perplexed mind asks how its presence can be compatible with the infinite perfection of loving wisdom, power, and provident purpose that is necessarily attributed to him.

Such perplexity can turn to agnostic doubt about the very nature of God. The enigma of evil is taken by some as grounds for concluding that there is indeed mutual contradiction between the perfections attributed to him, between his loving and provident wisdom on one hand and his omnipotence on the other. Since evil exists and abounds in this world, they object, either he does not will to exclude it or he cannot. On the former hypothesis, he is not perfectly loving, provident, and wise; on the latter, he is not omnipotent. They therefore reject the notion of an all-perfect God as a self-contradictory illusion.

Others, recoiling from an all-determinant divine will, which they conceive as arbitrary and cruel, react to the experience of physical evil by embitterment and estrangement from God and deny his loving care for his children. Such embitterment is not rare. I remember often a good friend and brave soldier with whom I served in war, an observant Christian since childhood, who suddenly shut the book of faith and turned his back on all religion when his beloved twin brother, who was his *alter ego*, was killed in action. I also call to mind, with affection and sadness, a Jewish academic colleague who told me it was impossible for him to believe in God after the Holocaust, especially in view of the cruel irony of history that the door was opened for the return of the Jewish people to the land of Israel only after they had been decimated in the gas chambers. Underlying such reactions is a sorely mistaken understanding of the doctrine of divine providence, which pictures God as a despotic puppeteer pulling the strings of human destiny by arbitrary decree, heedless of the resulting harm and pain.

Fatalism and Flawed Theodicies

The questions that perplexed minds have asked throughout human history are summed up by *The Catechism of the Catholic Church* in these words:

Is the universe governed by chance, blind fate, impersonal necessity, or by a transcendent, intelligent, and good Being, namely God? And if the world does come from God's wisdom and goodness, why is there evil? Where does it come from? Who is responsible for it? Is there any liberation from it?[5]

In all societies religious thinkers wrestle with the problem of the existence of evil. Widely diverse and conflicting speculations are proposed concerning it. Some conclude that the arbiter and determinant force of the cosmos is necessary fate, indifferent to whatever good or evil may befall. They view the world as a hostile environment and human life as a lottery of good or bad fortune, having no correlation with good or bad deserts. Fatalism, ancient and modern, inclines the mind to pessimism and nihilism when it is divorced from any religious interpretation of reality. Those who see themselves caught in a web of inexorable fate still seek ways to cheat it. Shamans, wizards, and astrologers claim to have power to decipher the baleful code of fate by divination and soothsaying, playing on pandemic superstition that ever seeks to conjure up good fortune or avert ill fortune by magical spells and charms.

Theology necessarily entails theodicy, the reverent vindication of God's goodness and providence against doubts and denials occasioned by the fact of evil, physical and moral. Just as there is a natural theology of human reason which is presupposed, transformed, and fulfilled by revealed theology, so likewise there is a natural theodicy which is perfected and surpassed by faith.

Theodicy, properly so called, is primarily a concern of the monotheistic religions, of that majority of humankind who conceive of deity as a personal, benevolent, and provident creator. Yet the weight of the problem of evil is felt also in other religious cultures, including the monist metaphysical systems of the East, which have only cloudy and distant conceptions of the divine Absolute. In their perspective, already sketched in earlier pages of this book, ultimate and impersonal necessity is conceived as an eternal and sacred law of the cosmos. Although they judge it pointless to pray to that ultimate principle, they accord it religious reverence. All men and women must, willy-nilly, submit to it. All are bound to conform themselves dutifully to the eternal law, reflecting it in their own lives according to the pattern fixed for each person within the community or caste into which each is born. Such an attitude of religious submission to sacred fate underlies the concepts of *r'ta* and *karma* in the religions of Indian origin and of the *Tao*, the Way of Heaven, in Chinese religion.

It was asserted by the sociologist Max Weber that the perennial human desire for a rationally satisfying theodicy, that is, for an explanation of "the basis of the incongruity between destiny and merit," led in time to the development of theological systems that attempted to satisfy that desire. Of those systems, he singled out three, which alone, in his view, provided such a rationally coherent theodicy:

> The metaphysical conception of God and of the world, which the ineradicable demand for a theodicy called forth, could produce only a few systems of ideas on the whole—as we shall see, only three. These three give rationally satisfactory answers to the questioning for the basis of the incongruity between destiny and merit: the Indian doctrine of *karma*; Zoroastrian dualism; and the predestination decree of the *deus absconditus*.[6]

In discussing these assertions, I resume themes that I broached in my fourth chapter. The first of the three systems of ideas singled out by Weber, which he names as "the Indian doctrine of *karma*," does indeed address the universal lament of humanity over the incongruity between destiny and merit. The solution offered by that doctrine, already outlined in those earlier pages, may be recapitulated as follows. As well as the inexorable law of *karma*, binding each soul with the ever enduring consequences of its past deeds, it postulates also the cosmic necessity of *samsara*, determining the transmigration of each soul through an endless cycle of deaths and rebirths. Those two principles, together with the ruling imperative of *dharma*, constitute the cosmic moral accountancy whereby all souls eventually reap reward of their merits and punishment of their demerits in due proportion. By that universal and impersonal system of sanctions, justice is redressed over aeons of time through innumerable reincarnations at higher or lower levels in the scale of life-forms, according to the balance of good or bad *karma* that souls have amassed by their deeds in previous lives.

One may remark that it is a misnomer to describe this theory as a *theodicy*. It is not dependent on the concept of a personal and provident God, but is common to all Indian religion, both theist and monist—in fact it accords more readily with the latter than with the former. Even in theistic Hindu belief, neither the law of *karma*, bringing eventual requital according to one's deserts, nor the ever turning wheel of *samsara*, proceeds from divine will, but both together are the eternal framework of necessity, in which the cosmic drama is enacted and in which the deity himself operates. Buddhist teaching is in continuity with this ancient theory; it presupposes *samsaric* metempsychosis as the setting of the universal predicament from which the Buddha's enlightening message gives release.

The second of the three systems of ideas that, according to Weber, offer the only rationally satisfactory solutions of the problem of evil, namely Zoroastrian dualism, had very wide currency in antiquity and still has counterparts today. It solves the problem of evil by positing the existence both of a supreme divine spirit, who is the author of all that is good in the world, and, radically opposed to him, an independently powerful malign spirit, who is the author of all that is evil.[7] The universe is seen as the arena of a struggle between those two rival principles and their adherents, visible and invisible, a struggle that will result in the final triumph of Ahura Mazda, the divine supreme spirit. Different from Zoroastrianism but with similarities to it were the creeds of other dualistic movements, Gnosticism, Manichaeism, and Catharism, in which matter itself was regarded as the evil element from which spirit had to be freed. Zoroastrianism can be seen as a basically monotheist religion centred on the primacy and perfect goodness of the deity who is worshipped as the source of universal good. In intent it is a theodicy, vindicating that deity from any responsibility for the existence of evil by explaining evil as the counter-creation of a demonic rival.[8] But it achieves this theodicy by postulating a deity who is not truly God, not the omnipotent creator of all things visible and invisible, not the source of all being and becoming, eternally changeless and all-perfect.

Similar theological contradictions are to be found in some modern theodicies which likewise postulate limitation and imperfection in the Godhead.

One such is so-called "process theology,"[9] according to which the deity himself is involved in and conditioned by the processes of cosmic evolution from the less to the more perfect. Another is the theory of a suffering God who, himself subject to and afflicted by the necessity of evil, can therefore compassionately share the affliction of humans. This "neo-theopaschitism,"[10] though favored today by some thinkers of renown, can be seen to be incompatible with traditional Christian faith, which teaches that while God incarnate, Jesus Christ, did truly suffer for the salvation of all, he could do so only in his assumed human nature, and that it is impossible to attribute any limitation, passion, or mutability to God in the infinite perfection of his divine nature.

"Voluntarist" Theology and the Problem of Evil

By the third of the three systems of ideas singled out by Weber as rationally coherent theodicies, namely "the predestination decree of the *deus absconditus*," he means the theological perspective that so exalts the otherness of "the hidden God" that in effect it excludes rational theodicy itself as being a futile attempt of the human mind to scrutinize and explain the wholly inscrutable decrees of the sovereign divine will. According to this radical solution, God, from all eternity and for his own inscrutable reasons, inflexibly determines whatever will come to pass, good and evil alike. What for men is good or evil, right or wrong, depends, like all else, solely on what he chooses to decree. While they are necessarily subject to the precepts and prohibitions that the omnipotent Creator has prescribed for them, his sovereign will is itself bound by no prior ethical code.

That conception of God's absolute mastery of human destiny, decreeing good and evil alike, underlies Islam's proclamation of absolute and unquestioning submission to the unfathomable divine will. In this sense is understood Allah's declaration of his will in the Qur'an: "Every adversity that befalls the earth or your own persons is foreordained before I bring it into being."

The same conception has been adopted by some Christian thinkers, whose theory of the utter inscrutability of the *voluntas Dei*, likewise conceived as beyond all our notions of good and evil, is accordingly called "voluntarism." It underlay the metaphysical theology of William of Ockham (1285–1347), who developed more radically the ideas of Duns Scotus.

Ockham systematized the implications of the voluntarist premise that God's omnipotent will does not have to conform to some necessary standard of justice and right, but justice and right are what he wills them to be. Although at variance with the mainstream of Catholic theology, Ockhamist voluntarism had considerable influence in the late medieval schools, and consequently (strange though it may seem to some) in the theology of the Reformation. Voluntarist thinkers could find in Scripture several texts which they could interpret in their extreme sense, adducing, for instance, the words of St. Paul: "But who are you, a man, to answer back to God? What if God, desiring to show his wrath and to make known his power, has endured with much patience the vessels of wrath made for destruction? . . . How unsearchable are his judgements and how inscrutable his ways" (Romans 9.20, 22; 11.33).

Ockham speculated subtly on the distinction between what God has actually decreed and what he could decree in his limitless freedom. On the one hand, there is the cosmic dispensation and law that his omnipotent will has actually ordained as valid in the present order of creation by his power as excercised through fixed decree (*"de potentia ordinata"*). On the other, there is an infinity of possible alternative systems of created reality, and of moral law, that he could ordain by his untrammelled absolute power (*"de potentia absoluta"*). Arguing from this ultra-voluntarist premise, Ockham concluded that acts which are evil and sinful for human beings in the present order could be good and meritorious if, in another order, God chose to account and accept them as such.

From the same premise Ockham inferred the incidental corollary that God could, *de potentia absoluta*, by a sovereignly free and effective decree of pardon from on high, simply confer his favor and salvation on a sinner worthy of damnation without any intrinsic change in the sinner himself and without the mediation of his grace through the priestly-sacramental Church. As a Catholic theologian following the dogmatic teaching of the Church, Ockham accepted that in the existing economy of salvation there is no such extrinsic justification merely by decree of the divine will, bypassing the divinely instituted instrumentality of the Church and her sacraments and leaving the pardoned sinner intrinsically unchanged by the grace he had received and acknowledged by faith. But what Ockham allowed merely as a hypothetical and unrealized possibility, Martin Luther later asserted to be the way in which God actually justifies the sinner. His affirmation of solifideist voluntarism became the basic principle of Reformation theology.

In that Ockhamist hypothesis may be discerned the germ of the Lutheran doctrine of imputed righteousness. Luther, who had imbibed Ockham's voluntarist ideas in his studies at Erfurt (while at the same time rejecting as "Pelagian" the optimism of the Scotist-Ockhamist schoolmen concerning the continuing goodness of human nature even after the Fall), could still say in old age, jocularly but truly, *"Ego Occamista sum"*—"I am an Ockhamist."[11] The phrase *deus absconditus*, cited by Weber to denote the third of his trio of coherent theodicies, was a usage favored by Luther.

The radically voluntarist answer to the problem of evil, namely unquestioning submission to the inscrutable will of the hidden God predestining his creatures to good or evil, to salvation or damnation, as he chose, was also adopted more generally in Reformation theology—especially in Calvinism, where it was developed with full logical clarity. Calvin's theology was thoroughly and inflexibly voluntarist. He taught a doctrine of "supralapsarian" double predestination, according to which God eternally foreordains some to salvation and everlasting life and some to doom and everlasting punishment, antecedently even to any consideration of the fall of humankind and the consequent culpable estrangement of sinners from himself. Calvin condemned as futile and sinful any attempt of human reason to measure God's decrees and acts by the same norms of right and good that God prescribes for men:

It is very wicked merely to investigate the causes of God's will . . . For God's will is so much the highest rule of righteousness that whatever he wills, by the very fact that he wills it, must be considered righteous. When therefore one asks why God has so done, we must reply: because he willed it. But if you proceed further and ask why he so willed, you are seeking something greater and higher than God's will, which cannot be found.[12]

Weber supposed ineptly that such extreme voluntarist theory is the only rationally coherent expression of Christian theodicy. It is not the teaching of the Catholic Church. According to that teaching, we have certainty that the moral values and noble qualities that human beings recognize as the norm and pattern for their own living exist in supereminent perfection in the divine exemplar who is their source. Thus Catholic theology attests that the goodness, love, justice, and provident wisdom towards which we are drawn by our human nature truly reflect the nature of God himself, in whose image and likeness we are created, and that we rightly attribute those perfections to God in supreme degree. His perfect freedom of will cannot contradict his perfect justice, wisdom, and love.

Here again, our reason's grasp of the analogy of being is, elevated by grace, ancillary to faith's understanding of what God has revealed about himself. It is true that God is *Deus absconditus* in the sense that his all-holy Being is veiled from our gaze and we glimpse his lineaments from afar, though truly, through the finite reflection of his transcendent Being by his creatures. That distant vision is made clearer by the light of revelation. But it is not true that God is *Deus absconditus* in the sense that his real nature and divine righteousness itself are wholly hidden from us behind the omnipotent decrees which mask his inscrutable will. Catholic theology rejects as false and blasphemous the notion that in decreeing our destiny and ruling our lives God deals out both good and evil with despotic arbitrariness, aloof from the principles of right and justice that he enjoins upon us.

In the face of the dark enigma of evil, the Church still resolutely attests that God cannot foreordain or originate moral evil and injustice. While always confessing the infinite power and wisdom of God, and the truth that he is the first author of our salvation, she has never accepted the notion of double predestination, according to which God deliberately creates some human beings for everlasting damnation, antecedently to any merits or demerits of theirs. A declaration made by the provincial Council of Quiercy (AD 853) illustrates this constant concern of Catholic faith in its interpretation of the scriptural doctrine of predestination to reject a false clarity that would attribute injustice to God, paradoxical though the mysterious truth must seem to human understanding: "That some are saved is the gift of the One who saves; that some perish is the just deserts of those who perish."[13]

According to rigidly voluntarist theology, the relationship of human beings to God is extrinsic to them, brought about by his word and decree; in authentic Catholic theology, it is also intrinsic, founded in their very reception of being from him, being that is transformed by his indwelling and transforming grace. That relationship is not merely notional but ontological.

Obedience to God's will and law is indeed the pathway we must follow to reach eternal life, but rigid voluntarism fails to distinguish between the positive precepts of his revealed law and the natural law he has inscribed in the human heart and in the structure of his creation, an inner law that his revealed will presupposes and brings to perfection. Certainly, Scripture shows many instances in which the divine will enjoins on men acts and observances additional to those that they are bound by natural conscience to perform, and likewise instances of prohibition of things that are not intrinsically evil. Christ gave to his Church power to declare and apply such divinely sanctioned precepts (Matthew 16.19; 18.18). Christians are thus subject both to the positive laws that faith enjoins and the natural divine law, which governs all humanity and which grace perfects. As a scholastic axiom has it: *"Quaedam sunt mala quia prohibita; quaedam sunt prohibita quia mala"*—"Some things are evil because they are forbidden; some things are forbidden because they are evil." Conscience itself tells us that distinction.

The Lesser Riddle: Physical Evil and Disorder

Both reason and faith ponder on the fact that God permits evil to exist. In the passage cited at the head of this chapter, the *Catechism of the Catholic Church* admits there is no easy answer to that "unavoidable, painful, and mysterious" problem, and asks once more the age-old question: "Why did God not create a world so perfect that no evil could exist in it? With infinite power, God could always create something better." What further light does Catholic theology throw on that universal problem of evil?

Less intractable than the problem of moral evil, which alone is evil properly so called, is that of the ills, adversities, and anomalies that we encounter in the created universe. The problem of so-called physical evil weighs heavily on our perplexed minds because our present perceptions of what is truly good for us, and likewise of what is truly harmful for us, are clouded and fallible. Those perceptions will be finally clarified only in the full light and beatitude of eternal life destined by God as the goal of our mortal wayfaring. Only there shall we be able to comprehend how the trials and tribulations of this earthly probation are woven into the tapestry of our lives according to his loving plan for bringing us to that goal. At present we see the pattern of that tapestry only from the underside, as a seemingly random miscellany of disparate threads and colors. From heavenly perspective we shall see it as it is, in its divinely crafted harmony and beauty. St. Paul uses the similitude of a child's growth to rational maturity to illustrate our growth in understanding of the mind and ways of God:

Once perfection comes, all imperfect things will disappear. When I was a child I used to talk like a child, and think like a child, and argue like a child; but now I am a man all childish things are put behind me. Now we are seeing a dim reflection in a mirror; but then we shall be seeing face to face. The knowledge that I have now is imperfect; but then I shall know as fully as I am known. *(1 Corinthians 13.10–12).*

The formative discipline given by parents may be hard for their children to accept, but when those children themselves become adults they realize that it was given for their true good and proceeded from their parents' loving care for them. We have to grow towards spiritual adulthood and fuller understanding of our heavenly Father's loving tutelage. Even in grievous travail we are given grace and strength to acknowledge and accept the divine pedagogy in the vicissitudes of our lives, though we cannot yet fully comprehend it.

God does not will as ends in themselves the physical adversities that befall us, but as means to the higher good that he intends for us and to which he draws us. He permits them to befall us inasmuch as they are conjoined in his loving design with good effects of immeasurably greater import. "We know that in everything God works for good with those who love him, who are called according to his purpose" (Romans 8.28). In sinners, physical ills may have penal, expiatory, and healing value; in the just, they serve to test and augment virtue. They are only truly evil in those who make them so. In the final audit, what we now see as physical evils may prove to be blessings bringing us to eternal life. How we respond to the test that they present pertains to our very relationship with God. It reflects the way we respond to the moral imperative that is in us by nature to acknowledge his all-holy sovereignty and our duty to orient our life to him.

But what of the indeterminacy, disorder, and destruction in the universe of matter, the play of random chance in its formation and change, the lethal hostility between living species, the fate of animals to suffer and be slain? How, it is asked, can the savagery and suffering that we see to be inherent in created nature be compatible with belief in the existence of an all-wise and providently benevolent God? On the emotional plane, this question parallels the objection, considered in the preceding chapter, of atheists who object that random disarray and disfunction in the natural world contradicts "the argument from design," which for many minds is the most cogent rational proof of the existence of God.

Catholic faith, seeking understanding, reverently acknowledges the fact that the world that has issued from the creative fiat of God is still in a condition of physical incompletion, change, and progression. In the words of the *Catechism of the Catholic Church* cited at the head of the preceding chapter, "The universe was created in a state of wayfaring toward an ultimate perfection yet to be attained to which God has destined it." The *Catechism* applies this truth to allay the disquiet we feel when confronted with the apparent ruthlessness and wastefulness of created Nature:

In his infinite wisdom and goodness God freely willed to create a world in a state of movement towards an ultimate perfection. In God's plan this process involves the appearance of certain beings and the disappearance of others, the presence of the more perfect together with the less perfect, of the constructive powers of nature together with the destructive. Thus with physical good there exists also physical evil, as long as creation has not reached perfection.[14]

We may find it disconcerting that the physical world as we know it is in an imperfect physical state; that, as well as clear evidences of purposeful design and direction, it also exhibits strange anomalies and an appearance of fortuitous disorder and futility. Yet none of those riddles, or any of the phenomena that we call physical evils, are veritable evil. They cannot argue defect in the infinite and unfathomable wisdom and goodness of the Creator, nor in his creative power. The divine first cause is all-perfect and indefectible. The secondary causality with which he empowers his creation is conditioned by the limitations and defectibility of the material universe, mysteriously destined to an ultimate transformation that will perfect it. We ponder wonderingly on that higher divine teleology that governs the created teleology intrinsic to the physical world. St. Paul writes of that mystery:

For the creation was subjected to futility, not of its own will but by the will of him who subjected it in hope; because the creation itself will be set free from its bondage to decay and obtain the glorious liberty of the children of God. We know that the whole creation has been groaning in travail together until now . . . *(Romans 8.20–22).*

Vatican II, speaking of that eschatological "time when the renewal of all things will come," reaffirmed, "At that time, together with the human race, the universe itself, which is so closely related to man and which attains its destiny through him, will be perfectly re-established in Christ."[15] Thus, although our sensibilities may be distressed by the destructive physical forces in created nature, we can realize that the existence of such a provisional and uncompleted order does not contradict the all-perfection of the Creator himself. God, sovereignly good and sovereignly free, freely creates a world that is good, very good; but he is not bound to create the most perfect of all possible worlds. We realize too that, although the created world is still in a state of imperfection, its present condition does not give licence to humanity to abuse the animal kingdom and the riches of the earth. Our awareness that the irrational creation has been ordered by God to serve the good of his rational creatures also entails acknowledgment of our duty to respect that good creation and to exercise aright our stewardship of it.

The Anti-God Enigma of Moral Evil

What we call physical evils are but the outer setting of the human predicament. Incomparably more grievous and more inexplicable than all physical disorder and affliction is the dark anti-God enigma of moral evil, rampant in his good world and present throughout the whole history of humankind. Sinful rebellion of rational creatures against the will of their Creator and against the law of good he has placed in their nature is the ultimate evil. The mystery of iniquity, permitted by God, defies our comprehension. It is an enigma of malice and unreason, a nether darkness seeming to overcast the divine goodness translucent in creation.

Christian faith traces the present predicament of humanity and its servitude to sin to a primeval fall prompted by diabolical malice: "Only the light of divine revelation clarifies the reality of sin, and particularly of the sin committed at humankind's origins . . . The whole of human history is marked by the original fault freely committed by our first parents."[16] But how can it be that the contagion of sin has been permitted by God to infect and condition human life so that the history of humankind is one of endless injustice, vice, fratricidal violence, and atrocious cruelty? How can it be that those made in the image and likeness of him who is infinite love possess this power to reject his love and alienate themselves from him by rebellious pride and self-love, thus bringing the greatest evil and harm upon themselves and upon one another? How can it be that they have become not only subject to that ultimate evil but also propagators of it? To these questions our reason, here at the limits of its range, can give only partial and uncertain answers. We look to divine revelation and faith for clearer light both on the problem and on its resolution.

Reinforcing the natural theodicy of humanity, the sources of revelation show us that God cannot be the source of moral evil, nor can he will it; that, as choice of right and rejection of wrong is the code of human conscience, so it is the law of the divine governance of the universe; that moral evil stems from perversion of the free will that God has delegated to his rational creatures, both angelic and human; and nevertheless that divine goodness and justice cannot be frustrated by the evil of sin that has entered into the world of his creation, but must ultimately be vindicated.

But if God is the first cause of all being and of all act, if from primary divine causality proceeds the secondary causality of created agents, how can moral evil contrary to his holy will come about? Seeking a rational answer, we may find some abatement of our disquiet in the reflection that moral evil is not positive being, but a negation of the goodness that is imparted to all things from their divine source. While all the being and actions of creatures are physically good in themselves, as proceeding from God's creative power that holds them in existence and from his causative concurrence with the agency of secondary causes, the wicked acts of rational creatures are morally vitiated by the evil intentionality given them by sinful choice. This dark mystery is opaque to our intellect because moral evil, not partaking in the goodness and intelligibility of created being but rather morbidly parasitical upon it, is a cosmic surd beneath rationality.

The faith that seeks understanding finds some comfort in other theological considerations that somewhat alleviate the grievousness of the problem of moral evil. We realize that the possibility of sin is linked to God's free choice, in his infinite and eternal wisdom, to create free beings in his own image and likeness, both angels who are pure spirit and humans who are spirit-in-matter, so empowering them to respond freely to his loving initiative and eventually to reach everlasting fulfilment and happiness with him. The true freedom of loving choice with which he endowed both angels and men implies the fearful alternative that they could refuse to use it

aright, could culpably fail their test, and could consequently turn away
from divine goodness into the negative darkness of evil. We, who cannot
comprehend the surpassing good that is realized by God's choice to create
intelligent beings other than himself and to draw them to share, by free and
loving response, in his own divine life, are not competent to weigh that surpassing good in a balance with the evil that arises from their misuse of the
power of free choice that he has delegated to them.

Pondering the mystery of God's will as expressed in what comes to pass,
speculative theology thus distinguishes between his will of good pleasure
and his merely permissive will. To the former we attribute all that comes to
pass through the operation of created causes acting in due conformity with
his sovereign plan of wisdom and love; to the latter, we attribute the effects
resulting from the sinful choices of rational agents. While not willing the
moral evil by which those choices are perverted, God permits their physical
consequences and works them into his master plan of love. As the *Catechism of the Catholic Church* testifies,[17] such evil cannot thwart his providence but is defeated by it:

He permits it because he respects the freedom of his creatures and, in a manner
mysterious to us, knows how to derive good from it . . . In time we discover that
God in his almighty providence can bring good from the consequences of evil, even
moral evil, caused by his creatures. From the greatest moral evil ever committed—
the rejection and murder of God's only Son, caused by the sins of all men—God, by
his grace "that abounded all the more" (Romans 5.20), brought the greatest of
goods: the glorification of Christ and our redemption. But for all that, evil never becomes a good.

In the light of faith, theological reasoning can probe far into the deeply
troubling question of the presence of evil and sin; but it reaches a limit beyond which it cannot penetrate. Ultimately its disquiet can be dissolved
only by absolute trust in the sovereign goodness and love of God, who is
the author and meaning of all and cannot will moral evil. Loving faith provides a vindication of his sovereign goodness and purpose that rebuts all
doubt and evil itself.

God has given us a conclusive resolution of the enigma of evil, not by
explanation but by act. Becoming incarnate in our human nature, he has
entered into our experience of evil and has borne its uttermost malice in
himself in order to deliver us from it. The sign of the Cross, which marks

our churches and our homes and which we trace on our bodies and in our lives, is the sign and pledge of that deliverance. By dying for us the God-man Jesus, our divine Lord and human brother, conquers evil and rescues us from the empire of sin and spiritual death. Risen, he fares forth with us in our Godfaring journey and is himself the way and its final end.

"Only in the mystery of the incarnate Word does the mystery of man come into true light," declared the Second Vatican Council,[18] in a passage on which Pope John Paul II comments:

Seen in any other perspective, the mystery of personal existence remains an insoluble enigma. Where else can human beings find answer to the questions that harrow their hearts—of suffering, of the afflictions of the innocent, of death—save in the light that shines from the mystery of Christ's passion, death, and resurrection?[19]

With Christ, St. Paul teaches, we suffer, with him we die and are buried, with him we rise to new life and eternal glory.[20] The way of the Cross, the expiatory suffering of evil both physical and moral, is the path that Christ trod for our eternal good and that he calls his disciples to follow daily in union with him. The profound meaning and spiritual value of their afflictions and sufferings—and those of all human beings, who are all within the sphere of his grace—is to be found in the communion of spiritual life and destiny which links the members of his Mystical Body to him, crucified and risen Lord of all. Through him, with him, and in him we have the ultimate answer to the problem of evil and the achievement of God's supreme design for us of love and final bliss.

Chapter 12

Conscience and Its Supreme Imperative

It is not the hearers of the law who are righteous before God, but the doers of the law who will be justified. When gentiles, who do not possess a law, do by nature what the law requires, for them, though they possess no law, there is a law. They give proof that the working of the law is written on their hearts, their conscience bearing witness.

Romans 2.13–15

In the intimacy of his conscience man discovers a law which he does not give unto himself but which he must obey. Its inward voice, ever calling him to love and do good, and to avoid evil, tells him in his heart what he ought to choose: "Do this, shun that." For, written in his heart by God, man has the law which is his very dignity to obey and by which he will be judged. His conscience is his most secret centre and sanctuary: there he is alone with God, whose voice resounds in his innermost being.

Vatican II, Gaudium et spes, §16

Of all God's works, the one of which I am most immediately conscious is myself. I reflect on that natural drive of my mind and will towards good and away from evil, which is called conscience. I reflect on its relation to my inward affirmation of God by reason and by faith. I come to realize that my sense of being drawn towards the right and the good is implicitly a bidding to acknowledge, obey, and worship him.

The moral law within us derives from "that supreme rule of life which is the divine law itself, the eternal, objective and universal law by which, in his wisdom and love, God orders, directs and governs the whole world and the paths of the human community."[1] Thus by reflection on the inward voice of conscience our mind may formulate a further rational argument for God's existence[2]—as it were, a "sixth way" to add to the traditional "five ways" under which Aquinas summarized the evidences of God gained from our experiential knowledge of the created world around us. Our awareness of the all-encompassing law of right and duty in our rational nature is a cogent argument for the existence of a personal Lawgiver. It is an argument that appealed with particular force to John Henry Newman:

Conscience is nearer to me than any other means of knowledge. And as it is given to me, so also is it given to others; and being carried about by every individual in his own breast, and requiring nothing beside itself, it is thus adapted for the communication to each separately of that knowledge which is most momentous to him individually . . . Conscience, too, teaches us, not only that God is, but what he is; it provides for the mind a real image of him, as a medium of worship; it gives us a rule of right and wrong, as being his rule, and a code of moral duties.[3]

Conscience belongs to our very rationality. In our natural power of reasoning and discerning truth about reality there are two modes or aspects, one speculative, the other practical. We do not come to rational consciousness with any preformed ideas or axioms, whether speculative or practical; but we do have by nature operative patterns of cognition and conation, according to which we are preconditioned both to interpret reality truly and to choose as we ought in the conduct of our life. As the directive power of speculative or scientific thought, our intellect enables us to seek truth and to discern what is objectively true. As the directive power of practical conduct, it sways us to seek moral good and enables us to judge rightly how we should live and act. The first principles of the speculative reason, such as the principles of contradiction, of sufficient reason and of causality, cannot be rejected by the sane mind, which necessarily has to follow them in all its rational judgments of reality. It is otherwise with the first principles of the practical reason, the promptings of conscience, which declare not the "is" but the "ought" in our experience. Recalcitrant free will, though it can never completely eradicate from the sane mind awareness of the difference between right and wrong, can subjectively reject the specific application of objective moral principle to itself in particular circumstances.

There are those who choose to reject as meaningless the concept of innate natural law, and to explain all statements of moral principle as either mere social conventions that are relative and replaceable, or as expressions of subjective emotion and personal preference, or at most as conventional precepts and prohibitions generally adopted to maintain order in society. Contradicting such moral nihilism is the universal human awareness of right and wrong in our life-attitude and life-choices, a universal imperative for right living that is individualized in each of us.

The Universal Sway of Conscience

The sway of conscience, inclining us to seek good and to avoid evil in the ordering of our lives, is antecedent to all our moral concepts and reasonings. It is not a ready-made set of right answers to moral questions, but a prompting to use our reason aright in the choices of our daily lives. It predisposes, but does not compel, the rational and affective processes by which we freely decide between right and wrong. We may have concomitant awareness of conscience by reflecting on those processes. Its inner imperatives are not merely theoretical rules elaborated by professors and divines; they are experiential truths grasped by Everyman in the exercise of moral choice.

Hence two aspects of conscience may be distinguished. First, it is a general orientation towards good and away from evil; second and more specifically, it is an aptitude and prompting to choose rightly in particular circumstances. In human beings by nature, conscience is tended and enhanced by nurture. The sense of right and wrong and of moral obligation grows clearer and stronger in the young within the seedbed of family and community. Conscience itself leads parents to guard and guide it in their children. As members of society, we acknowledge a common duty to instill and uphold moral principles and practice in our community life. The consensus of the plurality of human beings applying right reason to recognize specific moral obligations, especially the judgment and conduct of those endowed with exemplary probity and moral authority, provides for human society a common code to guide and confirm the judgments of the individual conscience—which nevertheless always remains personal and binding in each person.

Those who habitually heed the inner voice of conscience, cost what it may, acquire a moral sensitivity and nobility of character that gives them

clarity and sureness of judgment about right and wrong in all the circumstances of life. Conversely, habitual rejection of the bidding of conscience
brings a progressive moral obtuseness and proneness to self-deception that
is destructive of personal dignity. Those who deny and attempt to eradicate
the God-given moral law within themselves pervert their total life-
orientation. Systems of thought which deny the moral law itself are destructive of human society and are radically evil. "In every sphere," Aquinas reflects, "corruption of the principle upon which the whole depends is
the worst corruption. In the sphere of rational deliberation, the gravest
and basest error is that relating to those principles with knowledge of
which man is endued by his nature."[4]

Thus recognition of the specific dictates of the universal moral law of
our nature can be obscured, culpably or even inculpably, by various adverse
factors in oneself and in one's social circumstances. Its practical judgment
can be clouded by evil living, by self-deceiving laxity, by perplexity in complex situations, by anxious scrupulosity; also by bad example, by debased
social mores, by false ideologies. Right reason requires that we not only follow our conscience but also seek to keep it rightly informed, with sincerity
and prudence. In unclear circumstances we recognize our obligation to
weigh up the issues as best we can before deciding what to do, to seek coun-
sel where necessary, and to inform our conscience with the guidance that is
given by the consensus of right reason and by the moral teaching of God-
given authority.

All humanity hears the voice of conscience. Some religious cultures in-
tegrate its commands into an all-embracing system of sacred obligation.
Such is the religious law of Islam and of Judaism. Such is the observance of
dharma, the universal law of duty and right conduct which in Hindu religious culture binds all men and women according to their condition and
governs every detail of their lives, both as individuals passing through the
successive life-stages and as members of family, caste, and community.
Such also is *Asha*, the divine cosmic law hymned in the Zoroastrian *Gathas*.
Despite the many evils, aberrations, and defects to be found in the various
societies and cultures of the world, the elements of a common global ethic
can be formulated from the general moral convictions of the human race.[5]
The Second Vatican Council stresses the universality of the common conscience of humanity:

By conscience that law which is fulfilled by love of God and of neighbour is won-drously made known. Through fidelity to conscience Christians are joined to all other human beings in the search for truth and for the right solution to the many moral problems that arise in the life of individuals and of society.[6]

Pope John Paul II testifies likewise to the universal sway of conscience as a religious bond joining together all religions and believers: "In this witness to the absoluteness of the moral good Christians are not alone: they are supported by the moral sense present in all peoples and by the great relig-ious and sapiential traditions of East and West, from which the interior and mysterious workings of God's Spirit are not absent."[7] The faith and grace of Christ clarifies, elevates, and perfects the natural law of conscience, en-compassing it in the higher law of the Gospel and of loving obedience to God's revealed will.

The law of conscience is not absolute moral autonomy, as if our per-sonal judgment of right and wrong, self-law, were the ultimate norm; nor is it "heteronomy," a law-code imposed on us from without; but, to use the phrase preferred by Pope John Paul II,[8] it is "participated theonomy"—that is, an inborn inclination in our mind and will which assimilates the direc-tion of our lives to the divine law and wisdom that governs the universe. The law of conscience does not oppress our freedom but empowers and enhances it. Living by that law may entail suffering and distress, yet it is still the path of ultimate peace and happiness. In our life's course from youth to old age we find that duty and joy of spirit are not opposed but intertwined.

The Order of Conscience and Its Sovereign Precept

Reflecting on the exercise of that inner prompting of our practical rea-son, we may distinguish an order in its moral imperatives, corresponding to the different planes of our life-experience, bodily and spiritual, as individu-als and as members of society.

Like the irrational animals we are biologically preconditioned to self-preservation, to physiological development, and to sensory activity advan-tageous to our bodily well-being. Yet the motivation of human life is not mere animal instinct and conation. Our instincts and emotions are per-vaded and governed by our rationality and free will. The moral imperative within us inclines us to choose rationally and rightly in all those spheres of bodily activity.

While, like all living species, our race is naturally programmed to prop-
agate and preserve itself, the uniquely created human nature that draws us
towards being lovers, spouses, and parents does so with moral suasion and
sanction. Conscience governs all our choices and experience in that sphere
of sexual and familial responsibility. As essentially social beings we are also
bidden by the inner law of right and wrong to respect the rights of all others, to do well by them, and to succor them in their needs. That law also
bids us to cooperate with others for the common good, whether at the level
of the family, of the wider community to which we belong, or of human
society as a whole.

In all our conduct, whether as individuals or as members of family and
society, we are prompted by the dictates of conscience to live, speak, and act
truthfully, lovingly, justly, chastely, compassionately, generously, and pru-
dently, and to resist the disordered inclinations which tempt us to evil. The
common morality of the human race gives names to those disordered tendencies—such as anger, hatred, pride, lust, cruelty, envy, gluttony, dishon-
esty, avarice, or sloth; but we do not need to be able to name them to know
that in human living they go counter to the basic rule of our nature to shun
evil and to seek good. Sound and unstifled conscience is also self-
accusatory when we have transgressed its mandates and bids us to repent
and make amends.

While the inner dynamism of right reason inclines us to morally right
conduct at all levels of human experience, pre-eminently it inclines us to
seek truth and good at the highest level, that of rationality itself, which essentially distinguishes human from merely animal life. St. Thomas Aquinas, after treating of the sway of conscience at those levels of life-
experience which pertain specifically to our bodily nature, goes on to
consider "the inclination towards good according to man's nature as a rational being, which is proper to him." First and foremost of all the innate
dictates of the practical reason at that higher plane, he points to "the natural inclination that is in man to recognize truth concerning God."[9]

By the supreme precept of conscience we are implicitly bidden—but
not necessitated—to seek God as ultimate truth and goodness. That highest urging of conscience is not merely to pursue an intellectual quest but
to acknowledge and fulfil the primary purpose of our existence. To stifle
and disobey it is to fail the test of life. One who professes atheism may be

personally inculpable. His denial of God may be influenced by extenuating factors or based on a distorted idea of what is being denied. But deliberately asserted and chosen as a fundamental interpretation of reality and an orientation of one's life, atheism is a contradiction and rejection of that most basic dictate of human conscience and of the very meaning of human life.

To resume: conscience is ultimately an evidence of God, an imperative to seek him, and an invitation to meet him. It is an evidence inasmuch as it is a primary datum of inward experience from which we may infer, as we do also from the outward data of creation, his existence, sovereignty, and goodness. It is an experiential imperative, declaring the highest precept of our rational nature, which is to acknowledge and serve him. It is at the same time an invitation to respond to his love with our own. The prompting of our intellect to seek God is not only a moral imperative but also a drawing towards the fulfilment of our personhood and freedom, as Pope John Paul II testifies:

The religious impulse is the highest expression of the human person, because it is the highest reach of our rational nature. It springs from the profound human aspiration for the truth and it is the basis for our free and personal search for the divine.[10]

How Can Conscience Enjoin Faith?

Throughout the cultural history of humanity we find the linking of the innate moral sense with the intimations of the provident and law-giving God, which the human mind draws from reflection on the created world. Here too the light of natural reason is enhanced by and included in the higher light of divine revelation. As natural theology is purified, clarified, and surpassed by revealed theology, so the imperative of natural ethics in the conscience of humankind is purified, clarified, and surpassed by the grace of moral guidance that issues from God's direct communication of his sanctifying will through Christ and his Church.

Christian conscience bids us obey not only the natural law promulgated in creation but also the higher law of the Gospel revealed by Christ and faithfully interpreted to us by those whom he has vested with his authority. Conscience is, as Newman wrote, "a messenger of him who, both in nature and in grace, speaks to us behind a veil, and teaches and rules us by his representatives. Conscience is the aboriginal Vicar of Christ."[11]

But how can natural conscience bid us to assert the truths and to obey the precepts of supernatural revelation, which are surely above its reach? I recall here the deist-rationalist objection, referred to in Chapter 1 of this book, according to which any belief in revealed truth is an abdication of reason. It is an objection that is also applied in the field of ethics. Since the conscience which guides us to right choices springs from natural reason, how can it sanction choice of beliefs and values that cannot be established by natural reason?

The truths concerning God's being and his will that we are prompted to recognize by the fundamental moral inclination of our nature are indeed, primarily and most immediately, those that are attainable by our natural reason reflecting on the evidences of outward reality and inward conscience. Yet when, at the higher level of grace and faith, we make assent to the fulness of God's truth and commandments directly revealed in Christ and communicated through his Church, we are still acting in accord with that fundamental moral bidding of our natural conscience, though now in a sphere beyond that of natural reasoning. The law of our nature still bids us to embrace divine truth and goodness wherever we encounter it—both when shown by reason and when revealed to us by the higher light of faith, as the First Vatican Council observed:

Since man is wholly dependent on God as his Creator and Lord, and since created reason is essentially subject to uncreated Truth, we are obliged to render to God through faith the full submission of our intellect and will when he reveals his truth to us.[12]

By introspection I am aware that, in assenting by faith to the truths and commandments of revealed law, my mind is not assenting to them because of rational demonstration of their truth and rightness. Yet in accepting them I am conscious of still following the ultimate law of my nature, which is to conform myself to God's all-holy will. I am heedfully aware that, if I were to refuse or ignore faith's summons to believe and obey God's higher revelation and law, I should be contradicting the fundamental bidding of my conscience, which points me to seek his truth and to serve his holy will in all my life's experience. In the obedience of faith I do not have a sense of making an irrational leap in the dark, but rather of answering a call to journey trustfully into greater light. The highest exercise of our free will is to submit it to God in faith. In the words of Pope John Paul II, "Faith itself empowers each of us to express our freedom in a more excellent way. By believing, the human person performs the most significant act of life."[13]

Chapter 13

What Is "Religious Experience"?

Everyone moved by the Spirit is a child of God. The spirit you received is not a servile spirit rekindling fear, but a filial spirit moving us to cry out, "Abba! Father!" The Spirit himself testifies together with our spirit that we are children of God.

Romans 8.14–15

It must not be asserted that those who are truly justified ought to be wholly convinced in their hearts, without any doubt at all, that they have been justified. For while no right-minded person ought to have any doubt of the mercy of God, of the merits of Christ, and of the power and efficacy of the sacraments, anyone who reflects on himself and on his own weakness and waywardness can be doubtful and fearful about his own possession of grace. No one can know with the certainty of faith, with all possibility of error excluded, that he has obtained the grace of God.

Council of Trent, Decree on Justification, §9

Discussion of "religious experience" has developed and flourished during the past two centuries. It received a major stimulus from the writings of Friedrich Schleiermacher, who defined religion as "a sense and taste for the infinite" and as "the feeling of absolute dependence."[1] His experiential theology chimed in with the renewed yearning, in the post-Enlightenment age of Romanticism, for warmth and feeling in religion. Since his time "religious experience" has become a hackneyed term, though given different meanings by different authors.

In the debate about the meaning and possibility of religious experience there are two poles of discussion. On the one hand there are those who, following the lead of Schleiermacher, concentrate on the subjective aspect; that is, on the inner state of believers—on their feelings, hopes, fears, yearnings, and intuitions. Secularist sceptics indeed explain all so-called religious experiences as purely subjective emotions and states of consciousness without objective basis, or as projections of subliminal desires and anxieties, or as psychosomatic phenomena sometimes taking the form of group hysteria. On the other hand, there are those, notably Rudolf Otto, who give emphasis to the awesome attraction of the numinous "Other" which is the object of worship. In his work,[2] Otto developed the concept of the "numinous," a blend of awed fascination and reverence which seizes men and women in the presence of sacred mystery: the mystery, above all, of the transcendent supernatural reality apprehended as the object towards which religious attitudes and sentiments are directed.

Many use the term "religious experience" to emphasize the affective aspect of religion, as contrasted with the cognitive, the dynamic realm of seeking, acting, and suffering, as opposed to what they see as the static realm of dogma and theological theory, of abstract concepts, terms, and propositions about religion. Others indeed describe religious experience as cognition, but of a higher and richer kind than ordinary understanding, a special illumination of the mind bringing personal assurance of divine truth and purpose. Some would claim that it is direct perception of the power of God directing them, sensed as spiritual guidance, energy, and warmth.

Writers on mystical theology refer to an ineffable experience of divine indwelling that is not attained by active exercise of the intellect but by self-surrender to God in a blessed passivity. Others insist that religious experience is not a privileged state of the enlightened few, or an extraordinary happening, but that it is, in the words of the Anglican Archbishop William Temple, "the whole experience of religious persons." Not a few Christians see any claims to direct religious experience as suspect, even as derogatory to faith, which is said in Scripture to be "the conviction of things not seen" (Hebrews 11.1).

In the theological debate about the possibility and nature of religious experience two principal questions may be distinguished. One is to ask whether by their natural powers human beings can have direct awareness of God's presence and action in the world of his creation; the other is whether they can have direct awareness of God's grace supernaturally bestowed upon them. In this chapter I consider both questions, while giving principal attention to the latter. I draw here on what I have written elsewhere[3] on the elusive meaning of the term "religious experience," and on the possibility of "grace-experience" in particular.

It is common ground among Christian divines that finite human beings cannot have direct awareness of God in the infinite plenitude of the divine essence. If there is any experiential awareness of his presence in our lives it can only be through the means by which he communicates himself to us and leads us to himself. Regarding the possibility of any such religious experience, either by nature or by grace, there are significant differences between the teaching of the Catholic Church and the perspectives of Reformation and later Protestant thought.

First, there is the essential difference, referred to several times in these pages, that Catholic theology affirms and traditional Protestantism denies the natural power of human reason to have salutary knowledge of God's existence and attributes and of his creative action in the world and within ourselves. Thus on radical Protestant premisses, which deny the validity of natural theology, rational awareness of God's presence and action is antecedently excluded. On Catholic premisses, however, it is not. Indeed, although the exercise of reason that leads to knowledge of God's existence and attributes is inferential, it can be said to be, like all our conscious processes, experiential. "What is known is in a manner present to the knower."[4] I leave aside for the moment discussion of the further question of whether such natural awareness of God's presence can only be inferential and indirect, or whether there can be a direct "natural mystical experience," as some maintain.

Contrasting Doctrines of Grace

When we turn to the separate and more intricate theological question of the possibility of direct experience of God's grace, the perspectives of the Catholic Church and of Reformation Protestantism are again essentially different, this time because of irreconcilable differences in understanding of the nature of divine grace and of the way it is conferred upon humankind. It is of course a basic Christian belief, shared by both sides, that human beings stand in absolute need of God's grace and forgiveness, and that this is bestowed upon them by the sheer mercy of God.

Catholic theological teaching explains that the need of all sinful human beings for divine grace is not only under its aspect of *gratia sanans*, healing grace to repair the ravages of sin, both original and personal, but also under its aspect of *gratia elevans*, elevating grace to enable them to reach a supernatural end unattainable by their natural powers. That grace, which both justifies and sanctifies, originates in God's will to pardon sinners and to reconcile them to himself. "Uncreated grace," the presence of the Holy Spirit, comes to those who are justified. Consequent upon and issuing from that divine presence, according to Catholic doctrine, there comes the created grace that heals and elevates, a new intrinsic principle of supernatural life within them whereby they are regenerated, transformed, and ennobled. That inherent sanctifying grace gives, to those who are justified, co-filiation with Christ and thereby assimilation to the life and likeness of the triune God. It restores them to spiritual health and strength and endows them with the abiding theological virtues of faith, hope, and charity, by which they cleave to God and fulfil his will. It is (as the theology of the Orthodox Church also testifies with deep devotion) the restoration in the graced soul of the true image and likeness of God, preparing it for the ultimate "partaking of the divine nature" (2 Peter 1.4), which is the beatific union with God in eternal life.

Deriving from that inherent or "habitual" grace there is, according to Catholic doctrine, "actual" grace, illuminating the intellect and energizing the will for godly living. Transient actual graces, or grace-aids, can also be operative in unjustified sinners, to prompt them towards eventual repentance and conversion. Moreover, since God works all things together to achieve his loving plan for the whole human race and for each human being, the universal operation of divine providence in all its amplitude may be said to belong to the sphere of his actual grace. In that sphere are included not only the internal grace-aids, inspirations, and impulses given to individuals, but divine providence working together all external events and physical factors in the arena of salvation history. In the divine providential plan are also coordinated the consequences of sin and evil, out of which, even though they do not accord with God's antecedent will, he brings ultimate good.

The Catholic conception of the divine economy of salvation and of the meaning of Christian life may be described as "incarnational"; that is, Christ's living presence and action in his priestly-sacramental Church is seen as a perpetual extension of the purpose and work of his Incarnation.[5] Thereby he makes permanent and operative, for all generations of humankind until the end of time, the work of salvation that he accomplished once for all by his earthly life, death, and resurrection. His sanctifying grace dispensed through his Church, "the universal sacrament of salvation," is the new supernatural life-principle by which he lives and acts not only in the life of each Christian but also in his Mystical Body, the Church, as a whole. It empowers the members of that Body, according to their degree, to cooperate actively and meritoriously in his work of bringing humanity to salvation and eternal life.

Thus fallen humankind is not only redeemed by Christ's atonement but is raised up to active participation in the economy of salvation. He imparts to his Mystical Body a share in his ruling, teaching, and sanctifying power. Endowed with his priesthood, the Church through her sacramental ministry—above all, through celebration of the Eucharistic mystery, "the source and summit of the Christian life"[6]—ever transmits to humankind the fruits of his all-sufficient work of redemption.

Reformation Protestantism has a radically different conception of the meaning of grace, corresponding to its radically different understanding of the divine plan of salvation. For Luther and for Reformation theology generally, grace does not work an inward transformation in redeemed sinners, but is solely the divine decree of merciful pardon from on high, imputing to them the righteousness and merits of Christ and thus annulling the condemnation that was justly their due. Passively receiving that grace of pardon, they are incapable of cooperating with it. Even when released by divine merciful decree from the condemnation due to him, pardoned man remains radically vitiated by sin, *simul iustus et peccator* (at the same time justified and a sinner). According to the basic Reformation principle, the grace of divine pardon is certified directly to each of the elect through saving faith alone, not sacramentally communicated through mediation by the Church endowed with a share in the priesthood of Christ.[7]

Linked with that solifideist doctrine is the Reformers' understanding of the Atonement as the penal substitution of the innocent Christ in the place

of the guilty. This concept (not to be confused with the very different An-
selmian concept of vicarious satisfaction)[8] was stated by Calvin with his
customary clarity:

> Christ interposed, took the punishment on himself, and bore what by the just
> judgement of God was impending over sinners; with his own blood he expiated the
> sins which rendered them hateful to God, by this expiation satisfied and duly propi-
> tiated God the Father, by this intercession appeased his anger . . . Our acquittal is in
> this, that the guilt which made us liable to punishment was transferred to the head
> of the Son of God. We must especially remember this substitution in order that we
> may not be all our lives in trepidation and anxiety, as if the just vengeance, which
> the Son of God transferred to himself, were still impending over us.[9]

Different Answers to the Question of Grace-Experience

Those two opposing interpretations of the Christian revelation concerning grace and salvation give rise to differing perspectives on the possibility and manner of religious experience. From those different premises
follow different answers to the question: Can there be experience of divine
grace, of supernatural reality as such?

It might be supposed that the proponents of the Reformation doctrine,
holding that justifying grace effects no intrinsic change in man but subsists
solely in God's merciful decree, would not claim any direct and continuing
experience of it. The part of the saved, they taught, was simply to keep in
thankful remembrance the divine verdict of acquittal delivered once for all.
Conversely, it might be supposed that the Catholic theologians, holding
that the grace of justification was not solely the merciful decree of divine
pardon but also a created reality inwardly transforming and sanctifying the
one justified, would allow the possibility of experiential awareness of that
grace inherent within oneself. Yet neither supposition corresponds to the
actual course of theological speculation in the post-Reformation era.

In fact, the Protestant doctrine did not exclude all notion of experiential
apprehension of the fact of saving grace. Luther and his fellow Reformers
proclaimed, as the necessary counterpart of the merciful pardon decreed
by God from on high and declared in Scripture, personal reception of it by
justifying faith. That faith was not preached as merely intellectual acceptance of the truth of Christ's revelation and atonement, but as fiducial assurance of one's own pardon.

The nature of such assurance has been variously conceived by Protestant divines. Although personal fiducial faith as proclaimed by the founding fathers of the Reformation—namely, the certain and self-validating attestation of God's favor to each of the elect—could be described as experiential, they and their successors distanced themselves from those they called *Schwärmgeister*, fanatical enthusiasts who claimed that, to be genuine, the assurance of saving faith must be a charismatic experience of fervor and enlightenment testifying to one's possession by the Holy Spirit. (In controversy with their Romanist opponents, the "magisterial" Reformers were also critical of traditional legend-mongering, which, they protested, had fed popular religiosity on a diet of sensational miracle-tales, rather than on the pure bread of the Gospel).[10]

Claims to direct experience of saving grace were made not only by the "Spirituals" of the Radical Reformation but by other influential movements: by Lutheran pietism, by Wesleyan Methodism, and by other revivalist and charismatic groups. For John Wesley grace, if authentic, must be felt. In a letter to his mother in 1725[11] he wrote:

The Holy Ghost confers on us the graces necessary for an immortal nature. Now surely these graces are not of so little force as that we cannot perceive whether we have them or not; if we dwell in Christ, and Christ in us, which he will not do unless we are regenerate, certainly we must be sensible of it?

Such claims, however, remained controversial. Bishop Joseph Butler voiced a common distaste for them in his celebrated remark to Wesley himself: "Sir, the pretending to extraordinary revelations and gifts of the Holy Spirit is a horrid thing—a very horrid thing."

Such differences of opinion notwithstanding, the basic Reformation conception of fiducial faith presented a radical contradiction to the Catholic doctrine concerning grace and justification, and the manner in which Christ perpetuates his saving work through his Church. Reacting against that conception in its *Decree on Justification* of 1547, the Council of Trent condemned what it called "the preachment in our times of vain and wholly impious assurance" of personal righteousness.[12] The passage cited at the head of this chapter, in which the Council excluded the possibility of such fiducial certainty of one's own state of grace, was not framed in order to deny the possibility of any experience of grace. However, it subsequently seemed to many Catholic theologians that it necessarily implied such general denial. If someone professed to have a direct awareness of the presence of God's sanctifying grace in his soul, was that not tantamount to a presumptuous claim to be certain of his own justification, contrary to the teaching of Trent?

Moreover, as well as the Tridentine rejection of "vain and impious assurance" of grace, the development of Catholic theological understanding of the supernatural order, as essentially transcending the natural, also led to the conclusion that there cannot be experiential awareness of sanctifying grace as such. The *Catechism of the Catholic Church* states as follows this theological conclusion, at the same time recalling the motive for the well-founded trust that Christians may have that they are living in due obedience and union with God's will:

> Since it is supernatural, grace escapes our experience and cannot be recognized except by faith. We cannot therefore rely on our feelings or our works to conclude that we are justified and saved. However, as our Lord's words remind us, "By their fruits you shall know them" (Matthew 7.20). God's blessings in our life, and in the lives of the saints, offer us a pledge that grace is at work within us, and spurs us on to an ever greater faith and an attitude of trustful humility.[13]

Thus Catholic orthodoxy permits and encourages the faithful to have expectant hope that they are in the way of salvation. Although absolute certainty of one's own state of grace is ruled out, there are many valid signs in the life of the godly believer that give good grounds for inferring it. In this sense are interpreted the scriptural passages which encourage the faithful to take joyful delight in the action of the Holy Spirit within themselves.[14]

The age-old Catholic mystical tradition was thought by some to be at variance with the teaching of the Tridentine decree. In common with doctors of earlier centuries, some pre-Reformation mystics in the Rhineland and Low Countries, notably Eckhart and Van Ruysbroeck, used language which seemed to suppose that the graced soul could have mysterious consciousness of its own inner divinization, by which it was caught up into the eternal life of the Blessed Trinity. Likewise the spiritual doctrine of saints and mystics during the following centuries, pre-eminently St. Teresa of Avila and St. John of the Cross, both of whom were honored as Doctors of the Church, seemed to assert direct experience of the soul's communion with God. However, since those mystics also stressed the obscurity of that experience and the impossibility of adequately describing it at the ordinary level of conceptual consciousness, they could not be accused of claiming apodictic certainty of their own state of grace.[15]

Later Theological Speculations about Religious Experience

While Catholic orthodoxy precludes claims to direct experience of one's own possession of God's sanctifying grace, it would seem that to assert direct experience of his actual graces and providential aids should not necessarily be reckoned as spiritual presumption, since such graces may be operative not only in the just but in those not yet justified, prompting them towards repentance and response to God's loving mercy.

Even so, there still remains the diriment reason why, according to Catholic teaching, there cannot be experiential recognition of the presence and action within oneself of divine grace as such, whether habitual or actual: namely, that "grace escapes our experience and cannot be recognized except through faith," as the *Catechism of the Catholic Church* recalls in the passage cited above. As one cannot be certain, but can only infer with probability and humble hope, that one is in the state of sanctifying grace, so likewise one cannot have certainty that one is being moved by actual grace. While believers have sure faith that divine providential grace embraces and invites all human beings, they cannot be experientially sure that any particular insights and impulses that may come to them are in fact graces of the Holy Spirit. Such subjective perceptions, however fervent, must be submitted to the objective and prudent critique of faith and reason—what St. Ignatius Loyola calls "the discernment of spirits."

In recent times Catholic theologians have speculated anew on the possibility and reality of religious experience, whether natural or supernatural. Juan Alfaro suggested that just as the human spirit can be aware of its natural dynamism towards universal reality and truth, so it may be obscurely aware of the supernatural dynamism given to it in the realm of grace. On this view, while it is not possible to experience grace directly, a kind of indirect grace-experience is possible as a preconceptual awareness—what Alfaro called "a spontaneous and obscure awareness of one's active tendency towards God." Karl Rahner favored a similar view, holding that, "in a very anonymous and inexpressible manner" there may be a latent and indirect experience of the presence of grace in acts of altruism, renunciation, and love.[16]

Others have asserted the possibility for the human mind to have some deep awareness of the influx of created existence from its divine source, present and active within ourselves. Jacques Maritain spoke of a "natural mystical experience," which he described as a direct apprehension of our being as flowing from the creative power of God, an apprehension that can become connatural for the contemplative soul.[17] He made a distinction between two modes in the natural ascent of the mind to God. The first is by "ananoetic" contemplation, whereby the intellect mounts by analogy from created things to their divine source; the other is inward and direct, by the reflection of the intellect upon itself, in which one may have a mysterious awareness of one's own reception of being from divine Being. It is this latter mode which Maritain called "the natural mystical experience," and which he described as "an intellectual (negative) experience of the substantial *esse* of the soul."[18]

In appraising these insights of Maritain and of others who share them it is relevant to refer again to the significant development during the twentieth century, several times mentioned in these pages, in deeper theological understanding of the traditional distinction between the "natural" and the "supernatural." While that distinction is valid and important in Christian theology, it must not be taken to mean that there are two separate spheres in which human beings stand before God, one that of "mere nature," the other of grace. While human beings, by sinful misuse of their natural powers of mind and will, can be alienated from the supernatural life and efficacy of God's grace, whenever human beings (whether within the visible Christian Church or not) turn to God by right use of their natural powers of mind and will they do not do so without supernatural grace, bestowed on all humankind through Christ. Hence, while the mystical experience referred to by Maritain may rightly be called "natural," inasmuch as it proceeds from the natural potentiality of the human intellect, that does not mean that such experience must (or can) be "merely" natural. Elevated by grace, such reverent apprehension of the natural Godwardness of one's own created being would be in fact a supernatural grace, even though the one who has that awareness cannot be directly aware of it as such. The ineffable contemplation of the holy mystery of being, to which Maritain opaquely refers, is shared by countless women and men of every degree.

How does this discussion of Christian religious experience relate to the religious experience of the non-Christian majority of humankind? In earlier pages I have sought to express in many ways the insight that natural theology is the necessary forerunner to and companion of revealed theology. Here also it is relevant to recall what was said in the closing section of my fifth chapter, sub-titled, "Natural Religion Contained and Elevated in the Life of Grace." God's grace is the patrimony of all his children. It is operative in the religious wayfaring of all those who, though strangers to the Gospel of Jesus Christ, lovingly search for and find God in his created world and in themselves. With the higher supernatural finality given to it by divine grace their wayfaring leads them—albeit unawares—towards the eternal destiny of sharing in the life of the triune God revealed by Jesus Christ.

Chapter 14

The Truth That Pantheism Distorts

One who looks upon this visible world, and who considers the wisdom shining forth in the beauty of existing things, mounts by analogy (ἀναλογίξεται) through the things that are seen to the invisible beauty and the wellspring of wisdom whose flowing forth has formed the nature of these things.

St. *Gregory of Nyssa*, Homily XIII on the Song of Songs

The consideration of creatures sets the minds of men afire with love of the divine goodness. For whatever there is of goodness and perfection shared out partially among the different creatures is all universally united in him as in the wellspring of all goodness . . . If therefore the goodness, beauty, and sweetness of creatures so allures the minds of men, the goodness of God himself, the fount of goodness, lovingly traced through the rivulets of goodness found in all created things, will draw the minds of men, now aflame, wholly to himself.

St. *Thomas Aquinas*, Summa contra gentiles, 2.2

In this chapter I express in new form ideas already adumbrated in earlier pages, especially in my second and eighth chapters. Discernment of the divine signature in created reality is experiential wisdom shared by the peoples of the earth. I return to dwell again on that fundamental consensus. In all religions and cultures sages and seekers find in the natural world pointers to deity. Although the patterns of thought and language in which they express their speculations are very diverse, they yet give common witness to humanity's reverent awareness of the one holy reality that undergirds all things. Poets sing in many strains of "a presence which disturbs with the joy of elevated thoughts . . . A motion and a spirit that impels all thinking things, all objects of all thought, and rolls through all things."[1]

Nature is a cosmic symphony, all its parts concerted in one majestic paean of praise of the Holy One. There is nothing, however hidden or lowly, however vast or distant, which does not resound with that divine harmony to those who have ears to hear. Nature is a cosmic canvas, all things arrayed together in one masterpiece of color, line, and form. There is nothing, however small or shadowy, however strange or motley, which does not have its place and purpose in the master design.

This cosmos, this ordered whole, this realm of sacred being, is a universal frame of beauty which is the setting for the beauty of each part. We may seek and find God's glory, power, and splendor in the whole as in the parts, in the widest span of interstellar space as in the narrowest plot of earth, in the remotest galaxy as in the nearest blade of grass. However acutely scientists may apply the laws of mathematics and physics to interpret the structure and energies of the universe, however deeply they may probe into the secrets of matter, they may yet be blind to the deepest meaning and wonder of the material universe. That meaning the lowly and unlettered may discern by opening their eyes and hearts with wonder and reverent awe.

The mysterious truth affirmed by seers, poets, and philosophers in lofty words is grasped, less articulately but no less immediately, by the multitudes whose lives are set close to nature and whose work follows its rhythms. Nature speaks of divinity with special intensity to those who with reverent wonder and joy contemplate its beauty, power, and purposiveness, whose religion finds root in "the dumb certainties of experience." Although those who live enmeshed in a technocratic civilization may be less open to that awareness of God immanent in his creation, all have potency for it. The true beginning of wisdom is not to be found in an array of logical principles set forth in a scholar's study, but in humble awareness of the mystery of existence and a willed affinity with divinely ordered Nature.

"The heavens show forth the glory of God and the firmament declares the work of his hands" (Psalms 19.1). From our spinning globe, a minute speck in this universe of unheeding immensity, we look out into the bowl of space flecked with points of light. We come to know that they are myriads of suns in countless galaxies, unimaginably vast systems of molten matter and fiery gas hurtling through the endless corridors of space since time's beginning. Wonder stirs us to meditative reflection when we learn from scientists of the enigmatic origin and development of this material cosmos, governed by determinate physical laws and patterns of macrocosmic regularity that—despite apparent microcosmic indeterminacy—are universally operative throughout the measureless span of matter, space, and time.

The same wonder that is stirred in us by the marvels and mysteries of the cosmos is still more directly evoked by pondering on the manifold of reality that we directly encounter in our own life experience and on the meaning and purpose of this life. The awed wonder that is the antechamber to true wisdom is not mere curiosity; it is a prompting in our very nature to seek the meaning and purpose of all, God. It is a call to prayer.

Witness to the Holy One whose image is mirrored in all things comes most clearly from the monotheistic religions of the world, adoring him as personal Lord and Creator of all. Here Christians are joined in a special fellowship of reverence with Jews and Muslims, with Sikhs and Parsees, with Hindu *bhakti* devotees, with the millions in primal religions who honor the Great Spirit and Father, with all who worship and serve the one God under divers names. More distant and more opaque, but still reverent, is the witness of those systems of religious thought that regard the one and holy mystery as beyond form and personality: of Taoism, proclaiming the Way of Heaven as the pattern and rule of the universe and of human life; of Advaita Hinduism, declaring the cosmic unity of all with ultimate *Brahman*; of Theravada Buddhism, speculating subtly on what some sages describe simply as "that which is most precious," and others as eternal and enlightening Buddha-nature transcending the illusory world of *maya*; of Platonist mysticism, discerning in all earthly things the reflection of an ideal realm of perfect form, beauty, and goodness emanating from the One which is beyond all.

The many other religious ideologies of East and West, North and South, likewise find in and beyond the corporeal world in which human life is set intimations of a divine reality that gives meaning to all. The *Gayatri Mantra*, the dawn prayer of all Hindu religion, whether Dvaitin or Advaitin, expresses the natural reverence of humanity for that reality: *"OM!*—ye earth, sky, and heaven, we raise our minds to the glorious splendor of the life-giving Divine."

So God-like is the divine impress in the world that some mistake it for God himself, and construe divine immanence in a pantheist sense.[2] Recognizing the presence of deity in all things, most intensely in the human soul, they deny or blur the essential distinction between the divine Absolute and the created manifold that reflects him. In the history of the ceaseless yet often aberrant religious quest of the peoples of the world, pantheistic nature worship has been a besetting error in their concepts of deity, as Holy Scripture testifies:

> Yes, naturally stupid are all men who have not known God and who, from the good things that are seen, have not been able to discover THE ONE WHO IS . . . If, charmed by their beauty, they have taken things for gods, let them know how much the Lord of these excels them, since the very author of beauty has created them. And if they have been impressed by their power and energy, let them deduce from these how much mightier is he that has formed them; since through the grandeur and beauty of creatures we may, by analogy, contemplate their author. *(Wisdom 13.1–5)*

In proclaiming that the world is divine, pantheism grasps a fundamental truth, albeit while distorting it. For in truth the world *is* divine in the impress it bears. Pantheism is right when it finds God in all things and all things in God. It errs when it asserts that all things are God—most grievously when it asserts the identity of the human self with the divine Absolute, as in a celebrated passage in the Upanishads:

> In the beginning there was Existence alone—One only, without a second. He, the One, thought to himself: "Let there be many, let me grow forth." Thus out of himself he projected the universe, he entered into every being. All that is has its self in him alone. Of all things he is the subtle essence. He is the truth. He is the Self. And that . . . That Thou Art *(tat tvam asi)*.[3]

That ultimate affirmation of monist lore, *"tat tvam asi,"* may be seen as the ultimate blasphemy of the creature claiming self-deification. Alternatively, it may be seen as a forlorn attempt of human speech to refer to the ineffable union of the soul with God, which mystics experience in self-negating contemplation but cannot describe when they return to normal consciousness. Hindu monist mysticism may more precisely be described as panentheism—the doctrine that all things of our experience are in God as imperfect parts of a perfect whole. Yet a Christian interpretation could be given to the words attributed to the deity in the *Bhagavadgita* (6.30): "From one who sees me everywhere and sees everything in me shall I never part, nor shall he ever part from me."

Pantheism is right when it discerns the oneness of all finite being; it errs when it interprets that created oneness as the divine One, instead of his noblest image. "Every creature has its unique form according to which it shares in a particular manner in the likeness of the divine essence," writes Aquinas. But, he goes on to testify, "The totality of the universe more perfectly participates in the divine goodness, and shows it forth, than any single creature."[4] That is, while each individual form has its own perfection and beauty, creation as a whole has a unitary perfection and beauty that manifests supremely the One who is its source. There is one divine purpose that gives common purpose to all things, binding them together in one providential plan.

Those who interpret reality in a pantheist sense are attuned to hear the divine music and to discern the divine impress in all things. But they fall into the ultimate idolatry of revering all things as divine, of allowing what is made to lead them to God to keep them from God. The truth that pantheism distorts, grasped both by right reason and in a higher manner by faith is expressed in these words of Aquinas:

God is above all things by the excellence of his nature, and yet he is in all things, as causing the being of them all . . . He is in all things as he that contains them. The highest good in the totality of things is the universal order therein . . . Every creature tends towards its proper perfection; the divine goodness is what draws all. For this reason the world is one, because all things are necessarily combined in one order and to one purpose.[5]

The natural religion of humanity descries omnipresent divinity through mists, physical and moral, awaiting the clear vision that comes through God's personal revelation of himself. In the mists one may mistake the way, and at times stumble and stray; but all who seek to respond aright to the Godward prompting of their nature are already in the sphere of the supernatural and empowering grace of the Holy Spirit.

God is omnipresent not only in all that is, but also in all that comes to pass. All being and all becoming manifest THE ONE WHO IS, and who causes all else to be and to act. "Whoever sets his steps on the road to wisdom, spanning with his gaze and pondering in his mind all created things, begins to feel Wisdom showing itself to him joyfully in the way, coming to meet him at every turn of providence"—so testifies St. Augustine.[6] In her *Third Shewing* Julian of Norwich gives like testimony: "And thus he showed me blissfully, signifying thus: 'See, I am God; see, I am in all things; see, I do all thing; see, I never lift my hands off my works, nor ever shall, without end.'"

Awareness of the causal presence of God in his works, in all that is and in all that comes to pass, in all persons and in oneself, may become an abiding state of prayer and love. Through the sacrament of the present moment, holy communion with God's will is given to those who conform their will to his in whatever comes to be. That truly sanctifying grace is bestowed not only in times of peaceful contemplation but through all the business of daily life, in suffering of body or mind, even in spiritual desolation.

The Relation of Creatures to Creator

Discussion of the truth that pantheism distorts leads back to reflection on the analogy of being, resuming the meditation begun in my second chapter and continued in the eighth. What is most real in every created being is the Godward relation by which it participates in creative Being. That relation is unique; we can form no adequate concept of it. It is not simply a resemblance such as that of children to their parents or of a work of art to the idea in the mind of the artist who made it. Such resemblances are between effects that, once caused, exist independently of the agents that originated them. God's creatures are not sundered from him when they begin to exist; his sustaining of their being is continued creation. Without that unceasing influx of their existence from necessary Being, contingent beings would lapse into the nothingness from which they were called.

As Aquinas declares that the title, THE ONE WHO IS, is "the most proper name of God," so too he declares that "created being is his most proper effect." He continues:

God causes this effect in things not only when they first begin to be but as long as they are conserved in being, as light is caused in the air by the sun as long as its light remains in the air . . . Hence God is necessarily present most inwardly in all things.[7]

But while the relation of creatures to their divine source is more than a mere likeness to a separated exemplar, it cannot be the sharing of substance that there is between parts and their whole. Reason itself can recognize the falseness of pantheism's first premise.

The great metaphysicians of antiquity saw the attractiveness and the difficulties in both extremes of theory concerning the relation of creatures to the divine mystery. Plato spoke both of *mimesis*, imitation of the supernal reality, and of *methexis*, sharing in it. Aristotle saw the limitations of both concepts, but he could speculate no more clearly on the relation between the world of movement and the unmoved mover, between multiple potentiality and the unitary pure actuality. There were medieval thinkers, Jewish and Muslim as well as Christian, who veered towards one or other of those two opposing poles: merely extrinsic resemblance or intrinsic sharing of substance.

Perennial wisdom, while rejecting what is false in both those extreme views, draws from what is true in each. It rejects the error that makes univocal predication of being to God and his creatures alike, and that would accordingly imply that they are conjoined with his substance in a monist sense. On the other hand, it realizes that while God is infinitely transcendent, the influx of finite being that his creatures unceasingly receive from his infinite Being assimilates them to him ontologically, in a manner that, though beyond our capacity to understand, yet makes it possible for our intellect to have some true knowledge of his existence and perfections through contemplation of his created works.

The supposition of Rabbi Maimonides and also of some medieval Islamic metaphysicians that in speaking of God we can only use equivocal and metaphorical language, which cannot apply to him, leads logically to complete agnosticism about his being. Here I repeat what was said in earlier pages about the consequence of such a supposition. If, in this world, which is the arena of our experience and from which we draw all our concepts and the language that expresses them, there were nothing that had real connection with and reference to the creative origin and source of all the reality that we know, then we could know or say nothing true or meaningful about God. There would be no valid foundation for any human statement concerning God as he is in himself. Not only natural religion but revelation itself, which is necessarily expressed in human conceptual language, could convey nothing but meaningless word-spinning about an unknowable "X."

There must then be that mysterious third way of conceiving the relationship of creatures to God. We point to it when we say that the perfections of being that we perceive in the universe of our experience can be predicated supereminently of God in a true sense: not equivocally, nor univocally, but analogically. The analogy of being, as rightly applied in philosophical and theological thinking, corresponds to the procession of finite and contingent being from infinite and necessary Being. Since creatures can neither be simply separate from God nor simply one with him, there must be a unique manner in which they draw all their reality from him while he infinitely transcends them. God, with or without creatures, is the totality of Being: they do not and cannot add anything to his plenitude nor subtract from it. We ponder the obscure but not contradictory concept that there is a real albeit "one-way" relation between creatures and God, by which they derive all their being and becoming from him, while in no way affecting his eternal and unchangeable perfection. We grope for words to describe that relation.

The analogy of being is verily the ladder leading from earthly knowledge to heavenly wisdom. Our minds are made to recognize that the contingent being that we directly experience derives from the necessary Being who is the meaning and purpose of our lives and of all things. All created being is sacred because it proceeds from and manifests the All-Holy. Emboldened by scriptural precedent, we may even speak of created beings as "sharing" being from God, by virtue of the continuous reception of their existence from his. Created beings in their relationship to God have been described by Christian thinkers in terms that may seem to have pantheistic connotations; they have variously described creatures as participations, processions, emanations, or irradiations from God. Such words are all inadequate similes, but with due qualification they can bear an orthodox sense. Aquinas gives them such a sense when he says that the divine essence "is participated by created things, not as being parts of it but by diffusion and procession from it."[8]

From revelation we learn of the mysterious relation of all creation to the divine Logos who from his eternity is its exemplary originative principle and who, while eternally transcending that creation, has become incarnate in it in time. "He is the image of the unseen God and the first-born of all creation, for in him were created all things in heaven and on earth . . . All things were created through him and for him. Before anything was created, he existed, and he holds all things in unity" (Colossians 1.15–17). St. Thomas comments, "Because God knows in one act of intellect both himself and all things, his one Word manifests both the Father and his creatures."⁹ The highest degree in which it is possible for creatures to become "sharers of the divine nature" is indicated in the scriptural passage 2 Peter 1.4, where that phrase is used to refer to God's purpose to unite redeemed humanity with himself through Christ.

Sacred Being: Ontotheology and the intellectus fidei

These reflections on divine and human being link with the theme of "ontotheology" already discussed in earlier pages, most fully in my eighth chapter. The wisdom both of revealed theology and of metaphysical philosophy meditates on God as necessary and self-subsistent Being, *Ipsum esse per se subsistens*, whose proper name is "THE ONE WHO IS" and whose proper effect is to cause to exist. In Chapter 8 I have already noted how, in *Fides et ratio*, Pope John Paul II reaffirms and draws upon that traditional ontotheological wisdom, using the very terminology in which the Fathers and medieval masters expressed it.¹⁰ Now I return to dwell further on that teaching.

In his encyclical the Pope repeatedly emphasizes the central importance for Catholic faith and doctrine of what he calls "the philosophy of existent being."¹¹ In so doing he uses phrases that express the existential immediacy and dynamism of experienced *esse*, awareness of which leads us to acknowledge ultimate divine reality. In those Latin phrases, which lose some of their force when translated, he refers to that wisdom as *"philosophia respiciens 'esse,'" "veritas existentiae," "philosophia essendi," "philosophia actuosa seu dynamica."*¹² He extols it as pointing the path to *"veritas ontologica,"* ontological truth. Modern positivist philosophy has lost its bearings, he says, because it fails to direct its search *"in ipsum esse"*—"to Being itself." In the long development of the Church's understanding of the necessary relation of reason to faith, the Pope declares, "an altogether unique place belongs to St. Thomas Aquinas," whose "philosophy is of being itself, not merely of phenomena."¹³

In a passage unparalleled in the previous documents of the Church's teaching magisterium, the Pope expressly asserts that the true "philosophy of being" makes a necessary contribution to the *intellectus fidei*, that is, to faith's search for deeper rational understanding of the meaning of revealed truth:

> If the *intellectus fidei* is to integrate all the riches of theological tradition, it must have recourse to the philosophy of being (*philosophia essendi*). Set within the Christian metaphysical tradition, the philosophy of being is efficacious and dynamic philosophy that truly shows forth reality under its ontological, causal, and interactive aspects. Its motive force and perennial power is to be found in the fact that it is based on the very actuality of existing being (*quod actu ipso "essendi" sustentatur*). From that standpoint it is possible to gain a full and general vision of the whole universe of things, and thence, transcending all finitude, to attain to Him who gives to all things their fulfilment.[14]

While the faith that seeks understanding calls philosophy in aid, conversely, as the Pope also declares, "philosophy is enriched from its reciprocal concourse with the word of God."[15] While autonomous human reason can reach true philosophical conclusions independently of revelation and faith, nevertheless, in the process of reaching the most profound truths of philosophy, the dimmer and more fitful light of reason can be strengthened and guided by the higher light of revelation. Extolling "philosophical meditation which is vitally conjoined with faith," the Pope expressly cites, as a prime instance of such fruitful support given by faith to probing reason, the development of "the philosophy concerning *'esse.'*" The clarification of that profound philosophy has been aided, he says, by the knowledge that is surely given by revelation of the divine reality as "personal, free, and creator God."[16]

Voices for and against the Theology of Being

Thus the papal encyclical reaffirms the central place of ontotheological wisdom in Christian thinking. In the mid-nineteenth century it was thought by some that a cloud had been cast over that wisdom by the ecclesiastical censure passed on the so-called "errors of ontologists." At that time the speculations of certain contemporary Catholic thinkers concerning infinite and finite being were suspected of showing monist-pantheist tendencies. Eminent among those who fell under such suspicion was Antonio Rosmini, to whose opinions I have already referred earlier.[17] His leading idea was that of indeterminate and universal being, by intuition of which the human intellect could realize the procession of created beings from creative divine Being. His corpus of philosophical and theological writings (which reflect his profound study of the works of St. Thomas Aquinas and also of the insights of later philosophers, including Hegel) contained not a few singular propositions and expressions that not unnaturally gave rise to objections. Forty *"errores"* ascribed to him were censured by the Holy Office in 1887.[18]

Nevertheless, despite some obscure speculations and injudicious language, Rosmini's philosophizing about being was ruled by fervently orthodox faith and profoundly religious meditation on what I have called here "the truth that pantheism distorts." His reputation as a Catholic thinker is now fully rehabilitated by his inclusion in a group of five Western thinkers (which includes the two eminent "philosophers of being," Jacques Maritain and Étienne Gilson) whom Pope John Paul II names in *Fides et ratio* as "scholars who in recent times have, with noble diligence of mind, furthered the fruitful concourse of philosophy and the word of God."[19]

One must suppose that Pope John Paul would not include among such scholars the author of the anti-metaphysical book, mentioned in my second chapter,[20] entitled *Dieu sans l'Être—God Without Being*—the general thesis of which is in effect contradicted by the encyclical *Fides et ratio*. That book, by Jean-Luc Marion, has stimulated considerable interest and discussion. Since its perspective is very different from that of the papal letter (and from my own perspective throughout this book), and since consideration of its thesis provides an opportunity for further reflection on my present theme, I here digress once again to offer a brief critical comment on that controversial thesis.

When making previous mention of Marion's book I observed that its author, in developing his fideist and deconstructionist apologia, was much influenced by the secular existentialism of Heidegger, who in turn was influenced by the anti-metaphysical positivism of Nietzsche, and also, indirectly, by the fideist tradition in Protestantism. Marion cites with approval some words spoken by Heidegger at a colloquy in Zurich in 1951: "If I were to write a theology (as I am sometimes minded to) then the word 'Being' would not be found there. Faith has nothing to do with the concept of Being. When that is brought in, it is no longer faith."[21]

Marion likewise states his own intent as follows: *"libérer 'Dieu' de la question de l'Être"*—"to free 'God' from the question of Being." He inveighs against the central title attributed to God by Augustine, Aquinas, and the medieval masters, namely, *ipsum esse*, which they equated with the scriptural name of YAHWEH, THE ONE WHO IS. The coherence of the author's arguments is not always easy to grasp. Yet as one reads his devout expressions of faith, insisting that it is love, not being, that gives us true inkling of the nature of God, the vehemence of his diatribes against the traditional theology of divine *esse* seems mitigated. Even though his reductionist and fideist thesis is at variance with the ontotheological wisdom of the Fathers and doctors of the Church, and with the explicit teaching of the papal magisterium, the motivation of his writings may be sympathetically interpreted as a protest against what he conceives as lifeless metaphysical theory. In his work there is implicit witness to two cardinal principles of the Catholic theology of being: first, the necessity of due observance of the *via negativa* in all discourse about the Being of God; second, the truth expressed in the scholastic axiom concerning the transcendental perfections of being: *ens et bonum convertuntur*—"being and good are convertible terms." Being and loving may indeed be taken as synonyms to refer to the unitary and ineffable actuality of God. The "philosophy of existent being," which Pope John Paul extols, and which he describes as an "experiential and dynamic philosophy," is not a mere dialectical exercise but an opening to loving faith and adoration.

"Connatural" Knowledge of Divine Truth and Goodness

All human perception of what is true, good, and beautiful can be clarified and deepened by special sensibility for and dedication to the subject matter of what is known. For instance, those who have the mastery can intuitively grasp patterns of structure and harmony in a musical composition that others recognize only imperfectly or not at all. In human conduct, those who are attuned to moral good by long practice of virtue and selfless love immediately discern what is right and act accordingly, while the judgment of those who are accustomed to stifling the prompting of conscience is clouded. Such a manner of intuitive insight, both in practical and speculative grasp of the good and the true, becomes, as we say, "second nature" for those in whom it is habitual. Aquinas observes, "Sure judgement can be reached in two ways: one by acute process of discursive reasoning, the other by a certain connaturality with the matter on which judgement is to be made."²² Such connatural knowledge of the ultimate meaning and source of the universe, and of the purpose of human life, is found in those who, in the light of faith and with the aid of grace, constantly and lovingly contemplate the goodness of God in his outward works and in their inward experience.

While all nature bears the impress of God, it is in human nature, the masterpiece of this created world, that his likeness is to be found in unique and highest form. Endowed with intellect, human beings are made in the image of him who is supreme intellect. Endowed with free will, they bear the likeness of him who is sovereign will and freedom. Made for interpersonal love, they resemble from afar him who (as we know not by reason but by faith) is infinite interpersonal love. In each and all of them is to be recognized and reverenced that image of God. Out there, spread across the globe in the ceaseless cycle of birth, life, and death, are the unknown billions of humankind. Yet they are not unknown to each of us. Near or far, they are our companions in our Godfaring. Strangers, they are yet our kin; we are all children of the same divine Father, all bearing his lineaments. In all faces is glimpsed the face of God.

Why is it, then, that the company of those kinsfolk in God's family does not lead us more easily to him? Why, rather, do contemplative souls often find deeper awareness of God's presence in solitude, away from human beings rather than in the midst of them? Why is it that the harmony, power, and beauty of the non-rational creation may seem to lift our minds and hearts to God more readily than the company of those who are made uniquely in his own image, who manifest his likeness in their intellect and free will, in their personal dignity, and in their capacity to love?

One answer to these questions is that contemplation requires singleness of heart and recollection of mind; it can be hindered by the mundane cares and distractions of human society. "Be still, and know that I am God" (Psalm 46.10). In the busy bazaar of life our minds are agitated by fears, desires, griefs, and antipathies. All of us need at times to go apart into a desert place to rest awhile in quietness of spirit. But there are also other and graver reasons for our spiritual myopia: above all, the somber fact of sin. The sin of our race and our own sinfulness mar the image of God in ourselves and in others. Our spiritual vision is blurred, making it difficult for us to discern that image in one another. Yet the truly pure of heart can find

God as readily—or even more readily—in the market-place, in the class-room or office, or in those dying destitute in the slums of Calcutta or Rio de Janeiro as in the desert or on the mountain top. Love for all and each of God's children truly opens the eyes of the soul to see in them his likeness and to reverence him in them.

In India there is an everyday gesture of greeting which is a mark of social and religious respect. The one who greets bows to the one who is greeted, placing both palms together and saying *"Namaste."* That common ritual greeting can be taken (so I have been told) to convey the meaning, "I reverence the divine Spirit within you." With any monistic connotation excluded, that gesture of greeting could well be adopted by Christians, and indeed by all believers, to honor the divine image and dignity that is in every child, woman, and man whom we encounter.

Chapter 15

Faring Homeward to God

It is in the face of death that the enigma of man's condition is most acute. Not only is he agonized by the pain and progressive disintegration of his body, but even more by the dread of forever ceasing to be. By a sure judgement coming from his inmost self he abhors and rejects the idea of the utter destruction and final annulment of his personality. The seed of immortality which he bears within himself, transcending mere matter, defies death.

Vatican II, Gaudium et spes, §18

Heaven is the ultimate end and consummation of the deepest human longings, the state of supreme, definitive happiness . . . To live in heaven is "to be with Christ." The elect live "in Christ," but they there retain, or rather find, their true identity . . . This mystery of blessed communion with God and with all who are in Christ is above all our understanding and representation . . . Because of his transcendence, God cannot be seen as he is unless he himself opens his mystery to man's immediate contemplation and gives him the capacity for it . . . In the glory of heaven the blessed continue joyfully to fulfil God's will in relation to other men and to all creation. There they reign with Christ . . .

Catechism of the Catholic Church, §§ 1024–25, 1027–29

Every human life is a progress towards the final goal that gives purpose to it as a whole. Spread out in time, this life is a continuum of personal experience, unified by the unique self who lives it. Each of us has abiding self-awareness not only of the "I" who thinks, wills, and acts at every conscious moment, but of the unchanging identity of that self through the whole timespan of personal life-experience as recorded and perpetuated by memory. Through all the successive stages and vicissitudes of a lifetime, from childhood to old age, I have that continuing awareness that I am the self-same personal agent, accountable for my whole life, past and present. We do not choose to begin this mysterious journey of life, but from the first dawning of the light of reason to its eventual dimming and extinguishment we are responsible for how we progress towards the journey's end. On that probationary progress our eternal destiny depends.

Through this life the knell of mortality sounds ceaselessly. Sooner or later all of us must come face to face with the challenge of death. The loss of those we love, the impact of sudden tragedy, the ceaseless roll call of lives ended, our own advancing age and infirmity—these bring to the forefront of our minds questions that are not merely speculative but urgently practical and personal. In our youth and in the prime of life the truth that we shall one day die may seem notional and remote, but eventually there comes experiential realization that the sands of life's hour-glass are fast running out and that it is urgent to make ready for the inevitable hour.

By nature every sentient creature fears death and instinctively seeks to avoid it. Rational creatures are not exempt from that instinctive dread. Our reason itself resists the seeming finality of death and seeks to probe beyond it. It attests the natural yearning of humanity for immortality and for a final fulfilment unattainable here. The spiritual self that seeks ultimate meaning in its existence has a profound sense that it cannot be annihilated by bodily death but must in some manner survive. But without faith and trust in divine purpose and benevolence, such survival remains a somber mystery.

The sad incertitude of the human heart fearfully musing on what lies beyond death was voiced in a poignant little verse addressed by the Roman emperor Hadrian to his departing soul as he lay dying in his villa beside the Bay of Naples in the year AD 138:

> Little wayward tender soul,
> Guest and partner of this body,
> To what realms must you now go forth,
> Pale, palsied, and stripped bare?
> There you will no more be merry, as here you have been.[1]

In the course of his eventful life, holding together in an iron grip an empire of many different races and faiths, Hadrian had heard much of the religious quest of humankind and of the many diverse forms in which it was expressed. He was familiar with the civic cults of Rome and Greece, in which his own *genius* was accorded a share of divinity. He had seen how the homely cult of the guardian spirits of hearth and field pervaded the lives of the countryfolk of the Mediterranean lands. He had admired the great monuments that Egyptian state-religion, fixated on the afterlife, had reared above the flat lands of the Nile. He had heard of the savage gods of the Germanic tribes east of the Rhine, in those dark primeval forests where once a whole Roman army had been destroyed. He knew too of the Celtic divinities brought under Roman law, first in Gaul and then in the island of Britain, where he had raised a great frontier wall from the Tyne's mouth to the Solway Firth.

Hadrian had considered the speculations of the philosophers about metaphysical and divine reality. He had heard the whispered claims of the mystery religions of the Greco-Roman world, promising to their initiates spiritual enlightenment and other-worldly bliss: the cults of Dionysus, of Attis and Cybele, of Isis and Osiris, of Mithras, and the Eleusinian Mysteries through which, Cicero had said, "We have learned to live and die with a better hope." He knew of the militant piety of the Zoroastrians, worshippers of Ahura Mazda, the good creator god and lord of all good, in the Parthian empire beyond his eastern frontier. Doubtless he had heard something of the wisdom of India, and of its belief (parallelled by some speculations in the West) in the transmigration of souls and of the quest of its sages for ultimate release and absorption in the Absolute. He had faced and forcibly solved problems with the Jews, a people unlike all others, intransigently loyal to their God and to their ancestral customs. He had marked the ever-widening spread within his empire of the secretive sect of Christians, who were ridiculed for worshipping as divine a Galilean carpenter executed by a Roman procurator a century previously, and whose religious nonconformity had brought them too to suffer the ruthless penal force of his imperial authority.

Now for the mighty ruler of the Roman world everything he was and had, all his power, wealth, pleasures, learning, planning, and his life itself, was ending. When he wrote his desolate deathbed verse the only other-worldly survival he could envisage was as a joyless, witless wraith shivering helplessly in a shadowy netherworld. His melancholy lines express the plight of the self left finally alone in a desert of doubt and foreboding without having found the meaning and purpose of life.

Akin to Hadrian's dismal expectations of the after-life are the ancient Greek concept of Hades and the ancient Hebrew concept of Sheol. Loftier but still dim and joyless are the metaphysical expectations of those Eastern religious thinkers, referred to several times in these pages, who envisage the destiny of the soul after death as the cessation of conscious identity and as absorption of the self in the All. In its most impersonal form, this conception is found in the Buddhist yearning for Nirvana, which is conceived as the final realization of *anatta*, non-self: "The one who enters Nirvana ceases to exist—but Nirvana exists." The conception of Hindu monism, if less stark, is not dissimilar; the enlightened self, already aware of its identity with divine *Brahman*, passes through death to final engulfment in that oneness.

The religions of humanity commonly offer their adherents a deeper hope than that of survival as a ghost in the eternal sadness of a bleak underworld or that of the disappearance of the self into an ultimate sacred void. Natural religion yearns for personal survival and fulfilment beyond the grave, for an ultimate vindication of divine goodness and justice, and for a definitive judgment of human deserts. But the natural religion of human reason cannot part the veil drawn by death. Only divine revelation gives us clear assurance of what lies beyond.

Memento mori: *Life's Lessons Interpreted by Faith*

Life's road has many twists and turns, and rough places where in our frailty we stumble and fall. Yet always we have access to God's forgiving and healing grace, to raise us up and set us on the way once more. Each life story is a potential masterpiece of his grace, a unique pattern of conformity to his all-wise and all-loving will. Our sinfulness and selfishness may seem to have irremediably marred the divinely intended pattern. Yet, even at the eleventh hour and at the last moment of conscious life, God is able, in a manner beyond our comprehension, to make from the seeming wrack a still more wonderful masterpiece of his mercy, wisdom, and love.

However we have fared so far, whether well or ill, there still lies ahead that last defile, dark and daunting, through which we all must pass before we reach the end of our sojourn in time and emerge into eternity. While made by God to voyage through a mortal lifetime towards the goal of immortal life, we still instinctively dread the inevitable death of the body that must end our earthly wayfaring. It is part of our probation here to prepare for that final decisive moment when our bodily life will cease; while we still can pray, to offer our dying and death to the Creator of our life with the all-embracing prayer, "Thy will be done." In what manner and with what dispositions we shall enter the dark doorway of death we know not. Happily for us, safe passage through it to the eternal life beyond does not depend on whether or not we give edification to those around our deathbed by the manner of our dying but on the welcoming mercy of our loving Father.

It is an ideal not only of Christianity but of natural religion to devote one's old age to good works, contemplation, and the welfare of one's soul, severing oneself from worldly attachments in readiness for approaching death.[2] Alas, it is an ideal that few of us attain. Looking back on my life, I ask myself what lessons for my own dying I have learned through witnessing the deaths of others and sharing in the sadness with which death darkens human life and joy.

As a child, no doubt like countless other children, I was shown that on the palm of each of my hands, formed by the natural wrinkles of the skin, is inscribed the letter *M*. That twofold inscription *MM* could be taken, I was told, as initials signifying the Latin phrase *Memento Mori*, and so as a perpetual reminder of the truth that I like all others must one day die. Since hearing that quaint lesson in childhood I have been given, in the experience of a long life, more immediate reminders of that truth in personal bereavement and grief, in consoling the dying and those who mourned their dead, in often witnessing death both peaceful and violent.

Like others of my generation caught up in the carnage of war, I have seen men killed, have heard the sounds of wounded men dying, have buried the bodies of the slain. Often I was myself in imminent danger of violent death, and several times escaped it by a hair's breadth. In olden days devout Christians, like St. Jerome in his cell, would keep before their eyes a skull or the picture of a death scene as a reminder of mortality, of the impermanence of the world's pleasures, and of man's ultimate destiny. In the closet of my memory are many grim pictures of death that serve me as such reminder. In an Appendix to this book I recall one of them, a *memento mori* from a battlefield in North Africa that still stirs me to watch and pray.[3]

The time came when I was myself struck of a sudden by high explosive and experienced what I thought was the moment of my death. It was in the middle of the beachhead battle on the shores of the Gulf of Salerno in early September 1943. I was seeking a new site for our dangerously exposed battalion headquarters when an anti-tank mine blew apart the jeep I was driving, shattering my bones and rending my flesh, and hurling me, still conscious after the blinding impact of the explosion, into a dark void with an indescribable sense of violent dissolution. In my extremity I cried out to Jesus as somehow there beyond the darkness through which I seemed to be falling. A passage from my wartime diary, written in a hospital bed in Tripoli three weeks later, records the experience:

I stopped at the corner of a wood where a track led into it. I let in the clutch and turned to enter the track. There was a world-filling bang, and I felt myself falling forward towards a great flame at the foot of a pit of utter darkness. The explosion had hit me in a way I could not know in that moment of suddenness. My first thought was that my soul was on its way to eternity. I found myself crying out, twice, in a loud voice, "My Jesus I love you." Then the darkness cleared, and I found myself still alive and huddled in the wreckage of the jeep.

The memory of that experience has also remained ever vivid to me during all the years since then, as has thankfulness to my Savior, the Lord of eternal life, that he was at the center of my consciousness at that instant in which I felt certain that my soul was being hurled through the gateway of death.

Now, fourscore years of life gone by, the long delayed moment of my death, the end of my earthly Godfaring, draws near. Whatever the manner of it is to be, I pray to die in the love and peace of Christ. I pray for the grace and strength to kiss the crucifix that a beloved hand may hold to my lips, and to say with trustful faith the words of Scripture my Savior uttered as he died: "Father, into your hands I commit my spirit."

The Life of the World to Come

In figurative language the Gospel likens this mortal life to a journey, to running a race, to schooling and training, to warfare and combat, to the

growing of grain crops in the earth and their eventual winnowing, to trad-
ing for profit, to laboring in a vineyard for a wage determined by the will of
its master, to storing up provisions for the future, to preparing for a wedding feast, to a strict probation leading to forensic judgment, to the wander-
ing of an errant son returning in the end to dwell in the home and love of
his merciful father. Our Lord warns us to be always ready for that decisive
ending of our earthly probation.

"As it is written, 'What no eye has seen, nor ear heard, nor the heart of
man conceived, what God has prepared for those who love him,' God has
revealed to us through the Spirit" (1 Corinthians 2.9). Faith throws its beam
of light and love into and beyond the dark valley of the shadow of death, to
give us God's sure promise of what lies beyond. Faith makes it possible for
us to master the dread of death, and even to accept it gladly for the sake of
the higher good to which it is ordained in his loving plan. Christ has transformed the meaning of our death by dying and rising for us. With St. Paul
we can say, "For to me to live is Christ and to die is gain" (Philippians 1.21).
"Yes, the troubles which are soon over, though they weigh little, train us for
the carrying of a weight of eternal glory which is out of all proportion to
them" (2 Corinthians 4.17). With St. Francis of Assisi in his *Canticle of Creation* we can praise God for our sister death:

> Praised art thou, Lord, for our sister bodily death,
> from whom no living man can escape.
> Woe to those who will die in mortal sin!
> Blessed are they who will be found in thy most holy will,
> for the second death will not harm them.

In necessarily inadequate human speech Holy Scripture gives us some
true intimations of the nature of the life of the world to come, and of the
state of the self that survives bodily mortality. I resume here, in faith and
hope, the outline of revealed Christian eschatology that I sketched in my
fourth chapter as a counterpoint to my preceding survey of the teachings
of the other world religions on the goals and term of human life.

Christian revelation tells us in cryptic words of admonition, promise,
and hope of the mysterious realities that lie beyond: of the everlasting and
unimaginable beatitude of heaven (reached, if need be, through prior pur-
gatorial hallowing) and of the terrible alternative possibility of hell, self-

alienation from God for ever. It tells us of the final seal of divine justice on all human lives: under one aspect, a particular judgment for each at death; under another, the general judgment for all, when Christ, who by his dying has destroyed our death and by his rising has restored our life, will come again in glory to judge the living and the dead. Through that transforming final resurrection, the culmination of all human life and history, "the creation itself will be set free from its bondage to decay and obtain the glorious liberty of the children of God" (Romans 8.21), and the just will attain everlasting glory and joy in a restored unity of soul and transformed body. Heaven is, first and above all, final union with God. The eternal beatitude in his embrace for which we are destined is a deep mystery beyond our present understanding.

Some Christians, opening their arms and hearts to their non-Christian brethren, have found themselves able to accommodate the patterns of Hindu religious thought and language to express their own Christian hope for that ultimate union of the soul with God, while excluding the non-theistic presuppositions of Hindu monism. One who did so was a dear friend and colleague of mine, Frank De Graeve, a Belgian Jesuit priest who devoted much of his life to the sympathetic study of Eastern religions. He composed the following poem in English during a time of meditative seclusion in India a few years before his death:

Upanishadic Pilgrim

I am a spark of you, Light uncreated,
seeking my self in that momentary flash.
I am the search of you, the Seeker,
and, if I find, you are the One who finds.
You are the Seeker and the Sought,
You are the Thinker and the Thought.
I am the flashing, the passing of light.
Yet do I search, I, sourceless blindness,
pilgrim to your glory in my self.
And when I find you, Light, in what is lightning,
and finalize my matter in your Spirit,
I end my pilgrimage to your eternity
in which I, disappearing, find my self;
my light, returning to your Light,
is vanishing in white vibrations,
and you alone remain, you, blinding darkness.[4]

The ultimate destiny of human beings is not the cessation of personal identity by absorption in divine infinity—nor indeed was that the belief of the author of those fervent lines. While our promised destiny is to be "partakers of the divine nature" (2 Peter 1.4), heavenly bliss is also the perfecting of human nature, both for each person and for the whole community of the blessed. It is not passivity and unselving but sovereign actuality and perfect freedom.

Christian faith gives us certain assurance that our survival and continuity in that ineffable consummation, which we call eternal life, is not only individual but also social. In our earthly life we are called to love and relate to other persons, so to prepare for heavenly life which is essentially a community of love. It is communion in the interpersonal life and love of God, the divine Trinity of Father, Son, and Holy Spirit, and thereby with all the blessed. Faith assures us that it is in the sharing of the divine life that the members of redeemed and transformed humanity find their fulfilment and eternal bliss. Therein each and all of them eternally rejoice in communion with the God-man Jesus Christ in his glorified humanity. Pre-eminent in that heavenly communion of saints is his blessed mother Mary, spiritual mother of all humankind, who are his sisters and brothers. There they join company with the angels, created spirits resplendent with the glorious likeness of God, of whose tutelary aid on earth we are assured by Scripture. There the redeemed have everlasting reunion with those with whom they were joined on earth in kinship, love, and shared experience.

These truths of revelation I profess with certain faith and hope, though a cloud of unknowing veils from my present understanding the manner of existence that is eternal life.

Beloved, we are God's children now; it does not yet appear what we shall be, but we know that when he appears we shall be like him, for we shall see him as he is [1 John 3.2]. Now we are seeing a dim reflection as in a mirror; but then we shall be seeing face to face. The knowledge that I have now is imperfect; but then I shall know as fully as I am known [1 Corinthians 13.12].

This I believe: that I shall see the goodness of the Lord in the land of the living. (Psalms 27.13)

Epilogue

A Wayfarer's Prayer

God of mystery,
God within all things and beyond all things,
To you we bow down in awe and adoration.
Give us sight to see your inward imprint in all whom we meet and in all that
we look upon,
Ears to sense your music in all that we hear.
May our lives be a joyous pilgrimage to you and with you through this
world of your making.
Finding you in all, may we never cease to seek you above all.
Glimpsing you at every turn of the way,
May we never falter or stray from the long road that leads through light and
darkness to the final meeting point,
Where we are to see you no longer through created veils but face to face.
As each day we set our feet upon the way, staff in hand, we know that the
very earth we tread is holy ground,
And we kiss the imprint of your presence there.
Loving God, known and unknown, present and yet to come, draw us in
mind, heart, and body wholly to yourself.

Appendix I

An Autobiographical Endnote

The following summary (referred to in the Introduction) lists some stages and turning points in the author's journey through life.

Born 1919, the second child of loving and devoutly Catholic parents, both converts to the faith. On leaving my London grammar school I worked as a journalist until the outbreak of war in 1939.

Thenceforward a soldier on active service in the British Army: first in England, then via India to Iraq, thence to battle in North Africa and Italy. In September 1943, now captain and adjutant of the 8th Battalion of the Royal Fusiliers, severely wounded in action. Long convalescence, and a permanent legacy of pain.

In 1945 I entered a religious order, the Society of Jesus. There followed thirteen years of training as a Jesuit; studies and degrees in philosophy and theology. In 1954, I was ordained priest. In 1958, received doctorate in divinity from the Pontifical Gregorian University in Rome. In 1962, solemn religious profession. From 1959, professor of theology at Heythrop College in Oxfordshire; from 1963, also associate professor at the Gregorian University. Present in Rome during the Second Vatican Council, with occasional access to its sessions. Pastoral and spiritual ministries year by year; authorship and international academic activities.

In 1967, after a time of turmoil, a major change in my life's course: namely, withdrawal from my religious profession and priestly ministry. I was granted, by a direct personal decision of Pope Paul VI, "dispensation from all obligations arising from sacred ordination, including that of observing the law of consecrated celibacy." (The two-line papal dispensation, Protocol no. 2203/67, was unprecedented in making no mention of *reductio ad statum laicalem*.)

Return from Rome to England and a new way of life and work. In July 1968, I married Pauline (herself released from religious vows three years earlier) in the Cardinal Archbishop's chapel at Westminster. Our union has been, during the 32 years that have passed since that nuptial Mass, one of shared faith, love, and happiness. I never cease to thank God for my beloved wife, his peerless gift, for her love and devotion which is at the center of our family life, and for the blessing and joy he has given us in one another.

Returned to secular life and with our livelihood to earn, I worked for a while as a schoolmaster, next as visiting professor of theology at Fordham University, New York, and from the opening of the new Open University in the UK until my eventual retirement as head of Religious Studies there.

Joys and cares of our family life and (from 1970) parenthood, blessed with two daughters and a son, Antonia, Catherine, and Gregory. Engaged for several years in interreligious dialogue and collaboration, involving worldwide travels. Still, in old age, writing, counselling, lecturing in theology and history of religion. In November 1998, I was installed as a Founding Fellow of Maryvale Institute, Birmingham, UK, by Archbishop Maurice Couve de Murville.

Still a limping pilgrim, giving thanks, standing ready, praying to Him who walked with the troubled travellers on the way to Emmaus, making their prayer my own: "Stay with us, Lord, for it is toward evening and the day is now far spent" (Luke 24.29).

Appendix II

A memento mori *from a Wartime Diary*

The following account (referred to in Chapter 15, footnote 3) was published half a century ago in *The Shield* 54 (June 1950): 13–14. *The Shield* was a Church periodical in what was then Rhodesia. It reproduced a passage from my wartime diary in which I described the bloody ordeal of my battalion in early May 1943, when it made an unsuccessful night attack on a strongly fortified ridge south of Tunis. I related how four days later, after the enemy's eventual defeat and surrender, I went out with two others on a vain search of the battlefield for possible survivors:

"First we passed the burnt-out trucks which had been blown up by mines in our advance. Near them was the overturned carrier with a gaping hole in it below the driver's place, and several yards away the body of the driver himself, a huddled, shapeless heap lying as he had fallen when his soul was hurled to eternity. I remembered the awful humming whirr I had heard four nights before as the breath escaped from his crushed body. We went down across the valley to the minefield beyond the wadi bed, where the wreckage of another carrier showed up gauntly beside the track and a dismembered body lay nearby. On the way to the ridge corpses were sprawled here and there in the sand and scrub, their faces puffed and black. They were our men, London lads, what remained of them now swollen and bloated by several days' exposure to the African sun.

"As we climbed to the hill-top the noisome smell of corrupting flesh grew stronger. When we reached the groups of rotting bodies at the summit it seemed unbearable. To my dying day I shall remember that sight and that stench. All around was corruption. Mangled bodies were piled together, grotesquely distorted. The blackened flesh, bloated and splitting apart, was covered with vast swarms of gross, green meat-flies, feeding on the decomposing tissue and laying their eggs in it. My friend was there among the others. I could tell him only by his light hair and officer's brown boots. I knelt there amidst the grisly human wreckage and prayed in a confused way for the souls that had once given life to those putrescent heaps . . .

"It was two days more before I could return to the battlefield, this time to bury two of my men, close friends who had been killed by the same mortar bomb in the low ground at the foot of the ridge. The two extra days had wrought new ravages in the corpses. By now the maggots had hatched out and the dead faces and limbs were moving once more—moving with living streams of seething, loathsome worms. Rather, faces they were no longer but masks of slimy glistening creatures eating deeper and deeper into the rotting tissue. I stood by the body of the devout young man I had known and liked so well and watched with horror the teeming traffic of maggots flowing in and out of the holes that had been his eyes and nose and mouth, and round the gaping cleft in the back of his head made by the jagged lump of metal that had ended his life in a fleeting second . . .

We dug the graves, enfolded each of the worm-covered bodies in a blanket, and lowered them into the earth. The two padres were summoned and each in turn performed his duty. We shovelled in the earth, placed makeshift crosses in position, and went away."

Glossary of Religious and Philosophical Terms

Advaita Meaning "non-dual" in Sanskrit, the term refers to the basic tenet of Hindu monism that there is no distinction between the human soul, *atman*, and the sacred Absolute reality, *Brahman*. *Advaitin* monism was systematized by Sankara (around 800 AD).

Analogy of being The predication of concepts drawn from our experience of created beings to the infinite creative Being, founded on their mysterious ontological relation to him.

Ananoetic Adjective referring to the manner of knowing by which the contemplative soul rises by analogical inference from experience of lower realms of reality to higher spiritual realms, and eventually to knowledge of God.

Anthropomorphism The depicting of God in the likeness of man; applying to him human characteristics and limitations which cannot be attributed to the infinite and all-perfect Godhead.

Antisophical Descriptive of systems of philosophical thought that are contrary to true philosophical wisdom.

Apotropaic Supposedly having the power to avert ill fortune or to repel malign forces.

Atman The Hindu term for the human self or soul which undergoes successive reincarnations. In the teaching of the *Advaita* monistic sages, the term also denotes the universal soul, *Brahman*. Man's ultimate liberation is believed to lie in the realization of the identity of his *atman* with that Absolute Self.

Beatific Vision The direct knowledge of and blissful union with God, which is the eternal destiny of the blessed in heaven.

Bhakti The popular "loving devotion" of Hindu monotheistic religion to the deity as personal, provident, and gracious savior. In Vaishnavism, the Lord is worshipped as Vishnu, or one of his avatars (incarnations), principally Krishna and Rama; in Saivism, he is worshipped as Siva, or his female divine energy in different forms.

Bodhisattvas "Enlightened beings" who, in Mahayana Buddhist belief, have postponed their own passage to the bliss of Nirvana in order to manifest their compassion and wisdom by aiding suffering sentient creatures. They are invoked as savior-saints.

Brahman In Hindu monistic philosophy, the sacred Absolute reality. See **Advaita** and **Atman**.

Catharism A dualistic creed, akin to Manicheism, which had currency in the Middle Ages in Northern Italy and especially in Southwest France, where the Albigenses who held it were severely persecuted.

Communicatio idiomatum Translated somewhat opaquely as "interchange of the properties," this traditional phrase (which was used in the Tome of Pope St. Leo the Great in 441 AD) encapsulates the doctrinal truth that, while the divine nature and the human nature of Jesus Christ are distinct and incommensurable, their union in that one Person makes it legitimate to predicate of him in his human nature what is proper to his divine nature, and *vice versa*.

Conation Striving or willing to perform an action and to achieve an end; distinguished from cognition, which is acquisition of knowledge.

Conciliar Relating to Councils of the Church; in these pages, referring particularly to the Second Vatican Council (1962–1965).

Connatural knowing A clearer and deeper perception arising from personal affinity with and dedication to the subject that is under study.

Deists Those, especially in the 18th century, who based affirmation of the existence of God, and of religious truth and values, on reason alone rather than on revelation and faith.

Deontological Relating to obligation and duty.

Dhammakaya In Buddhist religious metaphysics, ultimate, impersonal, and formless reality.

Dharma In Hindu religion, the eternal and impersonal cosmic law that orders all things. As innate and operative in human life, it is the imperative duty governing society and all individuals according to their condition.

Dhikr In Islam, rhythmic recitation of Qur'anic verses and Names of Allah, especially as practised by Sufi mystics in whirling motion to reach a state of ecstatic trance.

Diriment Nullifying, rendering inoperative.

Dualism In the study of religion, the term is used in various senses. It can refer to duality and distinction between: (1) spirit and matter; (2) body and soul; (3) the good God and a rival power of evil; (4) the human soul and God (or the Absolute reality).

Dvaita The term means "dual" in Sanskrit. First applied to a South Indian 13th-century school, it is used more widely to refer to the theism of those who affirm, against the monism of *Advaita* religious philosophy, the real distinction between the human soul and God.

Ecclesial Having the character of the Church or of churches.

Ecclesiocentrism Term applied (by some modern critics) to the doctrine that affirms the central role of Christ's Church in the dispensation of God's saving grace for all mankind.

Ecclesiology Dogma and theological study relating to the Christian Church.

Economy of salvation The divine plan and effective means for bringing redemption and eternal life through Jesus Christ to the human race.

Empiricism In philosophical and theological usage, affirmation of the starting-point of all our knowledge in sense-experience.

Entelechy Holistic principle of organization and activity within each living organism, proactively promoting its survival, development and propagation.

Epistemology The philosophical and psychological study of human knowing, especially of the methods and validity of our processes of reasoning and understanding.

Eschatology Theological reflection and teaching on "The Last Things" (*eschata*): i.e. on death and immortality; on judgment, individual and general; on the final climax in the destiny of humanity and of all creation; on heaven and eternal life.

Exegetes Commentators on and interpreters of Holy Scripture.

Fideism A term applied to the traditional Protestant doctrine that only faith gives true knowledge of God, reason being powerless to do so. See **Solifideism** and **Fiducial faith**.

Fiducial faith A term applied to the Protestant Reformers' concept of faith as not only a confession of belief but as a personal assurance of and confidence in one's own reception of God's merciful pardon.

Final causality Cf. **Teleology**.

Gathas Hymns, probably written by Zoroaster himself, contained in the *Avesta*, the sacred scriptures of the Zoroastrian religion.

Gnosticism A dualistic creed offering secret knowledge and perfection, which became widely influential from the second century onwards. Its adherents contrasted themselves, as enlightened "spirituals" (*pneumatikoi*), with the fleshly multitude (*sarkikoi*), mired in the evil of the material creation. Similar in character were later gnostic movements such as Manichaeism and Catharism.

Heuristic Descriptive of questioning or teaching that encourages or allows the hearers to make discovery for themselves.

Hierogram Sacred inscription or symbolic sign.

Hypostatic Union The substantial union of the divine and human natures in the one Person (*hypostasis*) of Jesus Christ. The dogma was defined by the Council of Chalcedon (AD 451).

Impetration Prayer for divine aid or boons.

Imputed righteousness The Reformation teaching that human beings are justified and saved by the extrinsic imputation to them of the righteousness of Christ, without being sanctified by "inherent" or "habitual" grace, as the Catholic Church teaches. The two opposing doctrines are described and contrasted in the phrases, "imputed righteousness" and "imparted righteousness."

Jahiliyyah The term used in Islam to describe the times of ignorance from which the coming of Muhammad and the Qur'anic revelation brought liberation.

Justification This theological term refers to the merciful act and process by which God makes sinners just. It is also used to refer to the state of grace and righteousness of the pardoned and regenerated sinner. Justification is absolutely necessary for the sinful creature, estranged from God by sin, original and actual, to attain salvation and eternal life.

Karma The Hindu belief that all actions have their inevitable consequences, for good or evil, and will inevitably be requited by reward or punishment in the course of the eternal cycle of metempsychosis. It is conceived as a universal system of moral accountancy which necessarily restores and preserves cosmic justice.

Kenosis The "condescension" of God the Son when, becoming incarnate, he "emptied himself, taking the form of a servant" and "humbled himself and became obedient unto death" (Philippians 2.7–8).

Mahayana In Buddhism, the "great vehicle," or path to liberation dominant in Far Eastern Buddhism. It is contrasted with the "lesser vehicle" (Hinayana, otherwise Theravada). Influential in southern and northwestern India during the early centuries of the common era, Mahayana later became the prevalent form of Buddhism in Nepal, Tibet, China, Korea, and Japan. In contrast to the intellectualism and agnosticism of Theravada, it invokes the aid of heavenly protectors, and has a rich mythology and ritual culture.

Magisterium The teaching authority of the Catholic Church, exercised through Ecumenical Councils and through the Popes as successors of St. Peter.

Manicheism A radically dualistic and gnostic belief-system, founded by Manes in the Persian empire in the third century AD. St. Augustine was a Manichee for nine years before his conversion to Christianity.

Maya In Indian religious thought, the illusoriness and unsubstantiality of the world of phenomena, which deceptively conceals true reality.

Metempsychosis The transmigration of souls. See *Samsara*.

Mitzvoth In Judaism, the sacred obligations governing every aspect of life.

Moksha In Indian religious thought, salvation and liberation through release from the cycle of rebirths. See Samsara and Nirvana.

Monism The theory that all reality is one being, and that there is ultimately no distinction between the divine Absolute and the empirical world. See *Pantheism*.

Monotheism Belief and affirmation that there is only one God.

Mystical Body of Christ The name is applied to the Church, as signifying Christ's abiding presence in it and the unity of all Christians as members of that Body through his transforming grace.

Nirvana The central Buddhist doctrine of ultimate liberation from the state of suffering that is the lot of all sentient creatures, and from the cycle of rebirths that eternally renews it. *Nirvana* is conceived as an ineffable state of peace and bliss, beyond selfhood and form. It is to be attained by extinction of all desire and by final enlightenment.

Noble Eightfold Path The mental discipline indicated by the Buddha's teaching as the way to enlightenment. Its eight cardinal precepts are right understanding, right motivation, right speaking, right acting, right pursuit of livelihood, right striving, right mindfulness, and right meditative concentration.

Noetic Relating to the search for or attainment of understanding.

Numinous A word coined by R. Otto to refer to a sense of fascinated awe experienced in the presence of the Holy.

Obediential potency A theological term referring to a natural receptivity in human beings, which, while not giving them an innate necessity for or right to receive supernatural grace and gifts, gives them the capacity to be elevated to the supernatural plane.

Ontology Metaphysical reflection and teaching on being as such.

Ontotheology Theological reflection that applies "the philosophy of being" to illumine the relation of creatures to God, and to contemplate him as Being itself.

Orthopraxy Right religious practice (as distinguished from orthodoxy, right belief).

Panentheism The theory, a variant of pantheism, that all things are in God as imperfect parts of a perfect whole.

Pantheism The assertion of the divinity of all reality, in the sense that not only is God present in all things but that all things are ultimately parts of or identical with God.

Pelagian A term referring to the unorthodox teaching of Pelagius, a fifth-century Briton, according to which man can take the initial steps towards salvation by the power of his own free will, without the necessity for divine grace. The term is also applied by rigorist critics to those who affirm the essential goodness of human nature even after the original Fall.

Phenomena In philosophical usage, the term denotes objects of empirical experience, the objects of sensory rather than intellectual knowledge.

Piacular Expiatory, paying the due penalty for wrongdoing, making amends or atonement.

Process theology A contemporary system of ideas, pioneered by A. N. Whitehead, which proposes the notion that God himself is involved, proactively and reactively, in the evolutionary processes of the universe, and thereby shares in its throes and in the travails of mankind.

Pseudosophy False philosophy masquerading as true wisdom.

Ratiocination The discursive process of reasoning, as distinguished from and prior to intellection, that is, conclusive judgment.

Regnocentrism A term favored by some latter-day critics of Vatican II who challenge its teaching on the centrality of Christ's Church as "universal sacrament of salvation" in the divine salvific plan for all humanity. Instead they propose the theory that all religions, sharing in the wider "Kingdom of God," are independent channels of salvation and eternal life in their own right. See **Ecclesiocentrism.**

Rig-Veda The most hallowed of the early *Vedas*, containing hymns to the gods of the Aryan invaders of India.

R'ta In the *Vedas*, the cosmic principle preserving the order of the universe, which needed to be honored and maintained by cultic sacrifice.

Sacred tetragram The four Hebrew characters inscribing the Name of God, *YHWH* (vocalized as *YAHWEH*), revealed to Moses on Mount Horeb.

Salat The second "Pillar of Islam," the daily prayers of the Muslim faithful, who rhythmically prostrate themselves while facing towards Mecca.

Salvific Conducive to salvation.

Samsara In Indian religions, the transmigration of souls in an unceasing cycle of births and deaths at various levels of existence, bringing due reward or retribution according to one's *karmic* deserts in previous lives.

Sanatana Dharma "The Eternal Way," the Sanskrit name of the religious culture now called by the generic name of "Hinduism."

Sangha The community of *bhikkus*, Buddhist monks.

Sat-chit-ananda The threefold primary attributes of *Brahman*: existence, consciousness, and joy.

Satori In Buddhist meditative techniques, especially those of Japanese Zen, the breakthrough to sudden illumination.

Septuagint The Greek translation of the Old Testament, made in Alexandria during the third and second centuries BC.

Shekinah In Jewish Talmudic theology, the omnipresence and immanent indwelling of God in the world.

Solifideism The doctrine of Martin Luther and of Reformation theology generally concerning salvation by faith alone. See also **Fideism.**

Soteriology Theological teaching and study relating to salvation (*soteria*) and redemption.

Subsistent relations This phrase is used in Christian theology to refer to the ineffable mystery of the Three Persons of the Trinity in the unity of the one Godhead. They are not three different substantial entitites; they are differentiated only by their mutual relativity of origin within the divine unity.

Sufism The mystical and ascetical movement within Islam, originating in the eighth century.

Sunyavada In the teaching of the Buddhist sage Nagarjuna (c. 100 AD), it refers to the cosmic Void which is thought of as the womb and tomb of the illusory world, the ultimate "Emptiness" (*sunyata*).

Supralapsarian predestination The Calvinist teaching that God predestines the elect to eternal life and foredooms the reprobate to eternal damnation antecedently to any consideration of the original Fall (*lapsus*).

Taoism The ancient Chinese religious philosophy, with remote origins in shamanism, which developed between the fifth and third centuries BC and has been influential in Chinese life ever since. The famous Taoist sage Lao-Tzu was an older contemporary of Confucius. The Tao, "The Way," was conceived in monist terms, as conformity with the fundamental mystery of indeterminate and all-encompassing being, the dark cosmic womb from which all things issued forth and to which all would return. Meditative and magical-cultic techniques were practiced to attain oneness with that ultimate sacred reality.

Teleology Recognition of intrinsic purposiveness in the order of the universe, particularly in the development and activity of organic life-forms.

Telos Goal or term.

Theodicy Theological vindication of divine providence and justice in face of the problem of evil.

Theologoumenon A theological opinion that is tenable and reputable, but that has not been authoritatively approved by the Church.

Theomorphic Formed in the likeness of God.

Theophany A visible manifestation of deity.

Theonomy The law of God governing his creation, especially as manifest in the dictates of conscience.

Theopaschitism A name given to theories, both ancient and modern, that postulate suffering in the Godhead.

Theravada "The teaching of the elders," the form of Buddhism prevalent in Sri Lanka and South-East Asia. It claims to preserve more faithfully the orthodoxy of the original Buddhist canon. See **Mahayana**.

Torah "The Law" or "the teaching." The name given to the divine revelation to the Jewish people, and specifically to the first five books of the Hebrew scriptures (the Pentateuch). There is also "the oral *Torah*," namely, the traditional commentary on and interpretation of the written revelation.

Transcendental perfections of being The term refers to those universal notions that are applicable to being itself, transcending any limitation to particular beings or forms of being. Chief among the transcendental (or "pure") perfections of being are oneness, goodness, truth, beauty, actuality, causality, purposiveness. By the analogy of being the human intellect attributes them in supereminent degree to God, who is very Being itself—"*ipsum esse.*"

Tridentine Relating to the Council of Trent (1545–1563).

Triune Adjective referring to God revealed as Three and One.

Upanishads Hindu scriptures originating after the Vedas and mostly dating from between 800 and 300 BC Called "the end of the Vedas," and later systematized in the schools of *Vedanta*, they develop metaphysical religious ideas, particularly pantheist monism and the search for *moksha*.

Vedas The most ancient scriptures of Hinduism, preserving the sacred lore of the Aryans who invaded India during the second millennium BC. The earliest Vedas were transmitted by oral tradition. They were written down and substantially added to during the first half of the first century BC.

Via negativa The manner of knowing and speaking of God that necessarily negates attribution to him of the limitations of the finite beings, from which we draw our intimations of infinite Being.

Voluntarism A metaphysical and theological viewpoint (expounded by William of Ockham and also implicitly adopted by Luther, Calvin, and the other Reformers) that so exalts the sovereign freedom and inscrutability of the divine will (*voluntas Dei*) as to suppose that the concepts and standards of right and wrong that he decrees for his rational creatures cannot be attributed to him by them. Hence, since his will has absolute and arbitrary primacy, men cannot presume to question the justice of his predestinatory choices and providential control of all events. Theodicy is thus considered to be needless and futile.

List of Church Documents Cited

❈

Documents from Earlier Centuries

For documents dated before 1962 reference is made to the relevant texts given in *Enchiridion symbolorum definitionum et declarationum de rebus fidei et morum*, edited by H. Denzinger and A. Schönmetzer, 36th edition (Freiburg: Herder, 1976; = Denz.).

325—*Symbolum Nicaenum*: Definition of the Creed of the Council of Nicea. Denz. 125–26.

449—"Leo's Tome": The "Tome" of Pope St. Leo the Great on the Incarnation of the Word of God. Denz. 290–95.

451—*Symbolum Chalcedonse*: Definition of the Council of Chalcedon on the Two Natures, Divine and Human, in the one Person of Jesus Christ. Denz. 301–2.

853—Decree of the Provincial Council of Quiercy on Man's Free Will and Predestination. Denz. 621–24.

1215—Dogmatic definition of the Fourth Lateran Council on the Catholic Faith and on God in Trinity. Denz. 800–807.

1302—*Unam sanctam*, bull of Pope Boniface VIII on the unicity of the Church. Denz. 870–75.

1442—*Cantate Domino*, Decree (Reunion Decree for the Jacobites) of the Council of Florence. Denz. 1330–53.

1547—Decree and Canons of the Council of Trent on Justification. Denz. 1520–83.

1682—*Caelestis Pastor*, Decree of the Holy Office against the quietistic errors of Michael Molimos. Denz. 2201–88.

1690—Decree of the Holy Office against the errors of the Jansenists. Denz. 2304–6.

1855—Decree of the Sacred Congregation of the Index relating to the fideist and traditionalist propositions of Augustine Bonnetty. Denz. 2611–14.

1861—Decree of the Holy Office censuring "the errors of Ontologists." Denz. 2841–47.

1863—*Quanto conficiamur moerere*, encyclical letter of Pope Pius IX to the bishops of Italy. Denz. 2865–67.

1870—*Dei Filius*, dogmatic constitution of the First Vatican Council on the Catholic Faith. Denz. 3000–3045.

1887—Decree of the Holy Office censuring the opinions of Antonio Rosmini-Serbati. Denz. 3201–41.

1943—*Mystici corporis*, encyclical letter of Pope Pius XII. Denz. 3821.

1949—"Boston Letter" of the Holy Office. Denz. 2866–72.

1950—*Humani generis*, encyclical letter of Pope Pius XII. Denz. 3875–76.

Documents of the Second Vatican Council (1962–1965)

Official Latin texts in *Sacrosanctum Oecumenicum Concilium Vaticanum II: Constitutiones, Decreta, Declarationes* (Rome: General Secretariat of the Council, 1966). English translations in *Vatican Council II: The Conciliar and Post Conciliar Documents*, edited by A. Flannery (Dublin: Dominican Publications, 1992).

Ad gentes: Decree on the Church's Missionary Activity (Dec. 1965).

Dei Verbum: Dogmatic Constitution on Divine Revelation (Nov. 1965).

Dignitatis humanae: Declaration on Religious Liberty (Dec. 1965).

Gaudium et spes: Pastoral Constitution on the Church in the Modern World (Dec. 1965).

Lumen gentium: Dogmatic Constitution on the Church (Nov. 1964).

Nostra aetate: Declaration on the Relation of the Church to Non-Christian Religions (Oct. 1965).

Sacrosanctum Concilium: Constitution on the Sacred Liturgy (Dec. 1963).

Unitatis redintegratio: Decree on Ecumenism (Nov. 1964).

Recent Documents of the Papal Magisterium

The Catechism of the Catholic Church (CCC). The authorized English translation of *CCC* was published in 1994 (London: Geoffrey Chapman) "subject to revision in the light of the Latin *editio typica*." In these pages the 1994 English translation is cited with several minor changes of wording made in the light of the normative Latin text of *CCC* published by Libreria Editrice Vaticana in 1997.

Documents of Pope Paul VI

Address to the faithful in Rome, published in *L'Osservatore Romano* of March 23, 1966.

Evangelii nuntiandi: Apostolic Exhortation on Evangelization in the Modern World. Rome: *Acta Apostolicae Sedis* 68 (1976). English translation: London: Catholic Truth Society, 1976.

Documents of Pope John Paul II

Fides et ratio: de necessitudinis natura inter utramque. Encyclical letter on the Relationship between Faith and Reason. Latin normative text and English translation both published in Rome by Libreria Editrice Vaticana, 1998.

Redemptor hominis. Encyclical letter. Rome: Libreria Editrice Vaticana, 1979. English translation: London: Catholic Truth Society, 1979.

Redemptoris missio. Encyclical letter. Rome: Libreria Editrice Vaticana, 1991. English translation: London: Catholic Truth Society, 1991.

Veritatis splendor. Encyclical letter on Certain Fundamental Questions of the Church's Moral Teaching. Rome: Libreria Editrice Vaticana, 1993. English translation: London: Catholic Truth Society, 1993.

Notes

Notes to Introduction: Wayfaring and Wondering

1. A list of documents of the Church's magisterium cited in this book is given in the Index of Church Documents. For documents dated before 1962, which I translate from the Latin originals, reference is made to the relevant texts given in *Enchiridion symbolorum definitionum et declarationum de rebus fidei et morum*, edited by H. Denzinger and A. Schönmetzer, 36th edition (Freiburg: Herder, 1976; hereafter cited as Denz.). For documents of the Second Vatican Council (1962–1965), and for documents of the papal magisterium since 1965, readers may wish to refer to the following standard collections: *Vatican Council II: the Conciliar and Post Conciliar Documents*, edited by A. Flannery (Dublin: Dominican Publications, 1962); and *The Christian Faith in the Doctrinal Documents of the Catholic Church*, edited by J. Neuner and J. Dupuis, 5th edition (New York: Alba House, 1990). I acknowledge here the use I make of those two collections; but in many instances I adopt a different rendering of particular passages and phrases, following the original Latin texts. Likewise, my citations from the *Catechism of the Catholic Church* differ in minor respects from the official English version (1994), in order to take account of nuances of phrasing in the normative Latin text, issued in 1998.

2. The two phrases quoted here are from the encyclical letter of Pope John Paul II, *Fides et ratio*, §§ 85 and 4.

3. The encyclical was issued on 14 September 1998; the English translation was published by the Libreria Editrice Vaticana in the following month.

4. *Fides et ratio*, §§ 105–6. In some instances (as in the passage cited here) my preferred translation of the normative Latin text of the encyclical differs from the published English version not only in phrasing but in sense.

5. In a number of places in this book I incorporate, abbreviate, or adapt passages that I have written in other contexts. I give relevant references in footnotes, and here make appropriate acknowledgment to the respective publishers, who are named in each case.

Notes to 1. Knowing God by Reason and by Christian Faith

1. These words are from a sermon of Luther's, "Postil for Epiphany." His vehement polemic against the use of reason in theology was a constant theme throughout his

works, right up to his last Wittenberg sermon in 1546. Cf. Martin Luther, Works, vol. 51, edited by J. Pelikan and H. Lehmann (Philadelphia: Muhlenberg Press, 1959), pp. 374–79.

2. John Calvin, Institutes of the Christian Religion, edited by F. L. Battles (London: SCM Press, 1947), I.iii.3, I.v.1.

3. Notably by the nineteenth-century Parisian theologians A. Sabatier and E. Ménégoz.

4. Deist rationalism in its more thoroughgoing and minimalist form was propounded in England by J. Toland in *Christianity Not Mysterious* (1696); by A. Collins in *Discourse on Freethinking* (1713); and by M. Tindal in *Christianity As Old As Creation* (1730). It gained a more influential following in France, where it was propagated by Rousseau and Voltaire, by Diderot and many of the other Encyclopaedists.

5. Editions of Clarke's work were published in London in 1716 and 1738. The modern edition was edited by E. Vailati (Cambridge: Cambridge University Press, 1998).

6. Pope John Paul II refers to the defects of those two opposite theories in *Fides et ratio*, § 52. The "traditionalist" theories of A. Bonnetty were censured by Rome in 1855; cf. Denzinger and Schönmetzer, *Enchiridion symbolorum*, 36th edition (Freiburg: Herder, 1976; = Denz.), §§ 2811–14. His opinions were linked with the speculations of L. E. Bautain and others, which had come under episcopal censure some twenty years earlier; cf. Denz., §§ 2751–56.

7. The *errores ontologistarum* condemned by the Holy Office in 1861 (Denz., §§ 2841–47) were ascribed by some to G. C. Ubaghs of Louvain. The treatises of Antonio Rosmini-Serbati relating to ontology were also subjected to scrutiny and some censure (cf. Denz., §§ 3201–41). However, his reputation as a Catholic philosopher has now been vindicated by the honorable mention made of him by Pope John Paul II in his encyclical *Fides et ratio*. Cf. Chapter 14 below, notes 14, 15, and 16 and related text.

8. Chapter 2 and Canon 1 of the constitution *Dei Filius* (Latin text in Denz., §§ 3004, 3005, and 3026). Vatican I explicitly cites Romans 1.19–21. Relevant Old Testament texts are Wisdom 13.1–9 and Psalm 19.1–4.

9. The definition of Vatican I reflects a key passage from the *Summa theologiae* of Thomas Aquinas, I.1.1.

10. *Humani generis* (1950), § 561; Denz., §§ 3875–76. This statement of the papal magisterium resumes and amplifies the teaching of Vatican I, and likewise reflects the theological reasoning of Aquinas referred to in the previous footnote.

11. The passage cited is reproduced in full in § 37 of the *Catechism of the Catholic Church* (London: Geoffrey Chapman, 1994; = CCC).

12. *Fides et ratio*, §§ 19, 28.

Notes to 2. How Is Natural Theology Possible?

1. Aquinas, *Summa theologiae*, I.2.3.

2. Exodus 3.14. The meaning and historical use of the name Yahweh is futher discussed in Chapter 8.

3. Aquinas, *De veritate*, 10.8.

4. Ibid., 1.12 and 10.6. ad 2.

5. Aquinas, *Summa theologiae*, I.58.3.

6. Ibid., I.79.8.

7. Ibid. *"Ratio et intellectus in homine non possunt esse diversae potentiae. Quod manifeste cognoscitur si utriusque actus consideretur."*

8. Modern English translations of the two major works in which Kant expounds his critiques of pure reason and of practical reason are listed in the bibliography.

9. *Human Knowledge: Its Scope and Limits* (London: Allen and Unwin, 1948), chap. 9.

10. Michael Ruse, *Evolutionary Naturalism* (London: Routledge, 1992), p. 157.

11. *De veritate,* 1.9. *"[Veritas] cognoscitur autem ab intellectu secundum quod intellectus reflectitur supra actum suum; non solum secundum quod cognoscit actum suum, sed secundum quod cognoscit proportionem eius ad rem; quod quidem cognosci non potest nisi cognita natura ipsius actus; quod cognosci non potest nisi cognoscatur natura principii activi, quod est ipse intellectus, in cuius natura est ut rebus conformetur."*

12. St. Augustine, *Confessions,* trans. by Henry Chadwick (Oxford and New York: Oxford University Press, 1992), I.1.

13. Jean-Luc Marion, *Dieu sans l'Être* (Paris: Communion/Fayard, 1982). English translation, *God Without Being* (Chicago: University of Chicago Press, 1991 and 1995).

14. *"Mens est quodammodo omnia"* and *"in eo qui docetur scientia praeexistebat."* Other passages in which St. Thomas treats of the *a priori* endowment of the human mind with potential knowledge of all being include *Summa theologiae,* I.79.2 and I.14.2 ad 3; and *De veritate,* 1.2 ad 4 and 11.1.

15. Aquinas, *Summa contra gentiles,* I.11. ad 40. *"Desiderat autem illum [Deum] homo naturaliter, in quantum desiderat naturaliter beatitudinem, quae est quaedam similitudo divinae bonitatis."*

Notes to 3. Sources and Content of Natural Theology

1. Authors who proposed such views included Claude Saint-Simon, Herbert Spencer, E. B. Tyler, Auguste Comte, J. S. Mill, R. E. Marett, J. G. Frazer, *et al.*

2. E.g., Andrew Lang, *The Making of Religion* (London: Longmans Green, 1898), and especially the formidable 12-volume work of Wilhelm Schmidt, *Der Ursprung des Gottesidee* (*The Origin of the Idea of God*; Münster-in-Westfalen: Aschendorff, 1912–54). Based on a lifetime of anthropological fieldwork, it documents the general prevalence of a primitive monotheism. There is a much abridged compendium of the work, *The Origin and Growth of Religion,* translated by H. J. Rose (London: Methuen, 1931).

3. In this category were the theories of Ludwig Feuerbach, Karl Marx, J. H. Leuba, William James, J. B. Pratt, Sigmund Freud, and B. F. Skinner.

4. Words spoken by Lewis Wolpert in an interview reported in *The Tablet* 250 (1996): 818.

5. Jung had come to this change of position by the time of writing his major work (1923), *Psychological Types* (London: Routledge, 1992).

6. *CCC,* § 33. The quoted words are from Vatican II, *Gaudium et spes,* § 18.

7. *CCC,* § 32. The Catechism's repeated mention of "ways" alludes to what are commonly called the *quinque viae* of Aquinas, his five ways of reasoning that point to the existence of God. Cf. his *Summa theologiae,* I.2.3.

8. *CCC,* §§ 41, 43.

9. Decree, *De trinitate* (1215), Denz. § 806. So also *CCC,* § 42: "God transcends all

creatures. We must therefore continually purify our language of everything in it that is limited, image—bound, or imperfect, if we are not to confuse our image of God, who is 'ineffable, incomprehensible, invisible, unthinkable,' with our human representations." (The quoted words are from the Anaphora of the Liturgy of St. John Chrysostom.)

Notes to 4. *Religion and Religions*

1. *Nostra aetate*, § 2.

2. I adopted that threefold pattern of questioning as a pedagogical framework for the study of world religions in the Open University course *Man's Religious Quest* (= *MRQ*), for the overall planning and direction of which I was responsible. I explained it in *Seekers and Scholars* (Milton Keynes: Open University Press, 1977), the first of the 32 published study manuals for that course. I draw upon that text here. Other relevant study manuals written by several scholars for *MRQ* are also referred to in this chapter.

3. I cite Toynbee's fuller statement of what he considers to be the essential truths of religion, among several alternative statements by other authors, in my *Introduction to the Study of Religion* (Milton Keynes: Open University Press, 1980), p. 13.

4. For instance, this sense is manifested in the emotional awe of *mana* in Pacific primal religion, and of *kami* in traditional Shintoism.

5. Cited by Ninian Smart, *Hindu Patterns of Liberation (MRQ)* (Milton Keynes: Open University Press, 1978), p. 15.

6. *Isa Upanishad*, 8; cited by A. L. Basham in *The Wonder That Was India* (London: Fontana Collins, 1977), p. 254.

7. Pope John Paul II speaks with respect and hope of the Indian quest for ultimate truth and liberation. See *Fides et ratio*, § 72: "A great spiritual impulse moves the Indian mind to seek an experience in which the soul, freed from the bonds of time and space, would attain the absolute good. In the furtherance of this quest for liberation, systems of intensely metaphysical thought are developed. It is incumbent on Christians today, especially Indian Christians, to draw from that rich heritage elements that can be incorporated into their own faith, in such wise that Christian teaching will itself be enriched."

8. This is a fact stated by A. L. Basham, who amplifies it with a comparative comment of his own. See the *Concise Encyclopedia of Living Faiths* (London: Hutchinson, 1971), p. 224: "Hinduism is fundamentally monotheistic, and, from the point of view of the educated Hindu at any rate, the lesser gods have much the same status as the saints and angels of Catholic Christianity."

9. Joseph Masson, *The Noble Path of Buddhism (MRQ)* (Milton Keynes: Open University Press, 1977), p. 64.

10. Cf. J. Duchesne-Guillemin, *The Western Response to Zoroaster* (Oxford: Clarendon Press, 1958), p. 1. In Chapter 11, I give further consideration to the still influential theodicy of Zoroastrianism.

11. Cf. Kenneth Cragg, *Islam and the Muslim (MRQ)* (Milton Keynes: Open University Press, 1978), § 5, "Life under Law."

12. Cf. David Goldstein, *The Religion of the Jews (MRQ)* (Milton Keynes: Open University Press, 1978), chap. 5.

13. On one of the three occasions on which I have been privileged to speak one-to-

one with the Dalai Lama (it was at Eibsee in Bavaria in May 1986), I asked him whether he saw Buddhism as a missionary religion. His reply was: "Do I want everyone to become Buddhists? I see all the religions as different beautiful blossoms, making up together one beautiful bouquet."

14. This passage is from a paper presented by Dr. Awolalu at a congress of the International Association for the History of Religions held at Lancaster University in 1975, which I quote more fully in *Quest and Questioning (MRQ)* (Milton Keynes: Open University Press, 1978), pp. 47–48.

15. In what follows I draw on what I wrote in *The Christian Way (MRQ)* (Milton Keynes: Open University Press, 1978), § 4.

16. *Lumen gentium*, § 48.

17. *Fides et ratio*, §§ 11–12.

18. Cf. Denz., § 3005, note 1.

Notes to 5. *Natural and Revealed Knowledge of God*

1. While agreeing with Barth that only divine revelation and grace can bring salutary knowledge of God, Brunner argued against him that natural theology was a necessary condition for apprehending and expressing the Christian revelation. The controversial exchanges between the two authors (in 1926 and 1934) were published in an English translation by P. Fraenkel, *Natural Theology: Comprising "Nature and Grace" by E. Brunner and the Reply, "No!" by Karl Barth* (London: Geoffrey Bles, 1946). In later years (in the third volume of his *Church Dogmatics*), Barth somewhat moderated his hostility to natural theology.

2. *CCC*, § 36.

3. *Dei verbum*, § 13. The passage in quotation marks is from a homily of St. John Chrysostom.

4. *Fides et ratio*, § 66.

5. Vatican II, *Ad gentes (Decree on the Church's Missionary Activity)*, § 3.

6. *Gaudium et spes*, §§ 2, 3.

7. *CCC*, § 39.

8. Constitution, *Dei Filius*, § 2, "*De revelatione*," Denz., § 3005.

9. Cf. A. Tanquerey, *The Spiritual Life: a Treatise on Ascetical and Mystical Theology* (Tournai: Desclée, 1950), pp. 551–59, 624–34.

Notes to 6. *Natural Religion in the Divine Plan*

1. Relevant sources are cited, and the history of this long theological development of doctrine is outlined and acutely discussed by Francis Sullivan, S.J., in *Salvation outside the Church? Tracing the History of the Catholic Response* (New York and Mahwah: Paulist Press, 1992). I refer to that work of my esteemed friend and former colleague for fuller treatment of the themes summarized in this chapter. In what follows I make frequent use of his incisive study and of the documentation he has provided. A useful supplementary treatment of the history of the dogmatic axiom, *Extra Ecclesiam nulla salus*, is contained in Chapter 3 of the work of J. Dupuis, *Toward a Christian Theology of Religious Pluralism*

(Maryknoll: Orbis Books, 1997), which is discussed in the following chapter. A collection of relevant passages from documents of the magisterium is given in Chapter 10 ("The Church and the World Religions") of *The Christian Faith in the Doctrinal Documents of the Catholic Church*, edited by J. Neuner and J. Dupuis, 5th edition (New York: Alba House, 1990).

2. Denz., § 802.

3. References in Sullivan, *Salvation*, pp. 5–12, 18–43.

4. Denz., § 875; cf. also Denz., § 870.

5. *Reunion Decree for the Jacobites*, Denz. § 1351. The passage reproduces words from a sixth-century writing (*De fide ad Petrum*, § 36) by Fulgentius of Ruspe, a staunch proponent of the ideas of St. Augustine.

6. Aquinas, *Summa theologiae*, I.II.89, 6. "When a person reaches the age of reason, the first reflection that presents itself to him is to make a decision concerning himself. If he orders himself towards his proper end, he will through grace obtain the remission of original sin."

7. Aquinas, *De veritate*, 14.2 ad 1. In a number of other places St. Thomas puts forward similar considerations relevant to the present question. Cf. *Summa theologiae*, II.II.2.7 *ad* 3 and III.66.11; *In libros Sententiarum*, II.28.1.4 *ad* 4, and III.25.2.1 *ad* 1 and 2; *Quodlibetales*, 6.3.4.

8. Cf. Sullivan, *Salvation*, pp. 78–81.

9. An interesting speculation by De Lugo is cited in Chapter 7 below, at note 14.

10. E.g., in the statements of Alexander VIII (Denz., § 2305) and Clement XI (Denz., § 2426).

11. Denz., § 2866. The principle was also briefly mentioned in an encyclical letter of Pius IX to the bishops of Austria, *Singulari quidem* (cf. note in Denz., § 2865–67).

12. Cf. Denz., § 3821, *"inscio quodam desiderio ac voto."* The phrase is in the subsection of the encyclical entitled *"De salute hominum extra visibilem Ecclesiam."*

13. The declaration was sent to the Archbishop of Boston in 1949 to express Rome's censure on the exclusivist opinions of Leonard Feeney; Denz., §§ 3866–3872.

14. *Nostra aetate*, § 1.

15. Sullivan has penetrating observations on this question in *Salvation*, chap. 4 and 5.

16. *Lumen gentium*, § 48. The *Pastoral Constitution on the Church in the Modern World* expands the meaning of the phrase: "While the Church both serves the world and receives much from it, all that it does tends to one single end: that the Kingdom of God come and that the salvation of the whole human race be realized. Every boon that the People of God can offer to the human family during its earthly pilgrimage stems from the fact that the Church is 'the universal sacrament of salvation,' manifesting and making operative the mystery of God's love for men" (*Gaudium et spes*, § 45). Affirmation that the Church is the universal sacrament of salvation is also to be found in *Lumen gentium*, §§ 3, 9, 48, 52; and in *Ad gentes*, §§ 1, 5, 22. Cf. also the phrase in *Unitatis redintegratio*, § 3, *"generale auxilium salutis est."*

17. *Lumen gentium*, § 13.

18. Karl Rahner, *Theological Investigations*, vol. 14 (London: Darton, Longman, and Todd, 1976), p. 284.

19. The development of theological recognition of the sufficiency of implicit faith is surveyed by Sullivan, *Salvation*, in his chap. 4–7. Aquinas applied that principle to the question of the salvation of the gentile people living before the coming of Christ, arguing that their faith in God the creator and redeemer implicitly contained faith in Christ (*Summa theologiae*, II.II.2.7 ad 3, and 2.8 ad 1).

20. *Gaudium et spes*, § 22.

21. The salvific sufficiency of *"baptismus ex voto"* was formally declared by the Council of Trent in 1547 in its *Decree on Justification*, chapter 4; Denz., § 1524.

Notes to 7. Non-Christian Religions

1. *Gaudium et spes*, § 92.

2. The final sentence in the passage from *Ad gentes* repeats verbatim the Council's teaching in *Lumen gentium*, § 17.

3. *Nostra aetate*, § 2.

4. *Ad gentes*, § 11.

5. Apostolic exhortation *Evangelii nuntiandi* (1975), § 53.

6. The writings of John Hick have been influential in promoting the notion of such a "Copernican Revolution" in understanding of the interrelation between the world's religions. While radically disagreeing with Dr. Hick on the compatibility of such a theory with Christian faith, I express my cordial respect for him as a life-long seeker after truth, and appreciatively recall memories of interfaith dialogue in his company on the shores of the Bosphorus. A Catholic writer who shares his views, with further developments of his own, is Paul Knitter. Relevant writings of both authors are listed in the bibliography.

7. *Ad gentes*, § 7.

8. *Lumen gentium*, § 8.

9. Ibid., § 15.

10. *Unitatis redintegratio*, § 3.

11. *Nostra aetate*, §4; likewise *Lumen gentium*, § 16: "They are a people most dear for the sake of the fathers, for the gifts of God are without repentance." Both testimonies refer to Romans 11.28–29.

12. *Lumen gentium*, § 16.

13. *Nostra aetate*, § 3.

14. *De virtute fidei divinae*, disp. 12, nn. 50–51; cited by Sullivan, *Salvation*, pp. 94–98.

15. *Lumen gentium*, § 16.

16. *Nostra aetate*, § 2.

17. Sullivan gives a summary of recent theological speculation on this matter in the tenth chapter of *Salvation*, pp. 162–81.

18. In his eleventh chapter of *Salvation*, "Papal Teaching after Vatican II," Sullivan brings together and analyzes post-conciliar documents of the magisterium relevant to the present question. Dupuis does the same in his sixth chapter of *Religious Pluralism*.

19. *L'Osservatore Romano* (March 23, 1966): 1; cited by Sullivan, *Salvation*, p. 185.

20. *Evangelii nuntiandi*, § 53.

21. *Redemptoris missio*, § 29. This sentence in the Pope's encyclical of 1991 repeats verbatim a statement made by him in Madras in 1986, in an address to religious leaders in India.

22. *Redemptoris missio*, § 8.

23. Cf. Sullivan's observations about the opinions of Karl Rahner and others about such "mediations" in *Salvation*, pp. 179–81.

24. *Redemptoris missio*, § 5.

25. *Fides et ratio*, § 70.

26. *CCC*, §§ 842–843. In this passage the *Catechism* echoes Vatican II, *Nostra aetate*, § 1.

27. Maryknoll: Orbis Books, 1997.

28. These criticisms are already firmly stated in the author's sixth chapter, and are pertinent to his total argument throughout Part II of his book, where his own systematic theory concerning the theology of religious pluralism is expounded.

29. For instance, on page 307 he singles out one such phrase as coming from a source that he describes, in a critical and revealing aside, as "an unlikely witness"— namely, Pope John Paul II. He is referring here to the Pope's allowance of the possibility of "participated forms of mediation of different kinds and degrees," in the passage from *Redemptoris missio*, § 5, cited above. However, the Pope's immediately following explanation of that phrase excludes the sense that Dupuis would like to attach to it.

30. Among the reasons for its persistence Dupuis includes "the partial failure of the Christian mission, especially in the vast majority of Asian countries" (*Religious Pluralism*, p. 386).

31. Ibid., pp. 386–87.

32. Ibid., pp. 199–200.

33. Ibid., p. 385.

34. Ibid., pp. 22–23.

35. Ibid., p. 357.

36. "That society which is both hierarchically organized and the Mystical Body of Christ, which is both a visible congregation and a spiritual community, which is both the Church on earth and also the Church endowed with heavenly riches, is not to be thought of as two realities. But they form one unified reality, the divine and human conjoined" (*Lumen gentium*, § 8).

37. These citations are from the ninth chapter in Dupuis, *Religious Pluralism*.

38. Ibid., pp. 3–4.

39. Ibid., p. 388.

40. Ibid., p. 385.

41. Raimun Pannikar, *The Unknown Christ of Hinduism* (London: Darton, Longman, and Todd, 1964).

42. Dupuis, *Religious Pluralism*, p. 365.

43. Especially noteworthy is the review of Dupuis's book by Gavin D'Costa in *The Journal of Theological Studies* 49 (1998): 910–14. Cf. also the text of the letter of Cardinal Ratzinger to Cardinal König, which was published in *The Tablet* (March 16, 1999): 385. Therein the Prefect of the Sacred Congregation for the Doctrine of the Faith made mention of a request submitted confidentially to Fr. Dupuis by the Congregation, asking for clarification of the meaning of certain passages in his book.

Notes to 8. "THE ONE WHO IS"

1. Likewise entitled, "This name, 'HE WHO IS,' is the most proper name of God," that discourse was published in *Towards a New Humanity*, a *Festschrift* to mark the 70th birthday of Metropolitan Paulos Mar Gregorios, edited by K. M. George and K. J. Gabriel (Delhi: I.S.P.C.K., 1992), pp. 115–33. The Assisi interreligious conference at which my paper was first presented in May 1990 was sponsored by The New Ecumenical Research Association, to which I make due acknowledgment.

2. In my original paper for the Assisi conference, I followed the traditional rendering of the Latin "QUI EST" as "HE WHO IS." Reading that paper some years later, a student at Maryvale Institute, Birmingham, asked me why I translated the relative pronoun as "He" rather than "The One," which would be equally faithful to the Latin and linguistically more inclusive. I have adopted her suggestion.

3. Its absolute sense, namely "to exist," is the one with which this chapter is mainly concerned. Used copulatively in conjunction with a predicate, it indicates a particular manner of being, either permanent or transient. The English word "being" (like the Latin word *ens*, coined in post-classical times) is a present participle which is also used as a verbal noun, referring either to an individual entity or to existent reality in general. In other European languages the latter sense is often indicated, especially in philosophical parlance, by the infinitive used as a noun (*être, sein, essere, ser*). The Latin present infinitive *esse* is likewise used with special force to convey this sense of "being" as present existent actuality.

4. *De Genesi ad literam*, 16.57.

5. *De fide orthodoxa*, 1.9, in the collection *Patrologia Graeca* vol. 94 (Paris: J. P. Migne, 1857–66), p. 836.

6. "*Ipsum esse is se certissime, quod non potest cogitari non esse*" (*Itinerarium mentis ad Deum*, vol. 3).

7. Exordium to *De primo rerum omnium principio*.

8. This English translation (adopted in the Douay Version) of the words of the divine reply to Moses's question in Exodus 3.14 corresponds to the literal rendering of the Hebrew original in the Latin Vulgate: "*Ego sum qui sum. Ait: sic dices filiis Israel: QUI EST misit me ad vos.*"

9. *The Jerusalem Bible* (London: Geoffrey Chapman, 1985), p. 85, note g.

10. Cf. E. Gilson, *Being and Some Philosophers* (Toronto: Pontifical Institute of Mediaeval Studies, 1952), pp. 1–84; *L'Être et l'essence* (Paris: Vrin, 1948), chap. 1–4.

11. A classical statement of Aquinas's ontotheology and his insights on *esse* and *essentia* is to be found in E. Gilson's *The Christian Philosophy of St Thomas* (London: Victor Gollancz, 1957), chap. 1.

12. The distinction that Thomist wisdom discerns between *esse* and *essentia* in all creatures is a speculative insight which may aid faith in its search for some understanding of the central and most hidden mystery of the Christian revelation—that of the Hypostatic Union of divine and human natures in the second Person of the Blessed Trinity. Difficult as it is to express and assess, the sense of that insight may be briefly indicated as follows. The three divine Persons share together the unitary *esse* of the Godhead, in a manner that accords with the ineffable interpersonal relativity of each. In the Incarnation, the divine

esse as possessed by the Person of the divine Logos is directly communicated to the human nature in which he subsists as man (cf. Aquinas, *Summa theologiae*, III.2.6 ad 4). As in all his fellow human beings, so in the God-man Jesus of Nazareth there is distinction of *esse* and *essentia*. But, uniquely in him, the *esse* that actuates the human *essentia* (nature) is not finite *esse* concreated with it to constitute personhood, as in all other men, but it is the infinite divine *esse* of the Person of God the Son, directly giving existence to the human nature in which he subsists. This Thomistic insight, profound though it be, is not a dogmatic teaching of the Church, but remains a *theologoumenon* (speculative theological insight) open to reverent debate.

13. Cf. *Fides et ratio*, §§ 5, 73–76, 97.

14. In his study, *The Christian Intellect and the Mystery of Being* (The Hague: Nijhoff, 1966), J. J. Sikora reflects on the differing manner of the emergence of ontological awareness in different people and circumstances. Especially noteworthy are his observations on pages 115–20, "The Metaphysical Intuition of Being and its Affirmation."

15. Augustine, *Confessions*, VII.xvii (23). The scriptural allusion is to Romans 1.20.

16. Fernand Van Steenberghen, *Ontologie*, augmented 3rd edition (Louvain: Publications universitaires de Louvain, 1961), p. 1.

17. Cited by A. Keightley, *Wittgenstein, Grammar and God* (London: Epstein Press, 1976), p. 27.

18. Martin Heidegger, *Being and Time*, trans. by J. Macquarrie and E. Robinson (Oxford: Blackwell, 1952).

19. Cf. the comment on the ambiguous existentialism of Heidegger cited in Chapter 14 below, note 21.

20. Hazel E. Barnes, in the introduction of her translation of Sartre's *Être et le néant: Being and Nothingness* (London: Methuen, 1957), p. xxxiv.

21. Sartre, *Being*, p. 623.

22. Karl Jaspers, *Philosophie*, vol. 1 (Berlin: Springer, 1932), p. 302. He sets out his semi-agnostic (and Kantian) "Christian existentialism" in *Der philosophische Glaube angesichts der Offenbarung* (1962), English translation by E. B. Ashton, *Philosophical Faith and Revelation* (London: Collins, 1967).

23. *"Es ist denkbar, dass es gibt, was nicht denkbar ist"*: Jaspers, *Philosophie*, vol. 3, p. 38. Here Jaspers echoes St. Anselm's even pithier statement of the mind's power to apprehend the existence of reality incomprehensibly beyond its natural reach: *"rationabiliter comprehendit incomprehensibile esse"* (*Monologion*, § 64).

24. J.-P. de Caussade (1675–1751), *Abandon à la providence divine*. In English, *The Sacrament of the Present Moment*, trans. by K. Muggeridge (London: Fount, 1981).

Notes to 9. Matter and Spirit

1. This celebrated passage is in Russell's opuscule, *A Free Man's Worship and Other Papers* (London: Unwin, 1976).

2. Gerard Manley Hopkins, *The Wreck of the Deutschland*. In the preceding paragraph I recall some thoughts expressed long ago in one of my earliest published theological writings, an article entitled "Pantheism and Analogy," which appeared in *The Irish Theological Quarterly* 20 (1953): 24–38.

3. Romans 8.19, 22; Revelation 21.1; 2 Peter 3.13.

4. Richard Dawkins, *River out of Eden* (London: Phoenix, 1996), p. 14.

5. *Fides et ratio*, § 34 (the Pope quotes Galileo to the same effect).

Notes to 10.   *Theology and Teleology*

1. Aquinas, *Summa theologiae*, I.2.1.

2. Dawkins, *River*, p. xiii.

3. This prompts one to cite the scholastic aphorism: *"Ex absurdo sequitur quodlibet"*—
"From an absurd premise follows anything you want."

4. Dawkins, *River*, pp. xiv-xv. The same theme runs through his other works: *The Selfish Gene* (Oxford and New York: Oxford University Press, 1989); *The Extended Phenotype* (Oxford: Oxford University Press, 1982); *The Blind Watchmaker* (New York: W. W. Norton, 1986), *Climbing Mount Improbable* (London: Penguin, 1997); *Unweaving the Rainbow* (London and New York: Penguin, 1997).

5. The term has been coined by Dawkins. He explains the idiosyncratic meaning he gives to it in *Climbing Mount Improbable*, p. 4.

6. Dawkins, *River*, p. 123.

7. One of Dawkins's postulates was the existence of a gene possessing the specific property of recognizing rival genes, with the prior "utility function" of promoting the successful survival of its own pattern of DNA coding and of frustrating the survival of genes not bearing that pattern. Researchers have in fact found what neo-Darwinists hail as evidence of the existence of such a prescient and discriminatory gene in a South American ant. Reportedly, they found that red fire ants possessing a certain gene seek out and destroy queens not possessing that gene. From this finding, neo-Darwinists argue that those ants are moved to this fratricidal aggression by an ingenious gene, as Dawkins had postulated, which thereby seeks to promote the propagation of its own strain of genetic coding and to hinder the propagation of a rival strain.

8. Explained by Dawkins in Chapter 9 of *Unweaving the Rainbow*.

9. We need an English term to refer to that intrinsic principle of wholeness. A serviceable one is in fact available, namely "entelechy," a centuries-old anglicization of the Greek philosophical term *entelecheia*, which connotes such dynamic unity of *telos* in the living organism.

10. Dawkins, *River*, p. 111.

Notes to 11.   *The Dark Mystery of Evil*

1. My free translation of the famous line in Virgil's *Aeneid*: *"Sunt lachrymae rerum et mentem mortalia tangunt."*

2. E.g., John 8.44; 1 John 5.19; 1 Peter 5.8–9; 2 Thessalonians 2.3–10; Revelation 12.9.

3. *Gaudium et spes*, § 32.

4. *CCC*, § 395.

5. *CCC*, § 284.

6. Max Weber, "Major Features of World Religions," in *Sociology of Religion*, ed. Roland Robertson (London: Penguin, 1976), p. 28.

7. I here prescind from the scholarly debates about the more recondite points of Zoroastrian doctrine, which was variously presented in different ages.

8. This is well argued in the work of J. Duchesne-Guillemin referred to in note 10 of Chapter 4.

9. Stemming chiefly from the ideas of A. N. Whitehead and propounded by C. Hartshorne, P. Hamilton, W. N. Pittenger and J. B. Cobb. Other twentieth-century proponents of the notion of a limited God were H. G. Wells and C. E. M. Joad.

10. Theopaschitism was the name given to the doctrine of a Monophysite group in the sixth century who were accused of the heresy of asserting that the Godhead suffered in the Crucifixion. The term has a somewhat different usage when applied to the modern theories of a suffering God.

11. The influence of Ockhamist voluntarism on Luther was the subject of a radio lecture of mine which was broadcast annually in the United Kingdom by the Open University/BBC for some ten years from 1972 onwards under the title, "The Parable of the Monkey and the Kitten," as part of the Open University course *Renaissance and Reformation*. Here I draw on the text of that lecture. Cf. also § 21.3.9 of my *Luther and Lutheranism* (Milton Keynes: Open University Press, 1972, and later reprints), which was part of that course.

12. References to and discussion of the Geneva Reformer's teaching may be found in my *Calvin and Other Reformers* (Milton Keynes: Open University Press, 1972, and later reprints).

13. *"Quod autem quidam salvantur, salvantis est donum; quod autem quidam pereunt pereuntium est meritum"* (Denz., § 623).

14. *CCC,* § 310.

15. *Lumen gentium,* § 48.

16. *CCC,* § 387, 390.

17. *CCC,* §§ 311–12.

18. *Gaudium et spes,* § 22.

19. *Fides et ratio,* § 12.

20. Romans 6.3–5; 2 Corinthians 4.10; Galatians 2.19ff., 5.24, 6.14, 17; Philippians 3.10ff.; 2 Timothy 2.10–12.

Notes to 12. Conscience and Its Supreme Imperative

1. *Dignitatis humanae,* § 3.

2. "The deontological argument," as some call it, from a Greek participle expressing what ought to be.

3. John Henry Newman, *An Essay in Aid of a Grammar of Assent* (1870) (Garden City: Image Books, 1955), chap. 10. Pope John Paul II likewise extols "the dignity of the moral conscience as being the place, the sacred place, where God speaks to man" (*Veritatis splendor,* § 58).

4. Aquinas, *Summa theologiae,* II.II.154.12.

5. At an interreligious congress held in Chicago in 1993, a global ethical code was presented and given general assent, as expressing at least a statement of substantial moral principles commonly accepted by the religious traditions of the human race.

Attended by adherents of many faiths (myself among the multitude), the congress cele-brated the centenary of the so-called "Parliament of the World's Religions" convened in that city in 1893.

6. *Gaudium et spes*, § 16.

7. *Veritatis splendor*, § 94.

8. "Others speak, and rightly so, of *theonomy*, or *participated theonomy*, since man's free obedience to God's law effectively implies that human reason and human will partic-ipate in God's wisdom and providence" (*Veritatis splendor*, § 58).

9. " . . . *inest homini inclinatio ad bonum secundum naturam rationis quae est sibi propria, sicut homo habet naturalem inclinationem ad hoc quod veritatem cognoscat de Deo*" (Aquinas, *Summa theologiae*, I.II.94, 2).

10. *Fides et ratio*, § 33, note 28 (repeating words from an allocution of the Pope in 1983).

11. These words, from Newman's *Letter to the Duke of Norfolk*, are cited in *CCC*, § 1778.

12. Dogmatic Constitution *Dei Filius*, chap. 3; Denz., 3008.

13. *Fides et ratio*, § 13.

Notes to 13. What Is "Religious Experience"?

1. Friedrich Schleiermacher, *Reden über die Religion* (1799), translated into English as *On Religion: Speeches to its Cultured Despisers* (Cambridge: Cambridge University Press, 1996); *Der christliche Glaube* (1821–22), translated into English as *The Christian Faith* (Edin-burgh: T. and T. Clark, 1928).

2. Rudolf Otto, *The Idea of the Holy*, trans. by J. W. Harvey (Oxford: Oxford Univer-sity Press, 1950).

3. Francis Clark, "Grace-experience in the Roman Catholic tradition," in *The Journal of Theological Studies* 25 (1974): 352–72. In the present chapter I use and adapt parts of that article. I also recall here some reflections contained in Chapter 6 of my book, *Eu-charistic Sacrifice and the Reformation*, 3rd edition (Devon: Augustine Press, 1981; hereafter abbreviated as *ESR*).

4. "*Ipsum cognitum aliquomodo est apud cognoscentem*" (Aquinas, *De veritate*, 2.2).

5. Cf. Vatican II, *Sacrosanctum concilium*, § 7.

6. *Lumen gentium*, § 1324.

7. Cf. Clark, *ESR*, pp. 103–7. In recent years an ecumenical commission of divines, appointed by the Pontifical Council for Promoting Christian Unity and by the Lutheran World Federation, have devoted intense discussion to the meaning of justification and grace, in the hope of resolving the historic controversies. However, it has to be said that the radical divide between Protestant and Catholic theology on the subject has not been decisively bridged by the study-report resulting from that dialogue. This appears from the Holy See's response to the report, in the formulation of which the Congregation for the Doctrine of the Faith was closely involved (cf. *The Tablet* 4 [July 1998]: 886). While warmly praising it as a major enterprise of fraternal charity and mutual under-standing, the Vatican's official response made critical reservations on certain essential matters of doctrine which were not found satisfactorily clarified in the report. Some

parallel reservations were made in the official response of the Lutheran World Federation. The matters of doctrine in question are in fact those which were at the root of the doctrinal divide in the sixteenth century, as outlined in this chapter and in the pages of *ESR* cited above. That report, which is necessarily qualified by the Vatican's critical reservations, formed one part of the declaration of broad Catholic-Lutheran ecumenical agreement signed at Augsburg in October 1999.

8. Vicarious satisfaction, according to St. Anselm's concept, was Christ's making amends in the moral order for the offense given to divine honor by human sin. Finite and sinful mankind could not make due apology for that heinous affront to infinite divine dignity; only a person who, while true man, was also himself of divine dignity could make such amends on behalf of the human race.

9. Calvin, *Institutes*, II.16.2, 5. Cf. Clark, *ESR*, pp. 109–11.

10. For instance, Philip Melanchthon denounced the *Dialogues* commonly ascribed to Pope St. Gregory the Great, a collection of bizarre tales of prodigies performed by holy men, as a major cause of debasement of belief in the medieval Church. On the evidence of the fictitious miracle-stories and crude religious sensationalism of that book he scornfully referred to its author as "that Gregory whom they [the papists] call 'great,' but whom I call the dance-leader and torch-bearer of a theology falling into decay." I have set out the massive case for rejecting the ascription of that famous book to St. Gregory the Great in my two-volume work *The Pseudo-Gregorian Dialogues* (Leiden: E. J. Brill, 1987).

11. Quoted by R. Knox in his *Enthusiasm* (Oxford: Clarendon Press, 1962), p. 538.

12. Denz., § 1534; cf. also Trent's fourteenth canon on justification, ibid., § 1564. I give a summary overview of the Tridentine teaching on justification and grace in *The Catholic Reformation* (Milton Keynes: Open University Press, 1972), §§ 43.3.0–43.3.33.

13. *CCC*, § 2005.

14. E.g., John 6.45; Romans 8.15–16 and 9.1; Psalm 34.8.

15. Accusation of such presumption was brought against the Quietists of the seventeenth century, in particular Michael Molinos, whose errors were reproved by Pope Innocent XI in 1687 (Cf. Denz., §§ 2201–2269).

16. References to relevant writings of Alfaro and Rahner are given on p. 371 of my *JTS* article mentioned above in note 3.

17. "The Natural Mystical Experience," a special study republished as Chapter 10 of Maritain's *Redeeming the Time* (London: Geoffrey Bles, 1943), pp. 225ff. Cf. also M. Penido, *La conscience religieuse* (Paris: Vrin, 1935), chap. 4: "*L'intuition naturelle de Dieu.*"

18. Ibid., p. 247. There he describes the natural mystical awareness as "an experience of God *in quantum infundens et profundens esse in rebus.*"

Notes to 14. The Truth That Pantheism Distorts

1. Phrases from Wordsworth's poem, *Tintern Abbey.*

2. Here and in later paragraphs I again recall thoughts that I expressed in my article, "Pantheism and Analogy," referred to above in Chapter 9, note 2.

3. *The Upanishads, Breath of the Eternal,* selected and translated by Swami Prabhavananda and Frederick Manchester (New York: New American Library, 1957), p. 46.

4. Aquinas, *Summa theologiae*, I.34.3.

5. Ibid., I.8.1 ad 1 and 2; I.15.2; I.44.1; I.47.3 ad 1.

6. Augustine, *De libero arbitrio*, II.17.45; echoing Wisdom 6.17.

7. Aquinas, *Summa theologiae*, I.8.1.

8. Ibid., I.75.5 ad 1.

9. Ibid., I.15.2 and I.47.1.

10. I was indeed heartened to find that what I had written in that chapter about this central but too often neglected theme of patristic and scholastic theology accords with and is corroborated by the emphatic restatement of traditional ontotheological wisdom in the papal encyclical.

11. Cf. *Fides et ratio*, §§ 5, 76, 97.

12. "The philosophy that concerns being"; "the truth of existence"; "the philosophy of being-in-act"; "efficacious or dynamic philosophy."

13. Cf. *Fides et ratio*, §§ 43, 44. *"Eius vere est philosophia essendi et non apparendi dumtaxat."* St. Thomas's ontotheology is summarized by F. Van Steenberghen in his contribution to volume 13 of *Histoire de L'Église* (Paris: Bloud and Gay, 1956), pp. 270–80. In the Thomist synthesis, he observes (p. 277) that the metaphysical concept of God as *esse subsistens* is linked to the sublime truth divinely revealed to Christian faith: "The essential attributes of the Christian God (the saving mystery of the Trinity of persons) are thus found, at the highest reach of our metaphysical understanding, to belong to the supreme Being whose existence is affirmed as necessarily implied in the immediate reality of our experience of what is."

14. *Fides et ratio*, § 97.

15. Ibid., § 73.

16. Ibid., § 76.

17. Cf. Chapter 1 above, note 7.

18. Cf. Denz., §§ 3201–41.

19. *Fides et ratio*, § 74.

20. Cf. Chapter 2, note 13 above.

21. Marion, *Dieu sans l'Être*, p. 93, note 15. However, there is a puzzling alternation, remarked on by many, in Heidegger's attitude to being. "Before he did not speak of God. God did not appear in the light of human existence but was concealed, presumably in the encompassing darkness of being. Now, while still speaking very little of God, he speaks of being with reverence. He calls it 'holy'; he hails it, invokes it, thanks it" (John S. Dunne, *A Search for God in Time and Memory* [London: Sheldon Press, 1975], p. 200.)

22. Aquinas, *Summa theologiae*, II.II.45.2.

Notes to 15. Faring Homeward to God

1. *Animula, vagula, blandula,*
Hospes comesque corporis,
Quae nunc abibis in loca
Pallidula, rigida, nudula?
Nec ut soles dabis iocos.

My literal translation of those five lines of elusive Latin does not compete with the poetic renderings which Byron and many others have made of them. A copy of

Hadrian's deathbed stanza can be seen today displayed at the heart of the great mausoleum beside the Tiber made for his burial, now called the Castel Sant' Angelo. I repeat here some reflections that I wrote in *Quest and Questioning*, pages 9–12, the concluding volume of *Man's Religious Quest*.

2. Aristotle refers to that practice, in a passage which Aquinas cites with approval. Traditional Hindu religion presents as the ideal, after the duties and business of life are done, to become in old age a meditative forest-dweller (*vanaprasthya*); and even, in extreme old age, a homeless beggar mystic (*sannyasi*).

3. See Appendix II: "A *memento mori* from a Wartime Diary."

4. I am indebted to Professor Catherine Cornille, of the University of Leuven, who sent me the unpublished text of this poem for inclusion in a memoir of Fr. De Graeve that I wrote for the newsletter of the Interreligious Federation for World Peace, New York, in 1993.

Bibliography

Augustine of Hippo, Saint. *Confessions*. Translated by Henry Chadwick. Oxford and New York: Oxford University Press, 1992.

Baltasar, Hans Urs von. *Dare We Hope That All Men May Be Saved?* San Francisco: Ignatius Press, 1988.

Barnes, Michael. *Christian Identity and Religious Pluralism*. Nashville: Abingdon Press, 1989.

Basham, A. L. *The Wonder That Was India*. New York: Taplinger, 1968. London: Fontana Collins, 1977.

Brunner, Emil. *Natural Theology: Comprising 'Nature and Grace' by E. Brunner and the Reply, 'No!' by Karl Barth*. Translated by P. Fraenkel. London: Geoffrey Bles, 1946.

———. *Revelation and Reason*. London: SCM Press, 1947.

Calvin, John. *Institutes of the Christian Religion*. Translated by F. L. Battles. London: SCM Press, 1961.

Capéran, Louis. *Le problème du salut des infidèles*. Toulouse: Grand Seminaire, 1934.

Caussade, Jean-Pierre de. *The Sacrament of the Present Moment*. Tranlated by K. Muggeridge. London: Fount, 1981.

Clark, Francis. "Pantheism and Analogy." In *The Irish Theological Quarterly* 20 (1953): 24–38.

———. *Eucharistic Sacrifice and the Reformation*. 3rd ed. Devon: Augustine Publishing Company, 1980.

———. "A new appraisal of late-medieval Nominalism." In *Gregorianum* 46 (1965): 733–65.

———. "Grace-experience in the Roman Catholic Tradition." In *The Journal of Theological Studies* 25 (1974): 352–72.

———. *Origins of the Reformation*. Milton Keynes: Open University Press, 1972.

———. *Luther and Lutheranism*. Milton Keynes: Open University Press, 1972.

———. *Calvin and Other Reformers*. Milton Keynes: Open University Press, 1972.

———. *The Catholic Reformation*. Milton Keynes: Open University Press, 1972.

———. *Seekers and Scholars*. Milton Keynes: Open University Press, 1977.

———. *The Christian Way*. Milton Keynes: Open University Press, 1978.

———. *Quest and Questioning*. Milton Keynes: Open University Press, 1978.

———. *Introduction to the Study of Religion*. Part 1. Milton Keynes: Open University Press, 1980.

———. "This name, 'He Who Is', is the most proper name of God." In *Towards a New Humanity*, edited by K. M. George and K. J. Gabriel. Delhi: I.S.P.C.K., 1992, pp. 115–133.

————. *The Pseudo-Gregorian Dialogues.* Vols. 37 and 38, *Studies in the History of Christian Thought.* Leiden: E. J. Brill, 1987.

Clarke, Samuel. *A Demonstration of the Being and Attributes of God, the Obligations of Natural Religion, and the Truth and Certainty of the Christian Revelation.* Edited by E. Varlati. Cambridge: Cambridge University Press, 1998.

Cragg, Kenneth. *Islam and the Muslim.* Milton Keynes: Open University Press, 1978.

Damascene, Saint John. *De fide orthodoxa.* In *Patrologia Graeca.* Vols. 94–96. Paris: J. P. Migne, 1857–66.

Daniélou, Jean. *The Salvation of the Nations.* South Bend: University of Notre Dame Press, 1962.

Dawkins, Richard. *The Selfish Gene.* Oxford and New York: Oxford University Press, 1989.

————. *River out of Eden.* London: Phoenix Books, 1996.

————. *Unweaving the Rainbow.* London and New York: Penguin Press, 1998.

D'Costa, Gavin. *Theology and Religious Pluralism: the Challenge of Other Religions.* Oxford: Basil Blackwell, 1988.

Duchesne-Guillemin, J. *The Western Response to Zoroaster.* Oxford: Clarendon Press, 1958.

Dupuis, Jacques. *Jesus Christ at the Encounter of the World's Religions.* Maryknoll: Orbis Books, 1991.

————. *Toward a Christian Theology of Religious Pluralism.* Maryknoll: Orbis Books, 1997.

Gilson, Étienne. *Le Thomisme.* 5th edition. Paris: Vrin, 1948.

————. *L'être et l'essence.* Paris: Vrin, 1948.

————. *The Spirit of Medieval Philosophy.* London: Sheed and Ward, 1950.

————. *La philosophie et la théologie.* Paris: Fayard, 1960.

————. *Reason and Revelation in the Middle Ages.* New York: Charles Scribner's Sons, 1966.

Goldstein, David. *The Religion of the Jews.* Milton Keynes: Open University Press, 1978.

Hick, John. *God and the Universe of Faiths.* London: Macmillan, 1973.

————. *God Has Many Names: Britain's New Religious Pluralism.* London: Macmillan, 1980.

————. *Problems of Religious Pluralism.* London: Macmillan, 1985.

————. *An Interpretation of Religion: Human Responses to the Transcendent.* Basingstoke: Macmillan, 1989.

————. *The Metaphor of God Incarnate: Christology in a Pluralistic Age.* London: SCM Press, 1993.

————. *A Christian Theology of Religions.* Louisville: Westminster John Knox Press, 1995.

————. *The Rainbow of Faith.* London: SCM Press, 1995.

Hick, J. & F. Knitter., eds. *The Myth of Christian Uniqueness: Toward a Pluralistic Theology of Religions.* Maryknoll: Orbis Books, 1987.

Kant, Immanuel. *The Critique of Pure Reason.* London: Macmillan, 1929.

————. *The Critique of Practical Reason.* Amherst: Prometheus Books, 1966.

Knitter, Paul. *No Other Name? A Critical Survey of Religious Attitudes toward the World Religions.* Maryknoll: Orbis Books, 1985.

Knox, Ronald. *Enthusiasm.* Oxford: Clarendon Press, 1962.

Lang, Andrew. *The Making of Religion.* London: Longmans Green, 1898.

Lubac, Henri de. *The Mystery of the Supernatural.* London: Geoffrey Chapman, 1967.

Marion, Jean-Luc. *Dieu sans l'Être.* Paris: Communio/Fayard, 1982.

————. *Reduction and Givenness: Investigations of Husserl, Heidegger and Phenomenology.* Evanston: Northwestern University Press, 1998.

Maritain, Jacques. *De la philosophie chrétienne.* Paris: Desclée, 1933.

————. *Redeeming the Time.* London: Geoffrey Bles, 1943.

————. *The Degrees of Knowledge.* London: Geoffrey Bles, 1959.

Masson, Joseph. *The Noble Path of Buddhism.* Milton Keynes: Open University Press, 1977.

Meynell, Hugo. *God and the World. The Coherence of Christian Theism.* London: Society for Promoting Christian Knowledge, 1971.

Newman, John Henry: *An Essay in Aid of a Grammar of Assent.* Garden City: Image Books, 1955.

Otto, Rudolf. *The Idea of the Holy.* Translated by J. W. Harvey. Oxford and New York: Oxford University Press, 1950.

Penido, M. *La conscience religieuse.* Paris: Vrin, 1935.

Pieris, Aloysius. *An Asian Theology of Liberation.* Maryknoll: Orbis Books, 1968.

Rahner, Karl. "Christianity and Non-Christian Religions." In *Theological Investigations,* vol. 5, pp. 115–34. London: Darton, Longman, and Todd, 1966.

————. "Anonymous Christians." In *Theological Investigations,* vol. 6, pp. 390–98. London: Darton, Longman, and Todd, 1969.

————. "The One Christ and the Universality of Salvation." In *Theological Investigations,* pp. 199–224. London: Darton, Longman and Todd, 1979.

————. "On the Importance of the Non-Christian Religions for Salvation." In *Theological Investigations,* vol. 18, pp. 288–95. London: Darton, Longman, and Todd, 1988.

————. "Christianity's Absolute Claim." In *Theological Investigations,* vol. 21, pp. 171–84. London: Darton, Longman, and Todd, 1988.

Schleiermacher, Friedrich. *On Religion: Speeches to its Cultured Despisers.* Cambridge: Cambridge University Press, 1996.

Sikora, J. J. *The Christian Intellect and the Mystery of Being.* The Hague: Nijhoff, 1966.

Smart, Ninian. *Hindu Patterns of Liberation.* Milton Keynes: Open University Press, 1978.

Sullivan, Francis. *Salvation outside the Church? Tracing the History of the Catholic Response.* New York and Mahwah: Paulist Press, 1992.

Tanquerey, Adolphe. *The Spiritual Life: A Treatise on Ascetical and Mystical Theology.* Tournai: Desclée, 1950.

Thils, Gustave. *Présence et salut de Dieu chez les `non- chrétiens.'* Louvain-la-neuve: Faculté de théologie, 1987.

Thomas Aquinas, Saint. *Opera Omnia.* Multiple volumes. Leonine edition. Rome: S. C. de Propaganda Fide, 1882ff.

Van Steenberghen, Fernand. *Ontologie.* 3rd edition. Louvain: Publications universitaires de Louvain, 1961. English translation, *Ontology.* New York: Jospeh F. Wagner, 1952.

————. *Le mouvement doctrinal du XIe au XIVe siècle.* Vol. 13 of *Histoire de L'Église,* edited by A. Fliche & E. Jarry. Paris: Bloud & Gay, 1956.

Weber, Max. "Major Features of World Religions." In *Sociology of Religion,* edited by Roland Robertson. London: Penguin Press, 1976, pp. 19–41.

Zaehner, R. C., ed. *Concise Encyclopedia of Living Faiths.* London: Hutchinson, 1971.

Index of Names and Subjects

❧

Sankara, 42, 195
Sartre, J.-P., 23, 108, 214
Schleiermacher, Friedrich, 2–3, 155–56, 223
Schmidt, Wilhelm, 207
Second Vatican Council, *see* Vatican II
Septuagint, 12, 96, 102–3, 201
Shinto, 36, 208
Sikhism, 37, 107, 110, 168
Sikora, J. J., 214, 222
Siva, 13, 195
Skinner, B. F., 207
Smart, Ninian, 208, 223
Sociobiological theory, 18
Solifideism, 137, 159, 237; *see also* Fideism
Soteriology, 36, 44–45, 46, 93–94, 159–60, 201
Spencer, Herbert, 207
Suarez, F., 68
Sufficient grace, 10
Sufis, 107, 201
Sullivan, Francis, 209–12, 223
Sunyavada, 41, 201
Superstition, 34, 39, 57, 130

Talmud, 46, 201
Tao, Taoism, 36, 38, 40–41, 82, 101, 110, 133, 168, 201
Tanquerey, A., 209, 223
Teleology, 119–28, 141, 201
Temple, Archbishop William, 156
Teresa of Avila, St., 162
Theodicy, 31, 43, 132–39, 143, 201–2
Theonomy, 150, 201, 217
Theopaschitism, 135, 202, 216
Theravada Buddhism, 43, 45, 168, 198, 202
Thomas Aquinas, St., xi, 14–19, 23, 51, 67, 96, 99, 101, 109, 120, 149, 166, 170–71, 173–74, 177–78, 207, 210, 213, 223, and *passim*
Tindal, M., 206
Toland, J., 206
Torah, 44, 47, 202
Toynbee, Arnold, 40, 208
Transcendental perfections of being, 28–30, 59, 138, 172, 177, 202

Trent, Council of, 155, 161–62, 202–3, 211, 218
Trinity, 2, 56, 60, 98, 162, 188, 201, 203, 213–14, 219

Ubaghs, G. C., 206
Unam sanctam, 66, 203
Unitatis redintegratio, 204, 210–11
"Universal sacrament of salvation," 71, 83, 86, 88, 159, 200, 210
Upanishads, 41, 169, 187, 202, 208, 218
Utility function, 123–25, 215

Van Steenberghen, Fernand, 107, 214, 219, 223
Vatican I, 5–6, 51, 59–60, 153, 203, 206
Vatican II, xii, 9, 11, 33–34, 50, 54, 57–58, 62–65, 67, 70–71, 73–82, 84–86, 88–90, 94, 111, 118, 130–31, 142, 145–46, 149–50, 180, and *passim*
Vedanta, 40–41, 202
Vedas, 41, 200, 202
Veritatis splendor, 204, 216–17
Via negativa, 29, 177, 202
Vicarious satisfaction, 160, 218
Virgil, 215
Vishnu, 42, 195
Voltaire, 206
Voluntarism, 135–39, 202, 216
Votum sacramenti, 74

Weber, Max, 133–35, 137, 223
Wesley, John, 161
Whitehead A. N., 33, 200, 216
Wider ecumenism, 76–77
Wittgenstein, Ludwig, 107, 214
Wolpert, L., 27, 207
Wordsworth, 218

YAHWEH, THE ONE WHO IS, 12, 96–97, 99, 101–5, 169, 171–72, 174, 177, 200, 206
Yin and Yang, 39

Zeus, 13
Zoroastrianism, 38, 43, 107, 110, 133–34, 149, 182, 197, 208